THE GATEKEEPERS

The

GATEKEEPERS

Comparative Immigration Policy

Edited by

Michael C. LeMay

PRAEGER

New York
Westport, Connecticut
London

Library of Congress Cataloging-in-Publication Data

LeMay, Michael C., 1941–
    The gatekeepers : comparative immigration policy / Michael C.
LeMay.
        p.   cm.
    Bibliography: p.
    Includes index.
    ISBN 0–275–93079–3 (alk. paper)
    1. Emigration and immigration—Government policy.   2. Comparative
government.   I. Title.
JV6271.L45   1989
325'.1—dc19   88–17993

Library of Congress Catalog Card Number: 88–17993
ISBN: 0–275–93079–3

First published in 1989

Praeger Publishers, One Madison Avenue, New York, NY 10010
A division of Greenwood Press, Inc.

Printed in the United States of America

The paper used in this book complies with the Permanent
Paper Standard issued by the National Information Standards
Organization (Z39.48-1984).

10   9   8   7   6   5   4   3   2   1

This book, an offspring of my mind, is lovingly dedicated to my children: Jane, Steven, John, and Jill

Contents

Tables and Figures

FIGURES

Preface

MICHAEL C. LEMAY

THE IMPORTANCE OF IMMIGRATION POLICYMAKING

The Gatekeepers is the collaborative effort of a group of scholars on immigration policy. Students of public policy will hopefully find it a rich vein within which to mine insight into the policy process. Few public policy areas evidence such dramatic impact upon society as does that of immigration policy. Shifts in policy move to open or close the doors of a nation in ways that immediately impact upon the lives of tens of thousands of persons thereby allowed in or excluded. Immigration policy shifts can affect the economies of nations, and are viewed as integral aspects of a nation-state's economic policy.

Immigration policy, moreover, is a topic of substantive importance. As this book illustrates, it is also one which the several nations examined here have shown to be both of timely and abiding interest. The process of immigration, especially when that process involves mass movements of refugees, is a complex one. How those immigrants mix and intermingle with the population of their host nation is a compelling story of human interest.

Immigration policy, moreover, is the type of subject that affords a great deal of insight into the policy process. It exemplifies regulatory policymaking that involves the imposition of restrictions on the behavior of individuals and groups. Few areas of regulatory policy are as clear-cut in dramatic impact as is immigration policy. To cite but one example:

In the decade before the passage of the national origins quota system, over 8 million immigrants, nearly 71 percent of whom came from southeastern European countries, entered the U.S. This was the greatest number in the history of our nation. In the decade after passage of the quota system, our nation saw the smallest influx of immigrants for any decade since we began counting in 1820, and those from southeastern Europe nations had decreased to but 37 percent of that far smaller total. (LeMay, 1985)

The study of immigration policy is also useful in that it shows so well the impact of interest groups advocating or opposing changes in policy. In each of the nation-states examined herein, one sees the gatekeeping function of immigration policy having profound effects on which groups are permitted or denied entry to the country, and on social, economic, cultural, religious, and foreign policy concerns of the host nation. The policy reflects the pressures of internal groups pushing for restrictions or the easing of those restrictions as the needs of those groups change over time. The following chapters illustrate the *inherently political nature* of the immigration process and policy.

THE VALUE OF THE COMPARATIVE PERSPECTIVE

The study of immigration policy gains much from approaching it with a comparative perspective. A special richness of insight is afforded by comparing the similarities and differences in the ways various nations attempt to control their borders and who is allowed or refused permanent entry.

The Gatekeepers presents an interesting array of countries, which vary considerably in their fundamental approach to the question of immigration. Each of these studies, moreover, views that nation's immigration policy from an historical perspective, shedding light on how and why the policy shifted over time, and how such shifts affect the influx of immigrants to that nation.

In the chapters that follow, the reader will see that all six nations examined herein have adopted policies that not only attempt to control who can or cannot enter, but that in the process help to define the national character. Each chapter notes gaps between stated policy and the actual patterns of immigration that are at least tacitly allowed.

All of the countries examined herein have experienced relatively large-scale immigration in recent decades, yet they exemplify differing policy responses to that trend. They show, for example, a "guestworker" approach, as compared to policies aimed at permanent settlement. They include examples of large-scale "post-colonial" immigration as well as the recruitment of foreign labor with subsequent family immigration.

All of these countries, moreover, have experienced an international migration the scope of which was largely unforeseen and for which they were poorly prepared. Their policy reactions to this mass migration has been in part strikingly similar, yet in other respects dramatically different. All have evidenced increasingly restrictive policies. Active labor recruitment has stopped. Yet all have shown a number of improvements in the social and cultural situation of the immigrants.

The following chapters offer a number of parallels in the various nations' immigration policies. Both the United States and Venezuela, for example, struggle with the problem of controlling illegal immigration. Germany's lengthy experience with the problems of a guestworker program offers insight into what the United States might expect from a provision in its newest law. Australia and Great Britain are now experiencing the problems of coping with the assimilation of a much greater racial and cultural mixture of immigrants, akin on a smaller scale to the long history of U.S. immigration. Immigration policy, as examined herein, reflects the needs of nations of both the North and South; of both developed and developing nations; of both large and small countries; of both nations receiving large influxes, which often arrive in mass refugee movements, and of countries limiting that influx to a much smaller proportion of their total population and attempting to keep the stream one of a controlled inflow.

The following chapters also provide a number of intriguing contrasts. Each of the six nations examined can claim some "unique" aspects to its immigration process or policy. Australia illustrates the unique effect of its geographic isolation. Great Britain struggles with the impact of immigration flowing from its traditional Commonwealth political structure. That tradition results in some very pronounced limitations on British immigration policy. The United States is unique among major receiving nations in being a major economic superpower sharing a 2,000 mile border with a Third World nation. Germany exemplifies a nation espousing a "nonimmigration policy," yet struggling with the reality of a large number of foreign-born resident "guestworkers" and their families, who are in fact permanent immigrants. Venezuela faces the special immigration policy problems of the Third World developing nations. Israel provides a unique case of immigration policy based predominately on religious considerations.

AN OVERVIEW OF THE BOOK

The Gatekeepers, then, examines the immigration policies and politics of the United States, Australia, Great Britain, Germany, Israel, and Venezuela. Each chapter discusses its respective nation's immigration policy and politics by focusing on social and economic trends over time and how those trends help to shape and explain the resulting policy.

In Chapter 1, Michael C. LeMay examines U.S. immigration policy and politics. He stresses how shifts in policy reflect two conflicting value goals, causing policy to oscillate in varying degrees between them, variously opening or closing the door to continued influx. He distinguishes four major phases in U.S. immigration policy, underscoring the common social, economic, and political elements that have marked each shift in policy. Using that historical perspective, he then discusses the most recent trends in immigration to the United States, noting that the ebb and flow is marked by varying surges in massive refugee inflows, and by a marked shift from European sources to Asian and Latin American origins. After assessing the perceived problems with the existing policy resulting from these trends in the immigration flow, he discusses the alternative proposals to revise immigration law considered by the U.S. Congress during the 1980s. The chapter concludes with an analysis of the Immigration Reform and Control Act of 1986. It describes how that Act came to be passed with its particular provisions. It assesses the likely success or failure of the Act, concluding that the historical review of immigration policy leads one to expect that the new law will not be likely to achieve its primary goal of markedly reducing the influx of illegal aliens. It argues that the very compromises, ambiguities, and vague language necessary to get the bill enacted into law contain the potential seeds of the law's own problems. The chapter proposes that the enactment of the law marks a new phase in U.S. immigration policy that might well be called "the Revolving-Door Era."

In Chapter 2, on Australian immigration policy and politics, Gregory Tobin notes the many similarities between that nation's immigration experiences and those of the United States. But more importantly, he focuses on some striking contrasts, due to the two countries' different circumstances and profoundly contrasting geographies. He describes the colonial period of immigration policy from 1788 to 1901. The timing and nature of Australia's political development constitutes one of the major contrasts with the U.S. experience.

He notes, too, the facts of political geography, which provide another sharp contrast. Australia, having no contiguous border with any other nation, has been able to rigidly control its borders and access. This isolation of an island continent has heightened the local community's sense of ability to control entry. Illegal immigrants have never been a serious problem nor vexing concern of its immigration policy. As Professor Tobin notes, "Few countries have enjoyed the luxury of such a level of control of the inflow of population from beyond their borders, and such a degree of detachment from the conflicts that have generated so many exiles and refugees—advantages that seem all the more ironic when seen in the context of the origin of the society that enjoys them."

As in the chapter on the United States, Professor Tobin identifies and describes distinct phases in Australian immigration policy: the colonial period (1788–1900), with special emphasis on the goldrush era and free immigration during 1850–1900; the period of nation, empire, and commonwealth (1901–1945); the postwar era of "populate or perish," with its increasing reliance on non-British, European immigration, and the resulting problems for assimilation generated by the greater ethnic diversity; and immigration policy during the 1970s.

He closes the chapter with a discussion of the debates of 1983/84, when the question of non-European immigration suddenly resurfaced as a controversial issue, and of contemporary issues with which Australian immigration policy is faced in the late 1980s. He notes the profile of the nation's population at the end of 1986, which underscores the considerable social impact of the post-World War II immigration program. Nearly a quarter of Australia's almost 16 million population were foreign-born, with more than one-third of them British or Irish-born, and 100,000 being refugees from Vietnam. The recent influx included not only large numbers from Vietnam, but also from the Middle East, Latin America,

East Timor, Sri Lanka, Afghanistan, and Africa. He points out that a single year's immigration illustrates the two major themes underlying the overall trend in immigration policy since 1947—the continued reinforcement of the original British stock coupled with a progressive variation in the volume, and the composition of the non-British component. These trends point up the nervous uncertainty of Australian immigration policy as to just what combination of volume and content best serves the interests of economic growth and social cohesion.

In Chapter 3, Zig Layton-Henry analyzes British immigration policy and politics since 1945. Great Britain has traditionally been a country of emigration rather than immigration. Great Britain is also somewhat unique in that its immigration process and policy reflects the "Commonwealth" status of the ex-colonies of the British Empire. Its immigration policy concentrates on the immigration of British subjects from its former colonial territories, in particular from the "New Commonwealth" countries of the West Indies, India, Pakistan, and Bangladesh. As Professor Layton-Henry so vividly shows, "New Commonwealth" immigration has caused the greatest public concern and has dominated the thinking and actions of policymakers. He notes how much immigration flows have shaped changes in the British population. The influx of significant ethnic minority populations was neither planned nor anticipated by policymakers. Once the New Commonwealth immigration pattern developed after WWII, the government proved very reluctant to intervene with a policy of either management or control. Like the United States, British policy oscillated between two contrasting goals. While the government did not wish to be seen as encouraging New Commonwealth immigration, policies of control would have disrupted relations with Colonial and Commonwealth governments and would have reduced the flow of migrant workers at a time of severe labor shortage. As does Professor LeMay, in Chapter 1, he notes the interrelationship between foreign policy and economic concerns in British immigration policy. As in the United States, British unions have traditionally been suspicious of and hostile toward high levels of immigration. Yet the reactions of the trade unions toward New Commonwealth immigration has been surprisingly positive. The Trade Union Congress of 1955 welcomed such immigration and deplored attempts to erect color bars. However unions, for a long time, have allowed notices of exclusion and discrimination to operate at the local level.

Professor Layton-Henry notes also the somewhat unique relationship of the British social welfare system to the process and problems of the New Commonwealth immigration. At 18 percent of its GNP, the British social security system is among the largest such programs in the capitalist world. New Commonwealth immigrants, as British subjects, have been entitled upon arrival to the whole range of social welfare services. The British Nationality Act of 1981, however, means that Commonwealth citizens are no longer automatically British citizens as well. Those who are accepted for settlement are entitled to the full range of services. He describes the instruments of regulation and control, and analyzes the outcome of such in race relations, housing, employment, education, and inner-city policies. He discusses in particular anti-discrimination legislation passed since 1964, including the establishment of the Commission for Racial Equality in 1976. He critiques race relations policy as having been poorly defined and coordinated, noting that a wide range of government departments, local authorities, and organizations, such as the police, play important yet autonomous roles in dealing with immigrants and especially with ethnic minorities. He notes that even after fifteen years of aid to local authorities with large minority populations, no national policy on minority education has emerged. He traces the interrelationship between race relations policy and immigration regulation and control. He concludes that:

The major failure of British immigration and race relations policy concerns the lack of government action. Successive British governments have failed to give priority and resources to ensuring the successful settlement and integration of New Commonwealth immigrants or even to developing a policy on immigration before 1962, when the remedy adopted was control. Once settlement had occurred on a substantial scale, positive policies were again needed to ensure equal rights and opportunities. Little has been done, and it has been half-hearted and sporadic. The major problem facing future British governments will be to ensure that the second and third generations of black Britons are not alienated from their country of birth but feel full and equal citizens.

In Chapter 4, Marilyn Hoskin and Roy C. Fitzgerald discuss the politics of German immigration policy. As in the U.K. case, German policy concerns the problems associated with a labor influx. Indeed, the authors note that the inclusion of Germany in a comparative analysis of immigration policy is something of an anomaly in that all recent and current policy statements of the Federal Republic of Germany note that it "is not an immigration nation." Despite these disclaimers, however, they note that German policymakers face questions similar or identical to those at issue in classic immigration nations. Currently over four million non-citizens reside in the Federal Republic, most of whom have been there for more than ten years. Despite the halt in the recruitment of foreign workers in 1973, a significant number of their family members have joined them, which, combined with their higher birth rates, have produced a growing population of non-Germans in the overall population.

They note that the German case represents an intriguing variation on traditional immigration experience and analysis, yet one that is especially instructive in its reflection of the pressures increasingly faced by other nations. They pinpoint when and how key features of German immigration policy developed, and how they are maintained or challenged under current pressures to rethink and rationalize immigration policy generally.

As with the other chapters in this volume, they present a brief historical overview of immigration and its variations in modern Germany. They proceed to detail the evolution of policy out of that experience. They focus on a detailed analysis of popular sentiment toward immigrants, and offer some tentative conclusions about the prospects and limits of future absorption of foreigners into Germany, compared with other nations considered in this volume.

According to their analysis, German policy, like that of the United States, is dichotomized between an officially restrictive policy and an unofficial liberalness. They note that the political parties have abdicated their traditional leadership role, and less obvious groups have assumed primacy in pushing for official policy and implementing unofficial programs. Even in a case where strict new rules might be developed to confront an unanticipated influx that was not due to the short-sighted nature of previous policy, as in the dramatic case of asylum-seekers, conventional policymaking appears to be unable to meet the demand for a decisive objective and clear rules.

Their analysis of German public opinion shows surprising and increasing public support for the rights of those ethnic minorities, even when the economy has stalled and demands for social services were on the rise. This overall increase in public acceptance or sympathy has occurred even among groups harmed or threatened by the economic hard times.

They conclude that even when sanctioned by government or important groups, immigration rarely if ever evokes visible public enthusiasm and support. Yet government policymakers are almost the mirror-images of their constituents; they cannot confess to liking the influx of immigrants even while they often see advantages to their arrival or a real cost in trying to shut them out. And once foreigners have arrived, successive governments have found it easier to make room for them and accept their differences than to try to force them out. In the authors' words:

[p]ublic opinion and official policy are really two sides of the same coin on this seemingly volatile issue. Which side is examined first is largely irrelevant to the fact that the other will sooner or later be turned over and seen as similar. . . . The German case has allowed us to examine in some detail what has happened in the absence of clear policy. Public opinion has, gradually, made strides toward an acceptance of foreigners in the society that should ultimately allow the government to sponsor rigorous programs of naturalization. That it has not done so prior to this time is perhaps dismaying and perhaps reflective of governments that have been unwilling to take bold but necessary steps. On the other hand, it may also be reflective of a painfully slow but eventually less conflictual process through which foreigners are assimilated into societies that initially appear as especially unsuited to their integration.

In Chapter 5, Bat-Ami Zucker focuses on the Jewish identity of Israel's nationality policy. This chapter differs from the others in that its perspective is much more ideological. Yet that difference in scholarly focus reflects the fact that Israel's approach to immigration and naturalization is uniquely philosophical. As she notes in her introduction to the chapter:

One may ask why ideology should be relevant to the question of nationality when in order to acquire, for example, U.S. citizenship one does not necessarily invoke American culture, the national anthem, or a certain religion. This chapter will attempt to show that in Israel, as a direct result of the uniqueness of the Jewish state, the situation is completely different. Whereas U.S. nationality may lead to an American identity, in the state of Israel it is Jewishness that conditions automatic Israeli nationality. Jewishness, as both a religion and nationhood, had therefore to be legally defined so that the necessary ordinances and procedures concerning nationality could be enacted. Since, however, Israel is a secular, democratic state with a majority of nonobservant Jews, the attempts to legally interpret "Jewishness" led to ideological and legal controversy, often threatening the stability of coalition governments composed of religious as well as secular ministers.

Professor Zucker discusses Israel's nationality policy by first analyzing the Law of Return and the Nationality Law. Stressing the uniqueness of the Israeli case, she argues that status has been characterized by two dominant events in Jewish history during this century: the Holocaust and the establishment of the State of Israel. The disproportion of the influx of immigrants to Israel after the Holocaust is clearly the result of the state of emergency in which European Jewish refugees found themselves. Asylum was necessary as a quick solution to that vexing problem. The crisis nature prevented the luxury of time to deal with the enormous problems caused by such comparatively massive immigration. Important demographic, social, cultural, and economic questions had to be postponed. The major task was simply to absorb them: to provide them with food, lodging, and employment. Professor Zucker distinguishes two great waves of immigrants: the 1948–1951 period, and the more sustained influx since then.

She discusses in detail cases that have entailed interpretation of the Law of Return and the Nationality Law, emphasizing the six ways one can acquire Israeli nationality: by Return, by residence in Israel, by birth, by birth and residence, by naturalization, and by grant. She analyzes each way, to demonstrate the ideology behind the Laws.

Professor Zucker then discusses what she calls the unique character of Israeli nationality policy. She notes that while a definition of nationality is a political/legal relationship between a state and its citizens, creating rights and duties for both, Israeli nationality implies more. For a Jew, Israeli nationality means also belonging to a people—reflecting religious, traditional, historical, social and cultural ties. These factors, she maintains, have created an ideology and outlook peculiar to the Jewish people and the Jewish state. The fact that religion and nationhood are inseparable in Judaism has affected Israeli nationality policy. The secular State of Israel was obliged to adopt religious laws rooted in the *Halacha*—Jewish laws. In Israel, the most ancient of religious and ancient of peoples posed an unprecedented church/state problem of a peculiar kind. In Judaism, national aspirations took on religious forms and vice versa. As long as Jewish national aspirations were not realized, the question of sovereign secular power was less acute. Once the State of Israel emerged, however, the confrontation was inevitable. The status and place religion should occupy in Israeli law has been agitating public opinion and debates in the Knesset ever since the establishment of the State. As she notes, " . . . the question, 'Who is a Jew?', which might seem to be one solely of a legal/judicial context, has proved in Israel to be one that 'cuts to the heart of one's Jewish identity and self-perception.' " She then discusses and analyzes three cases that illustrate the perplexity of a secular society that cannot escape its traditional heritage without violating its identity, and the sometimes ironic implications of that problem.

Professor Zucker concludes that where other nations and faiths have long ago ceased to be troubled by arguments concerning national or religious status, accepting as final the rulings of their law codes, "Who is a Jew?" continues to be a dynamic matter in Israeli society where two conflicting definitions aspire to gain state recognition. The fusion of Jewish and Israeli identity, although not complete, demonstrates the unique character of Israel's nationality as against the concept of national identity in other national communities. She notes it is easier for a Jew to acquire Israeli citizenship for the simple reason that Israel is primarily a state for the Jewish people. This fact, however, does not totally deprive non-Jews. They may immigrate and may hold citizenship. And once Israeli nationality is obtained, non-Jews and Jews enjoy equal status as citizens and are guaranteed freedom of religion, conscience, language, education, and culture. Israel's policy of open-doors applies wholly to Jews, yet non-Jews who wish to cast their lot with Israel will find its gates are not wholly barred.

In the final chapter, Daniel Hellinger examines Venezuelan immigration policy and politics. He places his analysis within the explanatory framework of world systems theory. As with the earlier chapters, he discusses Venezuelan immigration policy in broad historical perspective, tracing the policy from its first law in 1831. He notes that the Venezuelan experience provides a relevant case study of immigration policy in Third World nations pursuing developmental goals. He notes, too, its parallel to immigration problems of many developed nations—that of undocumented and illegal immigration.

As a result of oil and the social transformations it wrought, Venezuela's relationship with other "peripheral" nations changed. The "boom/bust" nature of its economy shaped its immigration policy.

Professor Hellinger argues that while Venezuela's problems with undocumented aliens are comparable to those faced by the United States in its relationship with Mexico—caused by the gap in the levels of economic and social opportunities in the two countries—there are also important differences. The U.S.–Mexico case represents a periphery-to-center relationship (within the world system model), while that between Colombia and Venezuela is a case of an inter-periphery relationship. Immigrants to Venezuela are more likely to confront opportunities and limitations like those in their country of origin. And he notes that immigration policy alone, especially that of any one nation, cannot greatly influence international movements of populations in either case.

He then analyzes the evolution of Venezuelan policy—its goals, effectiveness, and impact during several periods, each defined by changes in Venezuela's location in the world system. Like the United States and Australian chapters, he distinguishes distinct periods: from colonial time to 1935; from 1935 to 1973; and from 1973 to the present, a period of boom and bust.

He concludes that the Venezuelan experience with immigration corresponds to the policy dilemmas of many of the core nations of the world economy—xenephobia, competition between foreign and native labor, and political manipulation of the immigration issue. He notes, also, a key difference. Immigration in the periphery is set in a context of a quest for development; most importantly, immigration policy is designed to increase the opportunities for the native population. As he sums it up:

Perhaps the similarities and differences are clearest in regard to undocumented immigration. On the one hand, the gap between Venezuela and its neighbors is pronounced enough to produce an immigration problem that North Americans can readily understand. However, if what the United States confronts in Mexican immigration is a steady flow of immigrants progressively rising above flood stage, what Venezuela has experienced is more like a flash flood, followed by slowly retreating waters. The Venezuelan experience adds to the evidence that immigration in the modern world obeys more the forces of the capitalist world economic system than it does the policies of individual states.

THE GATEKEEPERS

1

U.S. Immigration Policy and Politics

MICHAEL C. LEMAY

The effort made to restore the Statue of Liberty and celebrate its centennial, and the recent passage of the Immigration Reform and Control Act of 1986, have renewed attention on U.S. immigration policy. Since 1820, when the nation formally began keeping track of immigration, the United States has absorbed more than 50 million legal immigrants, born in some 155 foreign countries. Immigration policy is perforce controversial, since the immigration process raises serious questions about its cultural, demographic, economic, and social impacts.

Scholars dealing with this massive influx into the American "melting pot" have categorized the various periods of immigration into "waves." The nation's policies for coping with the massive influx have reflected the perceived needs of the nation as those needs shifted over time and in response to changing economic conditions. The policies have reflected reactions to the changing nature and composition of those immigrant waves, which, in turn, have influenced the nation's policies. Various economic, ethnic, foreign policy, and cold-war issues have all played key roles in the debates over immigration policy.

The shifts in policy reflect two conflicting value perspectives, which tug and pull at one another, causing policy to oscillate in varying degrees between them. On the one hand is the perspective that values the immigrant as a source of industry and renewed vigor, a desirable infusion of "new blood" into the American stock, enriching the heritage and spurring new economic growth. This perspective forms the traditional base for a more open immigration policy. Almost every president, from Washington to Reagan, has affirmed that the United States is a nation of asylum for which immigration expresses and reconfirms the American spirit of "liberty for all."

The other perspective calls for varying degrees of restriction. Its proponents fear an influx of strangers who are not, or in their view should not, be assimilated.

Those forces fear the dilution of American culture. They fear that so vast an influx will destroy the economy or at least severely depress wages and working conditions. During the period of the Great Depression, for example, the government, following this perspective, used the "likely to become a public charge" provision to keep immigrants out. Rather than giving immigrant minorities relief, local officials provided transportation for their return trip. One scholar estimated that over 400,000 Mexican aliens, and their American-born children, were "repatriated" during the decade of the 1930s alone (see Chiswick: 15).

FOUR PHASES OR ERAS OF U.S. IMMIGRATION POLICY

Immigration policy performs a gatekeeping function, and changes in that policy result in dramatic changes in the influx of immigrants, in terms of both the size and composition of the flow. That gatekeeping function suggests the imagery of "doors" to characterize immigration policy. We have described elsewhere in some detail four such phases (LeMay, 1987). Phase one, from 1820 to 1880, we called the "Open-Door Era." During this phase, policy involved virtually unlimited immigration. Practically all who sought entrance were allowed to do so. Indeed, official governmental policy was to reach out and seek immigrants. The second phase, the "Door-Ajar Era." lasted from 1880 to 1920. This phase saw the beginnings of limitations, even while the door was still clearly open to most. The third phase, the "Pet-Door Era," lasted from 1920 to 1950, a period when the national origins quota system formed the basis of U.S. immigration policy. Essentially a restrictive approach, it allowed in only the favored few. The fourth and most recent phase is called the "Dutch-Door Era." Spanning from 1950 to the present, this phase has entailed an increase in total immigration over the previous era, but with a decided bias favoring those who enter "at the top." That is, many were allowed in under special provisions and received favored treatment in comparison to the "old" and "new" waves prior to the Great Depression. Each phase is marked by some major events and policy enactments. Figure 1.1 graphically portrays these four phases and the major events or legislative highlights that help demark each phase.

The 1980s witnessed considerable renewed interest in immigration policy. After more than a half-decade of strenuous debate, the Congress finally passed, in October of 1986, the Immigration Reform and Control Act. It constitutes the most substantive revision of immigration law since 1965. One might well ask, "Is the United States entering a new phase or era in immigration policy?" An historical view of that policy suggests that the times and conditions are, indeed, ripe for such a new era. Such an historical review highlights several commonalities evident in each previous period marked by a major shift. All such elements are evident again today.

1. Each major shift was *preceded by a major recession or a depression*: 1873, 1893, 1920, the Great Depression, the early 1950s, and the early 1960s. The recession of

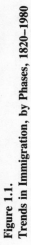

Figure 1.1.
Trends in Immigration, by Phases, 1820–1980

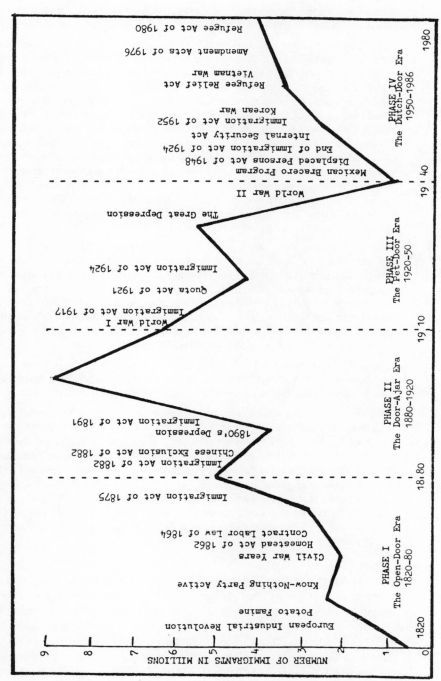

1980/81 was the most severe major downturn the United States has experienced since World War II.

2. Each major shift period was marked by *social unrest and anxiety*. The labor unrest and strife of the 1870s led to the first restrictions, imposed in 1882. The "Red Scare" of 1919 immediately preceded the imposition of the quota system in the 1920s. The cold-war era and the hysteria of McCarthyism ushered in the Immigration Act of 1952. The social turmoil of the civil rights era and the Vietnam War were reflected in the changes in the Immigration Act of 1965. In each postwar period—be it after the Civil War, World War I, World War II, the Korean War, or the Vietnam War—agitation led to substantial changes in our immigration policy. The Iranian hostage crisis and the national anxiety spawned by the recent resurgence of international terrorism engendered the rise in nationalist fervor that has contributed markedly to the movement to revise immigration policy. So too, the huge trade deficits and the spectre of increased economic competition from Japan has spurred a protectionist fervor in Congress that, at least in part, is also reflected in aspects of proposals to tighten immigration laws by imposing employer sanctions.

3. Each major shift in immigration policy in the past was enacted shortly after a *major shift in the composition of the influx of immigrants*. The influx of a new "Asian race" led to the first immigration restrictions. The change from Protestants from northwestern Europe to Catholics and Jews from southeastern Europe solidified support for the imposition of the national origins quota system. The need to deal with the "refugees" after World War II compelled another significant change in policy. More recently, the massive influx of Chicanos, Haitians, Cubans, and Vietnamese and other Asians has led to new demands to modify our current immigration law.

4. Each major shift in policy came after *one or more of the major political parties advocated such change as an important plank of that party's platform*. Immigration reform became a significant campaign issue before each major shift occurred.

5. Likewise, each major shift followed the *development of specific ad hoc interest groups* being formed to advocate such change. In the 1840s it was the Know Nothing Party. The Asian Exclusion League was the principal proponent of such change in the 1880s and 1890s. In the 1920s, the Ku Klux Klan, the American Coalition, the Immigration Restriction League, and the American Protective League of True Americans battled the Hebrew Sheltering and Immigration Aid Society and the Anti-National Origins Clause League. In the 1980s the Federation for American Immigration Reform [FAIR] and the Zero Population Growth movement have served as strong advocates of the need for change. Their efforts have been opposed by various Hispanic, black, and liberal groups.

This historical review highlights some *recurrent arguments*, like variations on a theme in a symphony, that are echoed and re-echoed by the proponents for a change in policy. Each major shift saw agitation over the impact of immigration on wages and working conditions. During each period of policy shift, cries bewailing the adverse effects of immigration on American culture, mores and politics were vehemently expressed. The recurrent theme of whether or not each new wave of immigrants *could be* or *should be* assimilated is a motif heard more distinctly during the period of each major shift—just as in the 1980s grave concern has been raised over bilingualism and the supposed "unassimilability" of the Chicanos or the Asians.

Each period of change saw its advocates touting some new *method* for restriction. Public policy shifted from a reliance on "excluded categories" to the "literacy test" and then on to the imposition of the "quota system." That was followed by an elaborate "system of preferences." Today's proponents advocate the use of "employer sanctions." While the method has been modified, a consistent pattern throughout is that each major shift in policy is associated with the advocacy of some "new method."

Historical analysis indicates that in each period the same *stable coalition of interest groups* generally supported the relatively unrestricted influx of newcomers while another such coalition of organized interests was pressing for increased restrictions on immigration. Time and again, various business and "ethnic" group coalitions in favor of unrestricted immigration battled a coalition of organized labor, the American Legion, and various "patriotic" associations who pressed for the adoption of some new approach to restrict the influx.

So too, the period of each major shift saw a spate of scholarly books, a mass media campaign, and a major governmentally-sponsored committee or commission that reviewed the then-current "problem" of immigration. Each such major movement to mold public opinion preceded a significant shift in public sentiment in the direction of the new immigration policy.

The long-term historical overview of U.S. immigration policy demonstrates that four main elements figure prominently in the formulation of such policy: economics, race, nationalism, and foreign policy considerations. These four main elements of immigration policy sometimes worked in harmony with one another, reinforcing each other in their impact on policy. At other times they worked in conflict with each other, as the forces contending to determine the primary thrust of immigration policy each stressed different elements. The policy eventually enacted reflected the then-current "balance" between and among these four key elements.

RECENT TRENDS IN IMMIGRATION

The 1965 Immigration Act ended the quota system and opened the way for forces that dramatically altered the immigration influx. It enabled the largest wave of immigration to enter the United States since the turn of the century. It altered the composition of that wave. Under the quota system, for roughly 50 years, immigrants entering the United States were overwhelmingly European. Today they come from Third World nations—largely from Asia and Latin America. Of the 544,000 *legal* immigrants who entered the United States in 1984, more than 10 percent (57,000) were from Mexico, followed by the Philippines (42,000), and Vietnam (37,000). British immigration, by contrast, at only 14,000, ranked ninth (*Time*, July 8, 1985: 26).

The 1980 Refugee Act's change in the definition of "refugee" increased the number of persons thus eligible from 3 million to nearly 13 million people (Leibowitz: 167; Ferris: 108). Although the question of refugee status is a complicated one with political, social, economic, as well as legal ramifications, the trends in Third World nations particularly have led to what has been called "the global refugee crisis" (Kritz: 157). The *1981 World Refugee Survey* places the number of refugees in the world today at 12.5 million. The vast majority of them are from Third World countries, seeking refuge in another Third World country.

The United States, as well as some other industrialized countries, will continue to grant asylum to those refugees with whom they have historic ties. For example, from 1975 to 1980 the United States took in 677,000 refugees—including Soviet Jews, Indochinese, and people from the Caribbean region. That was over three times as many as were taken in by any other country, and almost as many as all the other major receiving nations combined, as can be seen in Table 1.1, below.

The dramatic rise during the past decade in the number of potential immigrants has increased the pressure on immigration policy. The growing global interdependence and advances in transportation and communication make the United States more accessible than ever before. These pressures, moreover, result from causes largely outside the control of the U.S. government or policy. The worldwide population explosion, poverty, rising unemployment, and political turmoil, experienced in much of the Third World, have been added to ethnic and religious tensions and natural disasters as powerful push factors. The United States is unique among the industrialized nations of the world in having nearly 2,000 miles of its borders facing an adjoining Third World nation. These forces have led to increased economic migration and occasional mass refugee flows that have been large enough and sufficiently concentrated in a few localities so that the domestic impact of the refugee flow is of increasing concern to the American public and to Congress (see Knickrehm, APSA Paper, 1985: 14; and Peters and Vega, 1986).

The massive wave of legal and illegal immigration in response to these outside pressures raises some troubling questions. One such question concerns how many persons are actually entering our borders. In addition to the half-million annual legal immigrants, a substantial number of illegals are also entering. Estimates as to their number vary widely. In 1984 the Immigration and Naturalization Service (INS) apprehended 1.3 million undocumented aliens (many of them more than once) and the agency estimates that two to three times as many slipped through. In 1978, the census bureau estimated the total illegal immigrant population in the United States at between 3.5 and 6 million. A National Academy of Sciences study released in August 1985, however, denounced the INS figures and put the total number of undocumented aliens at between two and four million. These included everyone from persons deliberately overstaying their visas to the Haitian boat people who washed ashore in South Florida. But by everyone's standards, the majority of illegal immigrants are Hispanics, about two-thirds of

Table 1.1:
Resettlement of Refugees, 1975–1980

Country	Number	Country	Number
U.S.	677,000	Austria	4,300
China	265,000	New Zealand	4,100
Israel	105,700	Belgium	3,900
Malaysia	102,100	Argentina	2,800
Canada	84,100	Norway	2,700
France	72,000	Denmark	2,300
Australia	51,200	Romania	1,200
Germany (FRG)	32,100	Spain	1,100
U.K.	27,600	Italy	900
Tanzania	26,000	Chile	800
Hong Kong	9,400	Japan	800
Switzerland	7,500	Cuba	700
Sweden	7,300	Mexico	700
Netherlands	4,700		

Source: *1981 World Refugee Survey*, ed. Michael J. Sherbinin (New York: U.S. Committee for Refugees, 1981). Cited in Papademetriou and Miller: 264.

whom are Mexicans driven by poverty and unemployment across the highly porous 2,000 miles Mexican/U.S. border (*Time*, July 8, 1985: 27).

Other questions raised by this trend are how many of these new aliens can we absorb and at what rate; how many unskilled workers do we need in our increasingly high-tech society; do they drain the economy or enrich it; do the newcomers gain their foothold at the expense of the poor and the black; how possible and/or desirable is it to assimilate such large numbers and such diverse racial, linguistic, and cultural backgrounds; and will the advantages of such diversity outweigh the dangers of separatism and conflict?

Hispanic Americans, now estimated between 17 and 20 million in population, are a highly diverse minority. Indeed, the term is a catch-all phrase used to refer to all Spanish-speaking groups. The 1980 census data show Hispanics are comprised as follows (in percent): Mexicans, 59; Puerto Ricans, 15; Cubans, 6; Central/South Americans, 7; and all other Spanish-speaking, 13 percent. In 1980, all Hispanics shared one aspect in common besides their language—they are highly urbanized. Nearly 90 percent reside in metropolitan areas. About one-fourth of them (an estimated 3.5 million) live in the Los Angeles and New York areas alone. They are highly concentrated in six states: California, Florida, Texas, Illinois, New York, and Arizona (LeMay, 1985: 145).

A recent study released by the Population Reference Bureau estimates that the Hispanic population will reach 47 million by the year 2020, displacing blacks as the nation's largest minority group. A census bureau study shows Hispanics averaged 97.9 births per 1,000 women in 1981, compared with 83.6 per 1,000 for blacks and 68.1 per 1,000 for white women (*Parade*, September 4, 1983).

The border between the United States and Mexico is one of extraordinary contrast—exceeded in its starkness only by the Berlin Wall. On one side of a border stretching 1,936 miles is the world's greatest economic superpower. On the other side is a Third World country of widespread poverty and an enormous national debt. Across that border annually many millions of legal crossings occur. In addition, in 1984, over 1 million undocumented aliens were seized (up 50 percent from the previous decade). No one can firmly estimate the number who made it across illegally.

Resulting Problems

The increased size of the newest influx and its changing composition, coupled with the massive scale of the illegal flow, raise particular concern about a number of related problems. Can the United States control its borders? What about increased problems of morale and corruption within the INS? Can the United States maintain rights and liberties, yet search out and control the undocumented alien influx? Is bilingualism successful or will it contribute to separatism? What is the economic impact of immigration?

Milton Morris, the director of research for the Joint Center for Political Studies in Washington, D.C., recently pointed out the anomaly implicit in our national attitude toward immigration policy: "We are opposed to illegal immigration in principle, but we really object to the idea of the INS arresting some hardworking guy and taking away his chance to make a living" (*Wall Street Journal*, May 9, 1985:1). The war against illegal immigration often makes the INS an unpopular agency in a nation that proudly sees itself as a melting pot. *By keeping the INS weak we are simultaneously able to pursue two contradictory immigration policies: a stated policy of selective immigration, and an actual one of quite liberal immigration.* The very vagueness of some of the language of the Immigration Reform and Control Act of 1986, which seems to have been essential for its successful passage, retains the status of ambiguity in immigration policy.

And for those who do enter legally the INS has been unable to ensure that they obey the terms of their visas. The United States was embarrassed greatly by the deficiencies of the INS's recordkeeping during the Iranian hostage crisis in 1979. The President and the nation were shocked to learn that the INS didn't even know how many Iranian students were living here, let alone how many were doing so illegally. A good number of the Iranians that the INS identified as subject to deportation simply failed to attend deportation hearings or to leave the United States when told to do so (*Wall Street Journal*, May 9, 1985: 7; Crewdson: 117). The number of visa overstayers has been estimated to be in the several hundreds of thousands.

Problems of corruption flow naturally from the tremendous pressures for immigration coupled with restrictions of legal immigration and the inefficiency of the INS. Nor is the problem limited to the INS. The State Department and immigration lawyers share in the extensive nature of corruption associated with the whole immigration process.

Ambiguities in the new law and the lack of a secure and settled system of "documentation" for those who can be here legally and those who can work legally are likely to exacerbate, at least temporarily, problems of document fraud.

The underfunding of the INS compels it to engage in various secondary enforcement activities to locate illegal entrants: stopping traffic at checkpoints, watching air, bus, and rail terminals, inspecting farms, ranches, and areas of employment, and following up on specific leads. Such activities, however, pose more problems regarding the civil rights of individuals and numerous instances occur where such rights are likely to be abused. Enforcement begins to take on a perverse quality—we apprehend and return those aliens who are truthful; the ones who avoid apprehension and remain among us are the ones most likely to be those who can successfully dissemble (Bennett: 8). The 1986 law does increase funding and staffing for the Border Patrol but probably still insufficiently so to substantially reduce this aspect of the problem.

Another problem the current heavy immigration influx raises is the fear that the newcomers will be increasingly unassimilable. A central aspect of that concern is the growing program of bilingualism. More than 1.3 million students are currently enrolled in U.S. schools in federal, state, and local programs that provide instruction in their native tongues. These programs spring from the federal Bilingual Education Act of 1968.

By far the most controversial problem, however, the one that has stirred the greatest debate, has been the economic impact of immigration, particularly of the illegal influx. There are scholars and interests aligned on both sides of this hotly debated issue.[1]

Virtually all of the experts agree that illegal immigration is a boon for employers and consumers. Lower labor costs enable a business to be more competitive, earn healthier profits, and pass along some of those benefits to the consumer in the form of lower prices. All agree that illegal immigrants compete for many jobs involving unskilled labor—hurting some while benefiting others. The heated debate is over how many are hurt and how badly, against how much others are benefited.

Studies of the net impact of immigration on government finance are both sketchy and contradictory. A 1980 study by the Urban Institute found that California spent an average $3,254 on each Mexican immigrant household, both legal and illegal, in Los Angeles, and received only $1,515 in tax revenues in return. But a 1982/83 study by Weintraub indicated that Texas receives about three times as much revenue from illegal aliens as it spends on them. The Rand study found that fewer than 5 percent of California's Mexican immigrants were receiving any form of public assistance in 1980. This compares to an all-adult, statewide figure of 12 percent. Mexican immigrants' contribution to public revenues exceeds the cost of their service usage with the sole exception of education. The study concluded that they contributed less than the $2,900 it costs per year to educate a public school student largely because of their low income levels and the relative youth of the immigrants and their children (McCarthy and Valdez, May 1986).

Some of the confusion in this assessment is the result of using different methodologies and economic assumptions in the various analytical studies. The picture that emerges from actual jobs uncovered by INS sweeps substantiates that the impact is at the lower level of jobs and probably is concentrated in largely "undesirable" jobs. Such sweeps are, however, no doubt skewed samples of the total job displacement picture.

Nor is it so clear that illegals "drive down" wages. In those industries where alien workers are most heavily concentrated wages may already be about as high as they can realistically go. Some economists, like John Kenneth Galbraith and Marvin Smith, argue that such jobs are being filled at what is an "economical wage"—that is, a wage low enough to allow the employer to make a profit. When an employer is faced with the loss of cheap labor, there are other options besides raising wages to be considered: replacing workers with machines, moving the operation overseas, or simply going out of business. When the Bracero Program ended in California, only the lettuce and citrus growers raised their wages in an attempt to attract domestic workers. The tomato growers began using mechanical harvesters, the asparagus growers moved to Mexico, and marginal growers in all crops simply closed down and sold their farms.

Economist Walter Fogel counters, however, that the current inflow of undocumented aliens exacerbates the job and income problems of blacks, Hispanics, and other secondary-job market workers by reducing the number of such jobs available to them, depressing wages for those jobs they do hold, and generally undercutting working conditions as well (*The Unavoidable Issue:* 88).

RECENT PROPOSALS TO REVISE IMMIGRATION LAW

These problems, real or perceived, have led to several proposals to reform immigration law. Heightened concern over immigration-related problems was evident by the late 1970s, as demonstrated by media coverage and the number of federal task forces, committees, and commissions. During the 1970s immigration policy was the subject of five interagency task forces or cabinet committees in the executive branch. By the late 1970s the Carter Administration introduced a version of a Representative Peter Rodino bill, which contained a provision for employer sanctions and legalization. Both pro- and anti-immigration forces opposed the bill, however, and it never reached the floor (*National Journal*, March 7, 1981: 390). In 1978, Senator Edward Kennedy sponsored a proposal entitled "Contiguous Neighbors Act of 1978." It provided for more than doubling the legal ceiling on Mexican immigration within overall U.S. immigration, aspects of which were later incorporated in the Simpson–Mazzoli Bill (Teitelbaum, 1985: 41). Also in 1978, President Carter and Congress reacted by creating the Select Commission on Immigration and Refugee Policy to study the issue (Peters and Vega, 1986: 9; and Cornelius and Montoya: 33–34). In 1979, Congress established the Select Commission on Immigration and Refugee Policy.

The commission essentially recommended "closing the back door" to undocumented immigration while opening slightly the front door to accommodate more legal immigration, defining our immigration goals more clearly, and providing a more effective structure to implement them by setting forth procedures that would lead to fair and efficient adjudication and administration of U.S. immigration laws (*Final Report*, SCIRP). It maintained that immigration unquestionably served humanitarian needs, and that continued immigration was in the national interest. While the commission stated immigration entailed many benefits to U.S. society, it recognized our limited ability to absorb large numbers effectively. They held that "it is not the time for large-scale expansion in legal immigration, for resident aliens or temporary workers, because the first order of priority is in bringing undocumented/illegal immigration under control, while setting up a rational system for legal immigration." The commission recommended a "modest increase in legal immigration sufficient to expedite the clearance of backlogs—mainly to reunify families" (Introduction to the Final Report, SCIRP).

On March 6, 1981, President Reagan established a Task Force on Immigration and Refugee Policy. Chaired by the attorney general, the Task Force presented its recommendations to the President at three meetings in July 1981.

By late 1981, the House and Senate Judiciary Subcommittees on Immigration had finished their respective hearings on the Reagan proposal [S1765, HR4832]. The Chairmen of these subcommittees, Senator Alan Simpson (R.-WY) and Congressman Romano Mazzoli (D.-KY) emerged as the major proponents of the immigration reform issue. Virtually all the proposals since then have been variations of their bill—the Immigration Reform and Control Act of 1982.[2] That bill died in Congress in 1982, was re-introduced in 1983, and passed—in somewhat different versions in each House—in 1984.

The Simpson-Mazzoli Bill itself compromised the earlier Reagan proposal by including no provision for a guestworker program, substituting instead an expanded and streamlined version of the H–2 program with which it was deemed easier for employers to import temporary agricultural workers from Mexico. The 1982 bill incorporated the administrative rules that the Department of Labor used in the H–2 program during the years following the termination of the Bracero

Program. In committee, however, congressmen sympathetic to employer interests succeeded in incorporating changes designed to open up the flow of legal temporary labor through the H–2 channel, should other provisions in the proposed law effectively cut off the supply of undocumented workers. The Senate rejected an amendment proposed by Senator Hayakawa that would have included a large-scale guestworker program as well as one by Senator Kennedy that would have retained the H–2 program as it was. The bill that ultimately passed the Senate contained several provisions that would have affected the number and type of H–2 workers entering the United States for temporary employment, enabling a greatly expanded temporary worker program. The Senate version of the bill would also have greatly restricted the role of the Department of Labor (DoL) in the certification process. The 1982 bill would have converted the DoL certification from its current advisory status to a mandatory requirement. By eliminating this aspect, the Senate version allowed for the possibility that the INS, an agency less sensitive to domestic labor conditions, could ignore or overrule the DoL recommendations (see Cornelius and Montoya: 133).

In 1984, election-year pressure resulted in the Congress failing to find a compromise version for the two bills, and the measure died in Conference Committee, principally being stalled by Democratic opposition.[3]

In May 1985, Senator Simpson introduced a new version of his bill, this time without the co-sponsorship of Rep. Mazzoli, who declined to sponsor the bill without support from the Democratic House leadership and from the black and Hispanic legislative caucuses, all of whom strenuously opposed it.

Simpson's stated major goal for his new bill was to produce a compromise that would finally pass Congress (*Time*, July 8, 1985; see also "Simpson Tackles Immigration Reform Again," *Minneapolis Star and Tribune*, Monday, June 24, 1985: 10A). Such compromise was not then to be forthcoming.

Congressman Peter Rodino (D.-NJ), the influential chairman of the House Judiciary Committee, introduced legislation co-sponsored by Representative Romano Mazzoli (D.-KY) in July 1985 that was similar to the compromise version that died in the final days of 1984's conference committee. The Rodino–Mazzoli measure provided civil and criminal penalties for employers who knowingly hire illegal aliens and amnesty for illegals who arrived before 1982. To discourage discrimination against Hispanics, the bill created an Office of Special Counsel in the Justice Department, empowered to investigate and prosecute civil rights violators. Like the Simpson bill in the Senate, the Rodino–Mazzoli bill also strengthened the enforcement of immigration laws by increasing funding for the Immigration and Naturalization Service ("Immigration Issue Heats Up Again," *Washington Post*, July 28, 1985: A15).

Hispanic groups and the American Civil Liberties Union opposed both the House and Senate versions of the bill. Working through the Hispanic Congressional Caucus and the Black Congressional Caucus, they opposed the employer-sanction approach, fearing it would inevitably lead to increased discrimination against all Hispanics. In 1985, the Senate Judiciary Committee rejected all attempts by Senate Democrats to make the Senate version of the bill more like the House version.[4]

The Passage of the 1986 Act

After the Conference Committee was unable to agree on a compromise version of the bill, it seemed to be an issue on which the bill was "a corpse going to the morgue."[5] Simpson re-introduced his bill, which the Senate passed for a third time in September 1985. The House once again left the bill open to tinkering by submitting its version of the bill to six committees (see Peters and Vega).

The Judiciary Committee seemed deadlocked over the farm worker provision. It did not complete its drafting of the bill until the end of June, and then five other committees worked on it throughout the summer. When the House, late in September 1986, rejected a rule for considering a bill [HR3810], immigration reform seemed once again a dead issue (*New York Times*, October 13, 1986: A−16).

A small group of House members long involved with the issue, however, refused to let it die. Led by Rep. Charles E. Schumer (D.-NY), they put the pieces back together again. Rep. Rodino, chairman of the Judiciary Committee, and Hamilton Fish, Jr., its ranking Republican, aided Schumer in working out a compromise. Schumer met with Representative Howard Berman (D.-CA) and Leon Panetta (D.-CA) and the three hammered out a key aspect of the new compromise—the temporary farm workers provision. Extensive discussions with Rep. Dan Lungren (R.-CA), the ranking Republican, and Romano Mazzoli, the chairman of the Judiciary Immigration, Refugees and International Law Subcommittee, resulted in further fine-tuning of the bill's provisions. After the House members agreed on the new package of provisions—including numerous points designed to protect the rights of the temporary workers—they secured Senator Simpson's support as well.

In 1986 Congress was in a better mood to pass some sort of immigration law than in any previous year. As the Mexican economy deteriorated late in 1985 and early 1986, and the peso plunged in value, the INS caught a record number of illegal aliens attempting to cross. Their apprehensions rose by 31 percent during the fiscal year, to 1.8 million. The growing conservative mood of the country seemed to convince liberal opponents of the bill that continued resistance would only lead to even stricter legislation in 1987.

A key shift came when the Hispanic Caucus split on the bill—with five members supporting the new package and six opposing it. That split also enabled the Black Congressional Caucus to split on the bill. Reps. Robert Garcia (D.-NY) and Edward Roybal (D.-CA) continued to lead the opposition to the bill. Reps. Esteban Torres (D.-CA), chairman of the Hispanic Caucus, and Albert Bustamente (D.-TX), its vice-chairman, both voted for it.

The compromise on the temporary farm worker provision negotiated by Rep. Schumer also split the opposition among the growers. His compromise served to meet the demands among Western fruit and vegetable growers for foreign workers while allowing for sufficient protection of the workers against likely exploitation so as to win over enough of the Hispanic/liberal/union votes in Congress to allow passage of the bill. Rep. Schumer described the new bill as "a left-center bill," in contrast to the "right-center" version killed by the House Democrats in 1984. At that time they opposed it by a margin of 138 to 125. In the October 1986 vote, Democrats supported it by a vote of 168 to 61. The House passed the new compromise version on October 9, 1986 by a margin of 230 to 166 (*C.Q. Weekly Report*, October 18, 1986: 2612). Passage by the House once again necessitated a Conference Committee to make adjustments between the two differing versions.

The 1986 Conference Committee agreed on a series of compromises to settle those differences. The House agreed to the Senate version without the automatic end to sanctions in exchange for Senate provisions requiring Congress to review the program within three years, at which time the program could be terminated by joint resolution if the comptroller general determined that the employer sanction program had resulted in discrimination. The House also agreed to give up the Moakley provisions on Salvadorans and Nicaraguans in return for an administration pledge not to deport any Salvadorans to areas stricken by an October 1986 earthquake. In addition, Chairman Rodino promised to consider a bill on the subject early in the 100th Congress and Senator Simpson promised that he would not prevent Senate consideration of such a bill if it passed the House. The Senate agreed to accept the Frank anti-discrimination provisions and accepted, in slightly modified form, the free legal representation for H–2 workers. It was understood that such legal work would apply only to job-related problems such as wages, hours, and work conditions. The funding issue was resolved with a $1 billion appropriation for the next four years, with unspent money in one year being available in the following year. Any unused money at the end of fiscal 1990 could be carried over through fiscal 1994. The compromise funding version further specified that the amount of government payments for Social Security supplements and Medicaid would be deducted from the $1 billion appropriation. Finally, the Senate agreed to the House version of the amnesty program's starting date, that is, January 1, 1982.

The bill's tangled history helped make these compromises possible in 1986. Increased concern with the immigration problem meant that nearly everyone involved wanted a bill of some kind to pass. Previous fights meant that there was less need for "political posturing" this time. Congress desperately wanted to recess for the up-coming elections. The Conferees "didn't want to do this again" (*C.Q. Weekly Report*, October 18, 1986: 2596). In the words of Rep. Mazzoli, who urged its final passage: "It's not a perfect bill, but it's the least imperfect bill we will ever have before us" (*Washington Post*, Thursday, October 16, 1986: A–5).

The House passed the measure by a vote of 238 to 173 on Wednesday, October

15, 1986. The Senate approved it by a vote of 63 to 24 on Friday, October 17, 1986. President Reagan signed the bill into law on November 6, 1986.

CONCLUSION

What conclusions and assessments can be drawn, then, from this historical review and analysis of U.S. immigration policy? As in the past, the new immigration law involved achieving a new balance on the four main elements of immigration policy: economic, racial, nationalistic, and foreign policy.

Answering the questions of how effective the 1986 law is likely to be is a difficult task.[6] Certainly this review of the history of immigration policy enables one to predict one thing with a fair degree of certainty: that this major revision, as have all those enacted in the past, will surely have some unforeseen consequences, which will create new problems that will in turn sow the seeds for the next revision.

Critics note that what is being sold as a measure to punish employers will in fact more likely end up punishing workers. The bulk of research on employer sanctions indicates that they are at best ineffective, and at worst exacerbate the exploitability of both documented and undocumented workers. Initial reaction to the new law and to confusion over the rules adopted by the INS to implement the law have led to some instances of such abuse.[7]

The optimistic assessment of the ability of the "employer sanction" method for cutting down on illegal immigration, such as the one expressed by INS Commissioner Nelson, holds that such employer sanctions are essential to cutting off the immigration flow. Proponents of the approach argue that such a law may be relatively self-enforcing, much like the 55 mph speed limit with which they maintain, most motorists comply. They feel such a provision will significantly reduce the job magnet that now draws so many across the border. There are indications that some employers are, indeed, voluntarily complying with the law and actively cooperating with the INS. Other employers, however, are clearly willing to and actually breaking the new law.[8]

This author feels such a view is unrealistically optimistic. To use their analogy, those who economically gain from breaking the 55 mph speed limit (e.g., truckers) notoriously fail to obey it. The employer sanctions provision is much more likely just to give a boost to the phony-document industry.[9] It is, indeed, "no more likely to be effective than tough penalties have been in curbing the U.S. market for cocaine" (*Time*, July 8, 1985).

The employer sanctions provision exemplifies the failure of a policy to spell out procedures. It is weakened by the fact that its mechanism for enforcement, some sort of a secure worker-identification system, is left largely unspecified. The decision that we need a secure system for worker-identification is not enough. A clear method must be spelled out. We have a consensus to reduce unemployment, too, but we still often suffer from unacceptably high unemployment. The method chosen to ensure a "secure worker-identification" system will have major implications for various aspects of our national life. It will affect employment discrimination, the extent of document fraud, and even the integrity of various official documents issued, such as birth certificates and passports, and the cost of the system to employers. Many fear it will likely adversely affect civil liberties (see, for example, the *New York Times*, 1/15/87 and 2/21/87).

A review of how employer-sanctions laws have fared at the state level, or how successfully or not they have been used by other nations that have adopted them, would indicate that pessimistic assessments are more readily drawn from these experiences than are optimistic ones.

Eleven states and one city have passed employer sanction statutes since 1971. The main pattern that emerges from a study of the results of these state and local laws is of an almost perfectly consistent failure to enforce such sanctions. In large measure, the failure to enforce stems from the legal constraints imposed by the courts, which have consistently enjoined or discouraged agencies from administering the laws for a wide variety of constitutional and statutory reasons, including the employment rights of undocumented workers, the lack of proof that employers "knowingly" hired such workers, violations of Fourth Amendment protections against unreasonable search and seizure, and discrimination against aliens "authorized to work" by federal regulations even though they may not be "lawful residents" of the United States. Whether or not the new law's rather copious attempts to specify "guarantees" against such discrimination will be sufficient to avoid such legal challenge remains to be seen. Most probably, they will engender a good bit of judicial proceedings.[10]

The employer sanctions provision essentially makes the employer an immigration agent. But the lack of a clear method to ensure proper documentation leaves the employer on the horns of a dilemma. Under-zealous compliance could lead to fines and penalties being imposed. Yet overzealousness could lead to massive civil rights violations of due process and the citizens' rights to privacy. The new law is likely to develop a whole new line of case and administrative law from complaints by racial and ethnic groups of discrimination against the employer instead of the INS (*Washington Post*, 8/23/87:A–19).

Even though states that have large concentrations of undocumented aliens have passed such laws, employer penalties have not reduced the hiring of illegal immigrants and have often created additional problems. In California, not a single person has ever been convicted under the employer sanction law first passed in 1971. Nationwide, such state laws have only resulted in five convictions (Cornelius and Montoya, 1983: 143).

A major General Accounting Office report found in all 20 countries it surveyed that had national employer sanctions laws that such laws were not an effective deterrent to illegal employment, since employers were either able to evade responsibility or, when apprehended, were penalized too lightly to be deterred. Judges did not seem to treat employment of undocumented workers as a serious crime and were reluctant to impose penalties; the study also found that the more severe the penalty, the less likely it was to be applied, especially criminal fines and jail sentences (G.A.O., 1982; see also, Hammar, 1985; Krane, 1979; and Miller and Martin, 1982).

Such a review of state, local, and other nations' experiences with the employer sanctions approach on balance seems to indicate the following expectations. They are far easier to legislate than to enforce. They are not likely to work. They are likely to be expensive to administer and enforce. They may subject the undocumented to even more exploitation. They may result in discrimination against certain ethnic groups. They create a significant potential for abuse.

Insofar as employer sanctions are likely to fail to deter the employer, they are not likely to reduce illegal immigration. Far from reducing the number of such illegal aliens, the new law may ironically create a double "criminalization" of undocumented workers. To get a job now the immigrant will have to cross the border without papers and will also have to present the employer with bogus documents. Such workers will thus be even more vulnerable, potentially more susceptible to implicit or explicit blackmail by their employers. It is, indeed, predictable that the undocumented workers, and in some cases even the documented ones, will pay a price for the new legislation. Initially they will likely pay by layoffs, wage reductions, and up-front payment at the terms of employment. The employees will pay for the greater "risk" their employers assume in hiring them.

Thus the new law represents a compromise that allows for the reinforcement of anti-immigrant sentiment while avoiding any real change in the economic reality of immigrant employment.

The Mexican population is growing exponentially—at an annual rate of 3.2 percent, compared to the 0.9 percent annual growth rate of the United States. Mexican per capita income is $740, while the U.S. per capita income is over $6,000. Demographic projections estimate that Mexico will double its population every 20 years, reaching 150 million by the turn of the century. The political instability in Central America is likely to push migration northward, further increasing pressure on Mexico. Clearly, it will become increasingly attractive to cross the Rio Grande, legally or illegally, and work for whatever wages are available, as even the lowest U.S. wages will be far above those in Mexico. A number of scholars and Mexican politicians predict the new law will fail to stem the flow and may further strain U.S./Mexican, and possibly even U.S./Canadian relations.[11]

The special seasonal agricultural workers provision provides for up to 350,000 aliens who could prove that they have lived in the United States for at least three years and who could prove they had worked at least 90 days in U.S. agriculture in each of those years to qualify for temporary resident alien status. They could become permanent residents after two years. They would not have to remain in such agricultural jobs after they have received their temporary status. This essentially creates a whole new category of legal immigration, and a sizable one at that. Children born of such immigrants here in the United States will, of course, be citizens. The potential impact of this provision is far-reaching and was little-studied. Inasmuch as the provision allows for a "replenishment" of such farm labor for up to seven years, it will prove to be one of the most significant aspects of the new law in its impact on the nation's economy, immigration policy, and the relationship between this new way to legally migrate to the United States and other past ways. It certainly raises questions of justice or equity in the immigration policy inasmuch as other persons seeking entry who have patiently waited for many years to receive legal permission to do so are essentially now being "end-runned" by those temporary workers who came here illegally and within the last three years and have only worked for 90 days in agriculture (see *Newsweek*, 11/17/86: 12; Cohodas: 838–841).

Other critics fault the law on its legalization provisions. The amnesty provision is yet another example of a policy goal being stated with vague specifications as to the mechanisms to implement the goal. The amnesty proposal had strong political support. But the new law's legalization effort will necessarily require considerable intergovernmental cooperation and coordination with the private sector. Initial indications are that the manner in which the INS has decided to implement that process will pose severe problems for state and local government officials and has raised some opposition from local governments.[12] Yet the aspects of such a program have to be worked out. How many aliens will actually come forward to claim legalization is anyone's guess. The spur of phony documents to "prove" residency prior to 1982 is likely to be immense.[13]

Critics of the new law, which includes some in Congress who voted for it, have also faulted the INS decision to charge the immigrants fees to cover the cost of the legalization process. Those fees range from $185 to $420, with some families having to pay up to an additional $700 for medical exams. Additional medical costs will now be added in that they will now have to take (and, of course, pay for) an AIDS test.[14]

Likewise, the new law virtually ignores the entire area of naturalization law, the "stepchild of immigration policy," that as always, still needs attention.[15]

Another potential problem area involves the asylum issue and illustrates the elaboration of detailed procedures without stating a corresponding policy goal. What is the purpose of the new asylum procedures? Under what circumstances does the U.S. view itself as the country of first asylum? Having specifically trained people and elaborately detailed procedures to process asylum applicants does not constitute a policy response to the challenges to the very notion of asylum and refuge, nor do they imply policy to guide the nation on how to deal with instances of mass forced migration. Such movements constitute an assault on current international law and on the international apparatus of response to refugee emergencies. The elaboration of detailed procedures at least implies that the intention of the drafters of the new law was that the new asylum officers and procedures are really put forth in order to discourage applications for asylum.

The new law does involve increases in spending to improve the enforcement capability of the Border Patrol and the INS, and additional allocations to carry out the added duties for the INS imposed by the law. It does not, however, contain the degree of improvement warranted by the current status of the INS and the Border Patrol. Both need vastly improved levels of performance just to be brought into the 20th century. The lack of adequate computerization of recordkeeping, analysis of immigration data, and the correlation of such information is monumental (see Milton Morris or John Crewdson).

While the 1986 law entails some effort at upgrading the services, such improvements as are included remain far less than what seems so apparently necessary (see, for example, *Washington Post*, 9/28/87: A–18, and 7/26/87:21; and Morris: 144–145).

Although the data are still too tentative to assess the success of the new law in slowing the tide of illegals by an economic disincentive approach, the numbers to date seem to point toward a failure in that regard. Initially the numbers seemed to drop off markedly—a 27 percent drop within the first few months (*The Economist*: 22; *Washington Post*, 10/18/87:D1,4). Moreover, a shift toward increased illegals fleeing from the United States to Canada was also noted in the first few months after the new law was passed (*New York Times*, 2/21/87:30; *Cumberland Sunday Times*, 10/25/87: A–7). But after that drop-off in the initial months, the numbers of illegals entering the United States began to rise again. By mid-summer the estimated number of illegals entering the United States reached a record level (*Cumberland Times*, 8/25/87:A–7; *Milwaukee Journal*, 7/12/87: 1; *Cumberland Times/News*, 9/10/87: 14). So, too, the number of illegals applying for amnesty has been far less than anticipated. By the end of 1987 about one million had applied, but an estimated 2–3 million remained in hiding (*New York Times*, 11/6/87).

It would seem more productive to affect the immigration problems discussed here by upgrading fair labor standards. Such an approach would tend to make many jobs now held by illegal aliens more competitive, and would thereby deter illegal immigrants from entering the U.S. labor market by reducing the economic incentive to hire them. This would be especially the case in urban commerce, where the FLSA and comparable state laws apply more rigorously nationwide. The natural deterrence through the competitive forces of the free labor market seems to be at least as promising as attempting to militarize our borders or making the INS a "hit squad" against U.S. businessmen (Cornelius and Montoya, 1983: 97).

In the final analysis, then, this historical review of immigration policy leads one to conclude that the new law is simply unlikely to work. The compromises, ambiguities, and vague language necessary to get the bill enacted into law contain the very seeds of the law's own problems. Those problems will ultimately result, a decade or two hence, in the need for a new revision in U.S. immigration policy that will once again set off a "new phase" to replace what one might now call "the Revolving-Door Era" of U.S. immigration policy. [See Appendix III for a summary of the major provisions of the 1986 Immigration Reform and Control Act as highlighted by the *Congressional Quarterly Weekly Report*.]

NOTES

1. For a detailed discussion of the economic impact issue, see Kritz (ed.): 191–285; Chiswick (ed.): 251–358; Cornelius and Montoya, 1983; and North, 1978 and 1980. Additional viewpoints and elaborations on how to measure the labor impact are provided by: Bonacich, 1976: 34–41; Piore, 1979; and Geschwender, 1978.

2. See: H.R. 1510 and S. 2222; Peters and Vega, 1986: 10.

3. See: *Congressional Quarterly Weekly Report*, October 18, 1986: 2595; Hart: 8; Villarreal, 1985; *Time*, July 8, 1985.

4. See: "Trying to Stem the Illegal Tide," *Time*, July 8, 1985, Special Edition Section; "Immigration Legislation Voted Down," *Cumberland News*, September 14, 1985: A1; "Immigration Issue Heats Up Again," *Washington Post*, Sunday, July 28, 1985: 8; Jeffrey Hart, "Illegal Immigration," *Cumberland Evening Times*, Monday, July 22, 1985: 8; "Simpson Tackles Immigration Reform Again," *Minneapolis Star and Tribune*, Monday, June 24, 1985: 10A; and "Immigration Reform Elusive Goal," *Minneapolis Star and Tribune*, Monday, June 24, 1985, 10A.

5. See "Immigration Bill: How a 'Corpse' Came Back to Life," *New York Times*, Monday, October 13, 1986: A–16; *Congressional Quarterly Weekly Report*, October 18, 1986: 2595–2596; "Conferees Agree on Vast Revisions in Laws on Aliens," *New York Times*, Wednesday, October 15, 1986: A–1, B–11; and "House Passes Compromise Immigration Bill," *Washington Post*, Thursday, October 16, 1986: A–5; "Hill Revises Immigration Law," *Washington Post*, Saturday, October 18, 1986: A–1, 7–8.

6. For a thorough critique of the problems and prospects of the Simpson–Mazzoli approach, see: U.S. Commission on Civil Rights, *The Tarnished Door* (Washington, D.C.: U.S. Government Printing Office, September 1980); Cornelius and Montoya (1983); Chiswick (1982); Kritz (1983); Morris (1985); Papademetriou and Miller (1984); and Glazer (1985).

7. "Abuse of Immigration Law Feared by Some Hispanic Groups," *New York Times*, March 1, 1987: 31; "Immigration Law Backer Declares Success Amid Others' Doubts," *Washington Post*, November 6, 1987: A–12; Nadine Cohodas, "Immigration Law Brings Anxiety, Ambiguity," *Congressional Quarterly*, May 2, 1987: 838–841; "Immigration Rules Called Hard on Poor," *Washington Post*, April 9, 1987: A–22; "New Law Leaves Immigrants Confused and Fearful," *New York Times*, February 21, 1987: 29; "New Rules for a Human Tide," *The Economist*, January 17, 1987: 29; "State Panel Faults Enforcement of New Federal Immigration Law," *New York Times*, March 16, 1987: 15; "Suit Alleges Amnesty Law Puts Many Aliens in Limbo," *New York Times*, February 7, 1987: 6.

8. "Illegals Fill Day Care Jobs," *Washington Post*, August 16, 1987: A–1, 16; "Eight Maryland Companies Cited for Illegal Alien Violations," *Cumberland Times/News*, Monday, November 30, 1987: 3; "Immigration Reform, Control Act Impacts Farmers in the State," *Cumberland Times/News*, Thursday, September 24, 1987: 14; "Maryland Growers Assisting with New Immigration Laws," *Cumberland Sunday Times*, July 19, 1987: C–12; Alan Weisman, "Mexican Hearts, California Dreams," *Los Angeles Times Magazine*, September 7, 1987: 7–28.

9. See, for example: "Amnesty Program Means Phony Document Business Will Flourish," *Cumberland Sunday Times*, Sunday, November 2, 1986: A–16; "Reaction to Immigration Bill Is Sharply Split," *New York Times*, Thursday, October 16, 1986: B–

15; "Surge in Bogus Papers Predicted in Wake of Change in Alien Law," *New York Times*, Monday, October 20, 1986: A–1, 24; and "Immigration Reform: A Mess on the Border," *Newsweek*, December 22, 1986: 27.

10. See Carl Schwarz's analysis in Cornelius and Montoya: 83–97. See also: "Immigration Rules Called Hard on Poor," *Washington Post*, April 9, 1987: A–22; "State Panel Faults Enforcement of New Federal Immigration Law," *New York Times*, March 16, 1987: 15; "Suit Alleges Amnesty Law Puts Many Aliens in Limbo," *New York Times*, February 7, 1987: 6; "Waiting Anxiously: Amnesty Seekers Hope to Prevent Family Separation," *Dallas Morning News*, January 4, 1988: A–13, 15.

11. "U.S. Immigration Bill Assailed," *New York Times*, Sunday, October 19, 1986: A–12; "Illegal Migration's Fact of Life, Study Concludes," *Washington Post*, November 15, 1987: 18; Douglas Massey, "Understanding Mexican Migration to the United States," *American Journal of Sociology* 92 (May 1987): 1372–1403; Alan Weisman, "Mexican Hearts, California Dreams," *Los Angeles Times Magazine*, September 7, 1987: 7–28; "Immigration Law Alone Can't Work," *Chicago Sun-Times*, April 10, 1987: 1.

12. "Immigration Rules Called Hard on Poor," *Washington Post*, April 9, 1987: A–22; "Immigration Law Alone Can't Work," *Chicago Sun-Times*, April 10, 1987: 42; "State Panel Faults Enforcement of New Federal Immigration Law," *New York Times*, March 16, 1987; "Immigration Law Brings Anxiety, Ambiguity," *Congressional Quarterly*, May 2, 1987: 838, 840; "Successes Outweigh Failures in First Year of Amnesty Program," *Washington Post*, November 6, 1987: A–13.

13. "Trying to Reform the Border," *Newsweek*, October 27, 1986: 32, 35; "Abuse of Immigration Law Feared by Some Hispanic Groups," *New York Times*, March 1, 1987: 31; "Aliens Facing $185 Fee on Amnesty," *New York Times*, March 16, 1987: 15; "A Push to Delay Deportation of Aliens," *Washington Post*, July 26, 1987: 4; "New Law Leaves Immigrants Confused and Fearful," *New York Times*, February 21, 1987: 29; "Amnesty Sending Fearful Aliens for Help, Only Some of It Useful," *New York Times*, January 15, 1987: A–1; "Successes Outweigh Failures in First Year of Amnesty Program," *Washington Post*, November 6, 1987; Nadine Cohodas, "Immigration Law Brings Anxiety, Ambiguity," *Congressional Quarterly*, May 2, 1987: 838–841.

14. See, for example, *The Economist*, January 17, 1987: 29; *New York Times*, March 16, 1987: A–15; *Cumberland Times/News*, September 29, 1987: 2.

15. Cornelius and Montoya: 37–82; D. Bennett, 1985; Franklin, 1969; Weissbrodt, 1984.

2

Australian Immigration Policy and Politics

GREGORY TOBIN

At first sight, there are obvious similarities between the Australian immigration experience and that of the United States. Both societies had their origins in British colonizing activity, and both share lines of connection with British legal and political traditions. Both received the bulk of their immigrants from the British Isles during their years as colonial dependencies, and continued to draw on Britain as a source of population long after they established an independent national identity. Both have seen the Anglo-Saxon core of population augmented by large inflows of immigrants from Central, Southern, and Eastern Europe, and by smaller contingents from Asia. Both have in recent years confronted the problem of the unplanned movement of refugees, and both are currently debating such issues as the maintenance of ethnic identity and the relationship between immigration policy and the broader public interest.

Beneath these apparent similarities, however, there are profound contrasts, which can be traced to the different circumstances under which the two societies originated and to the simple facts of geography. The British government established its first colony on the eastern seaboard of the continent then known as New Holland in 1788, at a time when their former colonists in North America were preparing to launch a Federal Republic. A little more than a century later, the six Australian colonies were in the process of drafting their own Federal Constitution at the time when the United States and Spain were becoming embroiled in conflict over Cuba and when the United States had become an imperial power in its own right. For Australians, the colonial period extends from 1788 to 1901, and the National government dates from 1901. The Commonwealth of Australia came into existence in that year as a federation of six states with a combined population of 3.7 million, a figure not very different from that with which the United States entered the previous century. Unlike their American cousins, the Australian colonies arrived at national status without having to leave the British Empire, establishing the kind of constitutional relationship that some had canvassed as a possible solution to the crisis in the American colonies in the 1770s. Prior to 1901, the British Government had given each of the colonies a considerable measure of autonomy, and the problem confronting those who drew up the constitution for the Australian Commonwealth was not so much the establishment of independence as the design of a workable federal system.

Having achieved independence without the need for a break with the Empire, Australia has continued to maintain close legal, constitutional, and cultural links with Britain and with the British Commonwealth of Nations: the Queen of England is also, in constitutional terms, the Queen of Australia, and both the Governor-General of the Commonwealth and the Governors of the individual states are representatives of the Crown. Effective authority, however, is vested in elected Parliaments at both the State and the Federal levels. Since World War II, changing economic and strategic realities have eroded the basis of the traditional relationship with Britain, and what remains is a rather technical constitutional bond operating alongside deeply rooted social and cultural ties.

The timing and nature of Australia's political development constitutes one major element of contrast with the American experience; but even more central to that contrast has been what one Australian historian has described as ''the tyranny of distance.'' Even in the late twentieth century, the journey from Europe to Australia is tiring and time consuming. In the first half of the nineteenth century it was a major test of endurance, and one that could last for up to six months in the age of sail. It involved distances some four times greater than those across the North Atlantic, and subjected emigrants to extremes of climate and to long periods without the relief of landfall, with the prospect of shipwreck a very real one if vessels had to make their final approach to Bass Strait in poor weather. The fact that the British government supervised the emigrant ships heading for the Pacific more closely than those involved in the Atlantic trade appears to have reduced the incidence of illness and death among those making the longer voyage. By the 1850s a relatively small number of emigrants could take advantage of the speed provided by clipper ships, and spent as few as seventy days at sea compared to the more usual hundred or more. The arrival of iron-hulled ships, auxiliary steam power, and the opening of the Suez Canal in 1869 reduced the hazards and the duration of the voyage to more manageable proportions; but for most nineteenth century emigrants, the voyage to the South Pacific was an awesome undertaking, and one that had to be considered as leading to permanent exile; the distances were so great that few could expect that they would ever be able to make the return voyage.[1]

Finally, the facts of political geography provide one other major element of contrast. Australia never had a contiguous border with any other nation; as an island continent, it requires no border police, and the only access is via the air or sea routes. If distance has ensured that immigration is more commonly induced rather than spontaneous, the isolation of the continent has also heightened the

Table 2.1.
Percentages of Foreign-born and Native-born in the Australian Population, 1829–1984.

Yr	Total Population ('000s)	Foreign Born (%)	Australian Born (%)
1828	36.6	76.2	23.8
1841	176.4	76.1	23.9
1846	220.7	64.7	35.3
1851	396.9	65.9	34.1
1861	1152.2	62.8	37.2
1871	1662.6	46.5	53.5
1881	2250.0	36.8	63.2
1891	3174.4	31.7	68.3
1901	3773.8	22.8	77.2
1911	4455.0	17.1	82.9
1921	5435.7	15.5	84.5
1933	6629.9	13.6	86.4
1947	7579.4	9.8	90.2
1954	8986.5	14.3	85.7
1961	10508.2	16.9	83.1
1971	12755.6	20.2	79.8
1981	14854.9	20.8	79.2
1984	15555.9	21.1	78.9

Note: 1828 excludes Van Diemen's Land; 1841 excludes South Australia and Western Australia; 1846 excludes Van Diemen's Land and Western Australia; 1851 excludes Western Australia.

local community's sense of its ability to control entry. Border-hopping has never been a problem for governments, and until the 1970s even refugees were usually people known only at a distance, people about whom decisions could be make while the individuals concerned were in holding camps in remote countries. Although vast areas of the northern coastline are still unsettled and unpoliced, and theoretically open to illegal entry, there appear to have been no examples of any substantial inflow. The unheralded arrival of Vietnamese boat people in the northern port of Darwin in the mid–1970s created great interest precisely because of the novelty of the event. Illegal immigrants have tended to be the few who enter as stowaways, or the much larger number who enter as visitors and overstay their visa entitlement. Few countries have enjoyed the luxury of such a level of control of the inflow of population from beyond their borders, and such a degree of detachment from the conflicts that have generated so many exiles and refugees—advantages that seem all the more ironic when seen in the context of the origins of the society that enjoys them. (See Table 2.1.)

THE COLONIAL PERIOD, 1788–1900

The Convict Era: 1788–1850

The isolation of Australia from the sources of emigration in both the nineteenth and twentieth centuries accounts for one of the most distinctive features of its immigration experience—the heavy involvement of government both at the British and at the Australian end. It had been that isolation that appealed to the British government in the 1780s when it was considering ways of disposing of the surplus of convicts generated by a criminal justice system that placed so much emphasis on capital punishment for relatively minor offenses that courts tended to award long prison sentences. The government's preference was for a new penal colony as isolated as possible from Britain and capable of becoming self-sufficient. Captain James Cook's great voyages of exploration in the 1770s indicated that the eastern seaboard of the Australian continent could support settlement, and there was no doubt about its remoteness from Britain. On January 26, 1788, just over a thousand convicts, marine guards, and some dependents assembled at Sydney Cove to hear the foundation governor, Captain Arthur Phillip of the Royal Navy, read the proclamation establishing the penal colony of New South Wales. These members of the First Fleet were later to be considered the founders of a new nation, the counterparts of the Virginia Company at Jamestown, the Pilgrim Fathers at Plymouth, or the Puritans at Massachusetts Bay. Immigrants they were, but not by choice; they were part of a government project, and although in years to come others would travel to the new land of their own volition, the scale of the logistical problems involved ensured that government—especially at the Australian end—remained more central to the process of immigration than was the case on the North Atlantic route.

The British had only a sketchy idea of the size and nature of the continent on whose eastern rim they had established a penal colony. It would be some years before navigators were able to sketch the outline of the great island mass, roughly equal in area to that of the continental United States, and it was to take the best part of a century for explorers to compile even an outline portrait of the land itself and its resources. What eventually emerged was less than encouraging; as much as a third of the continent was desert, and another third semi-arid. Only in the coastal regions was rainfall at all reliable, and even those fertile areas could be devastated by periodic drought. The soils were difficult for Europeans to manage, the seasons were reversed, the fauna and flora peculiar to European eyes. This was clearly not a land flowing with milk and honey, a European-style landscape tempting the deprived and the ambitious to start life over again in a new setting. Both the convicts and their jailers were quick to note how unresponsive this new land was to the limited farming techniques they brought with them, and their descriptions of New South Wales as a difficult and strange land compounded the already unfavorable image of the colony as a remote prison operating under a particularly severe and often brutal regime. In the early decades of the nineteenth century there was little incentive for free settlers to make the long voyage to the Pacific. It was not until 1793 that the first group of 11 such settlers arrived, and of the 77,000 individuals who arrived in the colony between 1788 and 1830, only 10 percent were free immigrants.[2]

Despite its early trials and tribulations, the tiny colony gradually began to develop some measure of self-sufficiency. The small groups of free settlers were joined by time-expired convicts unable or unwilling to return home, and by others given conditional release. Gradually they learned how to adapt English farming techniques to the demands of a very different environment, and as the colony slowly extended out from the first settlement at Sydney, it began to take on the character of a mixed agricultural settlement. The discovery of a staple commodity—wool—then effected the kind of economic transformation that Virginia had experienced in its second decade. The introduction of the Spanish Merino sheep, and the discovery that the breed flourished in the Australian environment, combined to provide the new colony with a product much in demand in Europe and capable of being produced in substantial quantities. The demand for access to the large tracts of land needed for grazing pushed the settlers across the barrier of the Blue Mountains west of Sydney, and by the mid-point of the century the basis of a pastoral and mixed farming economy had been established in the southeastern segment of the continent, with extensions to Tasmania, South Australia, West Australia, and Southern Queensland. Over the course of half a century, the original penal colony had evolved into a community large enough to be given a measure of self-government by the British government, and with branch settlements sufficiently developed to be considered as self-governing colonies in their own right. In the 1830s these slowly evolving societies had been joined by the colony of South Australia, a venture unconnected with the convict enterprise and intended as a model, planned colony for the benefit of British settlers of modest means and proper religious convictions.

The gradual evolution of a penal establishment into a group of self-governing colonies geared largely to a pastoral economy did little to enhance the attraction of this remote continent to British or European immigrants. Although the great sheep stations (ranches) were not labor intensive, the winding down of convict transportation gradually reduced the amount of convict labor that the Governor could assign to the large landholders. Pressure on the government produced a system by which the income from land sales could be used to pay the fares of immigrants from Britain, a system that was to be the first of the many "assisted immigration" schemes that have come to be characteristic of Australian immigration. From 1830 onwards, the intake of free immigrants increased, although few of those who arrived could be induced to accept the lonely existence of the sheepherder on distant sheep runs.[3] Most preferred to stay in the small towns and find work in the small manufacturing establishments that were beginning to develop as the overall population of the colonies increased. By 1850, the convict era was over, although in the case of Western Australia it did not formally end until the 1860s. By 1860, natural increase had replaced immigration as the major source of population growth. What had emerged in the Australian colonies was a group of viable communities, some of them quite prosperous, and able to consider themselves distinct entities within the larger British Empire.

The Impact of the Gold Rushes and Free Immigration: 1850–1900

The early 1850s saw a dramatic and unexpected shift in the colonial economy and in the structure of the population. The discovery of gold in California had attracted some prospectors from the Australian colonies, and at least one of them realized that the gold-bearing terrain he came to know in California reminded him of areas he had seen in Australia. On his return, that recognition led to the discovery of gold near Bathurst, New South Wales, in early 1851, which was followed by even larger discoveries in the colony of Victoria, only recently separated from New South Wales. The gold rushes that followed proved to be the same kind of magnet to immigrants as they had in California. Initially, the rush mainly involved the transfer of population from the other colonies to Victoria; but as the news of the discoveries reached Europe, the costs and the distances involved were pushed aside and 95,000 immigrants reached the colonies in 1852, most of them from the British Isles, and most heading for Victoria.[4] In the next ten years, Victoria's population rose from 80,000 to almost 500,000 outstripping the older colony of New South Wales, and providing the basis for a further expansion of both the rural industry and the urban concentrations that, even by 1850, had become characteristic of Australian society.[5] By 1860 the population of all the Australian colonies had almost trebled, to 1,145,000—a tiny community in relation to the size of the continent, but large when compared to the tentative beginnings some seventy years earlier.

As the gold rush era gave way in the late 1850s to the less spectacular activities of mining companies extracting ore from deep shafts, the mining industry no longer provided sufficient work for the thousands attracted by the lure of easy riches. The emphasis swung back to agriculture, and to a complex and bitter struggle to give would-be farmers access to the lands held in large pastoral leases. The flow of immigration eased back, and in face of difficult economic circumstances the governments of the various colonies came to question the value of assisted immigration policies. By 1880 most schemes of assistance had been phased out, and the ebb and flow of free immigration was determined by reports reaching England of the state of employment in the colonies. At various points in the 1890s, a combination of drought and economic recession led to an excess of departures over arrivals. By 1879 the population had reached almost 3.75 million, and for the first time the majority were native born.

A review of the pattern of immigration over the colonial period to 1900 would show a gradual changeover from the coerced immigration of a convict population to the contrived immigration of free settlers. However, the latter process was one of peaks and valleys, as colonial governments responded to the demands of local employers for a docile labor force and the British Government took the opportunity to cull its surplus and disadvantaged free population in much the same way that it had culled its surplus prison population. As the colonial economies experienced the familiar boom and bust cycle, public opinion wavered in its attitude to immigration. The 1890s proved to be a searing decade; a series of fierce confrontations between labor and capital, and profound economic depression marked by spectacular bank failures, plus one of the most prolonged periods of drought ever recorded, made the Australian colonies an unlikely destination for prospective settlers. Only the gold fields of Western Australia proved capable of attracting migrants.

The decade of the 1890s was also a critical stage in the constitutional development of the former colonies, as their political leaders debated the wisdom of maintaining on the one continent six entities, each of them self-governing within the British Empire and maintaining separate defense forces and customs services. The problem was the familiar one of finding a constitutional arrangement that would allow the states to create a central authority to deal with matters of common concern, without at the same time losing their identity and their freedom of action. While the experience of the United States in operating a federal system was closely studied, the planners had to adapt that experience to the needs of communities that had no desire to break away from the Empire. The result was a federal commonwealth, in which six states federated and established a national government, while maintaining at both the State and Federal levels the traditions and practices of the Westminster model.

The new Constitution took effect in 1901, and since then areas such as defense, foreign policy, communications, and immigration policy have been the province of the federal government. The absurdity of six states trying to maintain individual policies in regard to immigration had always been a telling point in favor of federation, and the fact that the first statute passed by the new federal parliament was the Immigration Restriction Act of 1901 indicates how significant the issue of non-European immigration was at the time. From that point on, immigration policy was to be uniform across the continent.

NATION, EMPIRE, AND COMMONWEALTH, 1901–1945

Some efforts were made to restore the system of assisted immigration as the economy revived from the disasters of the 1890s, but with little effect until 1910, when the return of confidence in the infant nation's future and pride in its future role within the Empire triggered a campaign to boost the population by attracting more British immigrants. By 1914 some 200,000 new settlers had arrived, a remarkable intake compared to the grim years at the turn of the century. Industry was expanding in the urban areas, great hopes were held for the development of "closer settlement" schemes on tracts of land previously held for pastoral use, and the standard of living was rising. At that point the wider concerns of the Empire intruded.

The events of August 1914 triggered an immediate response in Australia. Britain's cause was automatically Australia's, and over the next four years thousands of Australian soldiers and sailors fought for the British Empire in the Middle East and France. Although the Australian voters refused to give the national government authority to draft citizens for military service abroad, some 330,000 volunteers presented themselves for duty and close on 60,000 lost their lives in the service of the Empire.[6] Given that the total population did not exceed 5 million until 1900, this was a substantial contribution to a distant war. Though increasingly conscious of the distinctiveness of their own national experience, most Australians took for granted that the nation's destiny would be worked out within the context of a powerful, familiar, and far-flung British Empire. Britain was the technological and financial hub around which the distant Dominions and dependencies revolved, and London was considered the undisputed cultural center of the English-speaking world. The problem of how best to strengthen the economic linkages that provided the concrete base for this sense of interdependence was one that had long concerned politicians both in Britain and in the Dominions. Two years before the outbreak of World War I the British Government established a Dominions Royal Commission to explore the whole issue, and its report—released in 1917, while the war was still in progress—included a recommendation that Britain take a more active role in encouraging the dispersal of British emigrants within the Empire, to stimulate the economic growth of the former colonies and strengthen the bond between the outlying regions and the homeland. No positive action could be taken while the war emergency continued, but in the early 1920s, an Empire Settlement Scheme was introduced in cooperation with the Australian Government, with the British Government contributing to the fares of emigrants leaving the homeland to begin farming on lands made available by the Australian States of New South Wales, Victoria, and West Australia. This was something of a departure from traditional practice;

in the nineteenth century, the British Government had limited its role to providing guidance for those considering emigration, and assisting in "the selection and dispatch" of emigrants whose expenses the colonial authorities were prepared to meet. In the 1920s, however, the British Government took a more active role in financing emigrants who were prepared to settle within the Empire; of the 282,000 settlers who left Britain for Australia in the period 1921–1933, some 212,000 were given financial assistance to make the journey.[7]

The outcome of all of this activity was not what the planners had expected. The costs involved in establishing British immigrants on Australian farms proved alarming, and defective planning at the State level led to many failures. The 1920s was not the best time to be expanding the rural economy, and the Depression of the 1930s made further activity of this type unlikely. In any case, official opinion in Britain had begun to change. Those who had seen emigration as one way of protecting the British standard of living by containing population growth noted that the declining birth rate already dealt with that problem, and those more concerned with Empire development found that in any case it was too difficult to match up the needs of both the British and the Australian economies. The onset of World War II meant the end of emigration for the time being, and questions of policy became meaningless at a time when Britain's survival as a nation was in jeopardy.

THE POST WAR ERA: A WATERSHED IN AUSTRALIAN IMMIGRATION POLICY

"Populate or Perish"

The fact that Australia originated as a group of British colonies, and that the transition from colonial to independent status was achieved without a revolutionary upheaval, meant that there has never been any abrupt change in the attitude of both societies toward the role of Britain as the major source of immigrants. Both societies took for granted that Australia would remain British-oriented in its economic, institutional and cultural life, and that both the colonies and the Federation that succeeded them in 1901 would continue to draw the bulk of their immigrant intake from Britain. In the nineteenth century very few immigrants were drawn from Europe. A small German community appeared in the colony of South Australia in the 1840s, a result of the efforts of the King of Prussia to tighten control over religious minorities in his territories. The only significant exception to the dominant Anglo-Saxon component was the large Irish community, which had its roots in the convict era and was reinforced by those escaping the Famine and others attracted to the goldfields in the 1850s. To some extent the Irish provided an obvious counterpoint to the overwhelming British tone of colonial life. As Catholics, and as bearers of a deep-seated resentment of British control of their homeland, the Irish constituted the major threat to the Anglo-Saxon ascendency; but as a group that aspired to respectability and modest prosperity in their new land, the Irish in time added their own brand of conservatism to many aspects of colonial life and adjusted their more radical inclinations to the realities of a social and economic order in which British values were clearly dominant.[8] By 1891, 83 percent of the vast majority of the almost one million born outside Australia had come from the British Isles. Apart from the small group of German origin in South Australia, and tiny groups of Italians and Greeks, Australia still had at the time of the outbreak of World War II a remarkably homogeneous population of almost entirely British stock. Yet by 1950 a transformation of Australian society had begun, and within a generation the ethnic composition of the Australian population changed dramatically.

The catalyst was the threat of invasion by Japan during the Pacific War. By the time of the attack on Pearl Harbor in December 1941, Australia had been involved in the European conflict for two years. Though less eager to enter a distant war than it had been in 1914, Australia maintained her traditional role as an ally of Britain and, despite the usual unpreparedness and the problems of an economy severely battered by the depression of the 1930s, dispatched an expeditionary force to the Middle East. Australian troops were heavily involved in the North African campaigns, in the defense of Greece, and in Syria. The entry of Japan into the war in December 1941 found Australia badly exposed, with its most experienced military, naval and air units engaged in the Middle East. The fall of Singapore meant the loss of an Australian division that had been hurriedly sent to Malaya, and the rapid spread of Japanese military and naval power through Southeast Asia meant that for the first time since European settlement, the Australian continent was under threat of invasion by a foreign power.

The recall of the divisions deployed in the Middle East, and the reverses suffered by the Japanese navy as the United States regained military supremacy in the Pacific meant that the threat was eventually removed. The shock, however, was massive and long-lasting; the small northern city of Darwin had been bombed by the Japanese air force in 1942, Japanese midget submarines had penetrated Sydney Harbor, and the Japanese had occupied key areas of New Guinea as part of an overall invasion strategy. All of this had shown how vulnerable Australia was in the face of modern means of warfare, and how difficult it would be to defend a vast continent with a population base of only 7.5 million. It had always been assumed that the armed strength of the British Empire would provide a shield behind which smaller members of the Imperial club could go about their business. The British presence in Asia, and especially the British naval base at Singapore, had always constituted a formidable element of forward defense, and Australia's involvement in Britain's wars was in part a way of paying one's dues as a member of a cooperative system of defense. The speed with which the Japanese cracked that defensive shield, and the inability of Britain to assist other members of the Empire at a time when Britain itself was fighting for survival, made it obvious that other arrangements would have to be made. The fact that Britain vacated its colonial possessions in South and Southeast Asia after the

World War II had ended put paid to any hope that the protective shield would be restored. The logic of the situation was obvious: Australia must encourage the British to do whatever they could to maintain security east of Suez, and to remain in place in those areas in the Middle East that guarded the sea routes over which Australia's trade passed to and from Europe. At the same time the United States, as the dominant force in the Pacific, must be encouraged to maintain an interest in the security of the Southeast Asia and South Pacific areas. Behind the cover provided by great and powerful friends—the one familiar, but experiencing decline, the other less familiar, but very much the rising super-power—Australia had to try to maximize its chances of survival in an increasingly dangerous world by expanding its industrial base, developing its economy, and above all, boosting its population. The only way to increase population to the levels required was by large scale immigration, and in the postwar years the nation turned again to assisted immigration; the scale of this operation, however, was to dwarf anything previously attempted.

Even before the war ended, the Labor Party government of Prime Minister John Curtin had begun to speak of the need for Australia to aim for a population of about 20 million rather than the current 7.5 million.[9] Initially it was assumed that, as in years past, the new immigrants would be drawn from Britain. The British government was known to be willing to pay the fares of veterans who wanted to emigrate; but the Australian government had begun to think in wider terms. Knowing that the birth rate had been low during the Depression years, the government realized that if an adequate level of population was to be achieved and economic development sustained, an unusually large intake of immigrants would be required, as many as 30,000 per year. A new federal Department of Immigration was established in 1945, with Arthur A. Calwell as minister, and by 1947 the British and Australian governments had agreed on a new program of assisted immigration, under which British veterans would be given free passage to Australia and other migrants would be required to pay ten pounds sterling per head for their passage. The Australian government paid part of the costs, and took responsibility for the selection of immigrants and their induction into the Australian community. Those immigrants who returned to Britain within two years had to repay the balance of their outward fare.[10] Under these arrangements, hundreds of thousands of British immigrants were to arrive in Australia between 1947 and the early 1970s.

In its initial stages, this program of assisted migration appealed to the British government because it provided a simple way of solving some of the problems involved in demobilizing some four million veterans at a time when the nation was making the painful transition to a peace-time economy. The fact that many who migrated were not veterans, but war-weary young couples looking for better opportunities for their children, was bound to cause some concern: the British authorities, for example, reserved the right to hold back individuals with skills vital to specific industries. Yet the transfer of population to countries such as Australia, Canada, and New Zealand could always be justified on the grounds that it was one way of maintaining British influence in former colonial outposts, and in an era when few could be confident that Britain would regain the military and political strength it had taken for granted before World War II, the preservation of such bonds seemed especially important. By the early 1950s, however, the flow of migration had developed a force of its own, and the British government progressively reduced its contribution to the cost of assisted passages.

Non-British European Immigration

At the Australian end, those who launched the postwar immigration program assumed from the outset that the incoming settlers would be drawn overwhelmingly from the British Isles, and that the Australian community would continue to be predominantly Anglo-Saxon, with just a dash of Irish and Scots. There was a suggestion that if the number of British applicants were insufficient to meet the target intake, immigrants from European countries could be used to make up the numbers. What was not envisaged was that within a decade the intake of immigrants from the European continent would constitute such a sizable component of the total inflow that it would bring about a profound change in the ethnic composition of the Australian population as a whole. Almost unwillingly at first, and then with considerable eagerness, Australia began to move away from the assumption that to be Australian was necessarily to be of British descent.

It was the presence in postwar Europe of hundreds of thousands of stateless persons and refugees that first led the Australian government to turn its attention to Europe as a possible source of new population. In the first instance the humanitarian factor was so compelling that the long-standing distrust of non-English speaking immigrants was pushed aside for the time being, and an initial group of 12,000 Baltic refugees was accepted in 1946/47 at the request of the International Refugee Organization.[11] The fact that it was easier to obtain shipping for refugees than for British immigrants meant that European immigrants could be used to make up any shortfall in the annual intake, and as the Australian authorities became accustomed to this new development, they realized that there were economic advantages to be gained. Refugees could provide skills that were in short supply in the Australian workforce, and individuals could be selected from specific age groups; but the main advantage of taking in refugees proved to be their value as a directed work force. In return for their passage, they were required to spend their first two years in whatever employment the government selected for them; they could be sent to wherever labor shortages were most severe, and they could provide the unskilled labor needed for public works and development projects. In return they received normal pay and the chance to resume something close to a normal life after years in refugee camps; the cost to the refugee was often loneliness, isolation, and lack of recognition of their skills. Between 1947 and 1954, some 170,000 European refugees reached Australia, paving the way for what was to become a growing stream of conventional immigrants.[12]

By the early 1950s the Australian economy had undergone profound changes, and although the greater part of the national income was still derived from agricultural exports, manufacturing had become much more significant than had been the case before the war. The threat of invasion by Japan had highlighted both the need for a larger population and the danger of isolation from the traditional sources of manufactured goods. In the face of a sudden war emergency, the country had had to produce its own warships, aircraft, weapons, and ammunition to supplement the limited supplies available from its allies and trading partners. It seemed obvious in the postwar years that some degree of industrial self-sufficiency should be maintained in the interests of national security, and by the 1950s industrial and urban growth had become key elements in the national economy. With half its population concentrated in metropolitan Sydney and Melbourne, Australia experienced the same kind of suburban expansion and rising demand for services so evident in the United States at that time. The increase in population stimulated demand for housing, school and hospital construction, for highway and dam building, and for goods and services. The immigrant inflow both added to the level of demand and provided part of the workforce to meet that demand, and the problem of estimating the size of each year's intake and relation to the state of the economy became part of national budget planning. Short-term recessions meant a quick downward adjustment to the target for the following year, as labor unions stressed the futility of introducing new settlers to compete for scarce jobs with the native-born. Indications of improved economic conditions would in turn lead to a return to earlier levels of immigrant intake. The fact that the Labor Government, which launched the immigration drive, lost office in 1949 had no effect on the general policy. The Liberal coalition government of 1949–1972 maintained a strong commitment to the broad framework established in 1947.

Once the link between economic growth and migrant inflow had been clearly established, it became evident that Britain could not be relied on to provide even half of the numbers required, let alone the high proportion anticipated when large-scale assisted immigration was resumed in the late 1940s. By 1953 the Department of Immigration had negotiated immigration agreements with West Germany, the Netherlands, Italy, and Malta, to facilitate the movement of skilled workers and their families to Australia.[13] In that year half of the unusually low target of 80,000 new settlers were to be drawn from Europe, including the wives and children of workers already in the country, while the older provisions for the acceptance of displaced persons were discontinued. Targets were increased in the late 1950s, and the Department of Immigration worked through its network of branch offices in Britain and the Continent to attract and screen potential immigrants. Their task became more difficult as the West German and Dutch economies revived and rising living standards in Northwestern Europe lessened the incentive to emigrate. Forced to spread its net wider, the Department became more active in Italy and Greece, which proved in the long run to be major sources of supply. By the late 1960s and early 1970s the search for potential settlers had reached the eastern rim of the Mediterranean, and the last reservoir to be tapped before the great era of migrant inflow came to an end in 1972 was Turkey. To some extent, the search for immigrants followed—though in a briefer time span—the kind of northwest–southeast axis across Europe that had been reflected in the earlier movement of settlers to the United States: Britain, followed by Northwestern and Central Europe, then Southern Europe, and finally the Eastern Mediterranean. By the late 1960s there were very few European ethnic groups not represented in significant numbers in what was rapidly becoming a large and diverse immigrant community. Greece and Italy were heavily represented, France and Spain hardly at all. Between those extremes Germans, Dutch, Hungarians, Poles, Yugoslavs, Maltese, and Turks brought to what previously had been a predominantly Anglo-Saxon society a lively mixture of cultures and life styles that startled a native-born population ill-prepared for sudden exposure to peculiar foreign customs.

ATTITUDES TOWARD ETHNIC DIVERSITY: THE EMPHASIS ON ASSIMILATION

Australia's isolation from Europe and the dominance of British attitudes and institutions in Australian life meant that the postwar waves of immigrants were met with some suspicion and unease. Australians had had little experience in coping with foreigners, and only a tiny minority had any facility in European languages. The decision to introduce displaced persons from Europe in the late 1940s had involved something of a calculated risk, and the first Minister for Immigration, Arthur Calwell, was so concerned about the possibility of a hostile reaction that he ensured that the first contingents chosen from European refugee camps were blue-eyed and blond, so that they would seem less foreign to most Australians.[14] When the public reacted favorably, the Department of Immigration began to cast its net wider and the large scale resettlement of refugees got under way. Both the federal government and the community in general agreed that the new arrivals should make every effort to blend into Australian society and to conform to Anglo-Saxon norms. The designation "New Australian" was introduced to provide a more pleasant term for a refugee or a European migrant than the range of abbreviations already in circulation by the late 1940s: "Balt", "Reffo", "D.P." (Displaced Person)—and other less attractive designations. The very choice of the term underlined the basic assumption of both the government and the community in general that incoming migrants would assimilate as quickly as possible. Conformity to Anglo-Saxon norms was taken for granted, and while the federal government readily accepted its responsibility to ease the entry of new settlers into Australian society, it discharged that responsibility largely by providing hostel accommodation for those who had no relatives or sponsors in Australia, and by providing some training in the English language.

Table 2.2.
Birthplaces of the Five Major Immigrant Groups, by Country, in Selected Years

1846	No. ´000s	%	1861	No. ´000s	%
England	69.1	48.4	England	342.8	47.4
Ireland	49.3	34.5	Ireland	177.4	24.5
Scotland	16.5	11.5	Scotland	97.2	13.4
Other Brit. Cols.	3.6	2.5	China	38.7	5.3
Other Countries	3.3	2.3	Germany	27.6	3.8
1891			**1933**		
England	456.7	45.3	England	487.9	54.0
Ireland	229.2	22.7	Scotland	132.8	14.7
Scotland	125.0	12.4	Ireland	79.2	8.8
Germany	45.3	4.5	New Zealand	46.0	5.1
China	36.0	3.6	Italy	28.8	2.9
1947			**1954**		
England	382.1	51.3	England	478.8	37.2
Scotland	103.1	13.8	Scotland	123.7	9.6
Ireland	45.1	6.1	Italy	119.9	9.3
New Zealand	43.6	5.8	Germany	65.4	5.1
Italy	33.6	4.5	Ireland	47.8	3.7
1961			**1981**		
England	556.7	31.3	England	915.7	29.5
Italy	228.3	12.8	Italy	283.4	9.1
Scotland	132.9	7.5	New Zealand	184.8	5.9
Germany	109.3	6.1	Scotland	156.5	5.0
Greece	77.3	4.3	Greece	150.6	4.8

Table 2.3.
Immigration to Australia: Birthplaces of the Five Major Immigrant Groups by World Region, in Selected Years

1861

Region	No. '000s	%
British Isles	630.1	87.1
E./S.E. Asia	38.1	5.4
N. Europe	37.2	5.1
Americas	7.1	1.0
S. Europe	2.4	0.3
Africa	1.6	0.2

1891

Region	No. '000s	%
British Isles	829.5	82.3
N. Europe	70.0	6.9
E./S.E. Asia	39.5	3.9
New Zealand	23.9	2.4
Americas	13.7	1.3
Pacific	10.8	1.1

1933

Region	No. '000s	%
British Isles	716.8	87.1
New Zealand	46.0	5.1
S. Europe	40.8	4.5
N. Europe	35.4	3.9
E. Europe	17.0	1.9
E./S.E. Asia	13.6	1.5

1947

Region	No. '000s	%
British Isles	543.8	73.1
S. Europe	52.8	7.1
New Zealand	43.6	5.8
N. Europe	32.4	4.3
E. Europe	24.3	3.3
Americas	11.6	1.6

1954

British Isles	666.6	51.8
S. Europe	175.5	13.6
E. Europe	174.0	13.5
N. Europe	145.4	11.3
New Zealand	43.3	3.4
E./S.E. Asia	21.5	1.7

1961

British Isles	757.8	42.6
S. Europe	361.2	20.3
N. Europe	258.5	14.5
E. Europe	227.8	12.8
New Zealand	47.0	2.6
E./S.E. Asia	37.0	2.1

1981

British Isles	1170.1	37.7
S. Europe	587.8	18.9
E. Europe	329.7	10.6
N. Europe	278.4	8.9
E./S.E. Asia	192.4	6.2
New Zealand	184.8	6.0

(See Tables 2.2 and 2.3.) It did not, however, regard the maintenance of the language and traditional culture of immigrant groups as something to be encouraged; national costumes were quaint and colorful when brought out for display on holidays and public events, but they were seen by the host community as relics of a past that the immigrants should now put behind them. As a considerable proportion of European migrants, and especially those from southern Europe, had been chosen from the unskilled and the less educated so that they could fill gaps in the Australia work force, it was unlikely that they would produce the kind of leadership that could have argued for assistance in preservation of immigrant language and customs. So the first major wave of non-British immigration flowed into a community that was at first uncertain whether it really wanted large numbers of aliens in its midst, and that expected the newcomers to shed their national identities as rapidly as possible and accept Australian values and customs as their own. The attitudes of the Australian community in the period from the late 1940s to the 1960s resembled that of many native-born Americans in the early years of the twentieth century, when the large intakes of southern and east European immigrants triggered debate about the "Americanization" of newcomers whose language and culture seemed so radically different from the American norm. While the image of the melting pot was not commonly cited in Australia, the notion that cultural differences would be soon obliterated was taken for granted.

It was an assumption that became increasingly difficult to sustain. With its origins in a worldview that had been shaped for so long by Anglo-Saxon perspectives, the Australian outlook toward non-British immigrants was shaped by the relative ease with which earlier generations of English, Scots, and Irish newcomers had adapted to the local milieu, and by the fact that previous immigrants from the European continent had been so few in number that their adjustment to local conditions had been a largely individual and unnoticed process. By the late 1950s, however, the size of the non-British intakes became large enough to create very considerable ethnic communities in the major cities, communities that were eventually to prove both capable of maintaining their cultural traditions and determined to do so. This became more evident as the revival of the Western European economies and the rise of the European Economic Community changed the context in which young people made decisions about their future. As Germany, France, and Switzerland began to develop guestworker schemes; which drew in labor from southern Europe, Australian immigration officers found that they were facing stiff competition in attracting migrants from what had become an important recruitment area. Although the annual intakes during the 1960s were high—100,000–185,000 per annum—this was in part due to a resurgence of interest in the United Kingdom, where the economic revival was far less evident. Despite these high annual intakes, the pattern of return migration had also changed, and northern European migrants were much more likely than their counterparts a decade earlier to return home after several years in the Australian workforce. The composition of the Southern European intake in the 1960s also changed, and the drop in Italian immigration would have cut the totals considerably if it had not been for a compensating increase in the number of immigrants arriving from Greece. By the late 1960s, the Department of Immigration was looking to Turkey, Yugoslavia, and South America for the numbers needed to meet the intake targets.[15]

The fact that Australia had to search more vigorously for new settlers meant that the character of the exercise had changed. Although some of those who reached Australia in the late 1950s and the 1960s were refugees from Hungary and Czechoslovakia, most could not be classed as being grossly disadvantaged in their homeland. Their decision to move was based on rational decisions about their future economic prospects and the opportunities for their children. They were to some degree upwardly mobile, and their problem was to choose between several options, of which transfer to Australia was one. That in turn meant that those who did migrate were less forcibly separated from the culture of their homeland than were the refugees or those depressed by the economic climate in Europe after World War II. The later generation of immigrants had less need to be grateful to the host community, and less inclination to respond to suggestions that they put their cultural heritage behind them. By the late 1960s, such immigrants were arriving to find that quite extensive migrant communities were already in place, and their own capacity both to meet the minimum requirements of life in the new land and to maintain their own ethnic identity and cultural linkages was considerably enhanced. Whether it liked it or not, the native-born Australian community had to recognize the fact its migrant communities were less prone to assimilate fully than had been expected.

The Acceptance of Ethnic Diversity

At the same time, attitudes within the host community itself began to show signs of change. In the decades following World War II, changes in transportation and communications technology had if anything a more dramatic effect on Australia than on countries in the northern hemisphere. The physical isolation of the continent, which had for so long promoted insularity of outlook and suspicion of foreigners, now began to break down. The ships that brought thousands of European immigrants to Australia provided relatively cheap fares for thousands of young Australians to visit Europe as tourists, students, or temporary workers, and they returned with a heightened awareness of the diversity and richness of European cultures. Rapid developments in air transportation and in telecommunications reduced the gap in both time and distance even more dramatically, and the rising generations of the 1960s and 1970s were far more in tune with attitudes and mores beyond their own continent than their parents and grandparents had been.

Even more striking, however, was the impact of the immigrants and their children. By the late 1960s, native born Australians—the vast majority of whom live in urban environments—had had more than a decade and a half of contact with immigrants from many European societies in their workplace, in their churches, and in community organizations. European immigrants had become a familiar part of the urban landscape, and their impact on fashion, design, music, business—and even eating habits—had been widely acknowledged. Moreover, an increasing proportion of the native-born were themselves the children of immigrant parents, and therefore sensitive both to the demands of the new land on immigrants and to the continuing significance of an attachment to the culture of the homeland. The fact that the immigrant communities were not physically separated from the native-born tended to enhance the interaction, both between ethnic groups and between those groups and the host society. While some sectors of the cities came to be identified with ethnic groups because of the high proportion of shops and restaurants owned by immigrants and servicing local ethnic communities, the degree of concentration was rarely high enough to bring about ethnic segregation. The locally-born reacted with initial suspicion toward the growth of what appeared to be ethnic enclaves, but the steady impact of suburbanization meant that nothing close to permanent ethnic ghettoes emerged.

While the federal government made some efforts to promote contact by providing classes in the English language and promoting a national system of "Good Neighbour Councils", the most effective contact between the native-born and immigrants probably occurred within the school system, both public and parochial, in the churches, and in the workplace. By the late 1960s, community attitudes toward European immigrants were a great deal more tolerant than in the late 1940s, and the fact of postwar immigration had come to be accepted as one of the defining characteristics of the nation's recent history, something to be referred to as a considerable social achievement. Only in recession years was the desirability of maintaining a high migrant intake questioned; even then, very little animus was shown toward those already in the country. While prejudice against immigrants and ethnic groups by no means disappeared entirely, it remained confined to a decreasing proportion of the population and appeared unable to generate significant social conflict.

Shifts in community attitudes were reflected in the gradual movement at the federal level away from the view that immigrants would lose their separate identity and merge into the local culture, and toward the view that integration could occur without loss of ethnic identity. By the early 1970s this shift had gone so far that the possibility of accepting, or even encouraging, ethnic pluralism was coming under discussion. By this time, the growth of interest among social scientists in the issues involved in the preservation of ethnic identity had begun to have an impact at the political level. The quantity and variety of the data now being made available, and the quality of the technical advice being given to administrators and political leaders were far superior to anything available in the immediate postwar period. Legislators and migrant leaders alike were made aware of changing attitudes toward the question of ethnicity in other societies, and began to relate the Australian experience of immigration to the wider international discussion of both the persistence of ethnic identity and value of encouraging ethnic pluralism. By the early 1970s political leaders at both the federal and state levels were aware of the significance of the ethnic vote in some localities, and the emergence within their own ranks of individuals with strong ethnic identification. The shift in emphasis can be seen in the renaming of government departments. The Federal Department of Immigration became the Department of Immigration and Ethnic Affairs, and most of the states with an administrative unit dealing with immigration matters also added "ethnic affairs" to its title. Funds became available for ethnic radio, multiculturalism became official policy, and by 1979 a specifically multicultural television channel—the Special Broadcasting Service (S.B.S.)—had been established with federal funds.[16] The first half of the 1980s saw multiculturalism become highly favored among politicians and academics, and the degree of outrage that followed the announcement of funding cuts for ethnic programs in the 1986 Federal Budget indicated the extent to which ethnic communities had assumed a permanent federal commitment to real rather than token acceptance of multiculturalism.

A Decade of Review: Immigration Policies in the 1970s

The shifts in both official and community attitudes, which in the early 1970s established the basis for an acceptance of cultural pluralism rather than complete assimilation, were part of a much wider review of social and economic policy. If the initial justification for a national immigration policy had been linked in part to humanitarian considerations and—to a larger degree—questions of long-term national survival in a dangerous world, the experience of the 1950s and 1960s had brought about a considerable change. In both the public and the official minds, the rise in levels of immigration had coincided with a period of economic expansion and general prosperity. Most Australians considered the postwar decades to have been a period of unprecedented prosperity, one that saw high levels of employment, low inflation, and a rising standard of living. There had been several short and disturbing recessions, but the general trend was considered to be unusually favorable. Both the federal and state governments scrambled to provide the services needed by an expanding (and predominantly suburban) population. The high immigrant inflow was considered a prime indication of the growing attraction of Australia as a land of opportunity, and at the same time a vital element in the growth of the economy. Immigrants contributed to the rising demand for goods and services, and they provided part of the labor needed to produce growth. By the mid 1960s, immigration and economic prosperity were inextricably linked in the public mind, and as long as growth was considered the predominant social objective, the status of immigration as a factor in national life remained high.

In the late 1960s and early 1970s that nexus was broken. Intellectuals and planners in Australia, as in much of the Western world, began to question many prevailing assumptions about the capacity of Earth's natural resources to sustain the pressure being exerted by the rise in world population and the increasing rate of exploitation. At a time when public attention was being drawn to the population explosion and its implications for the social and physical environment, it seemed no longer appropriate for a nation to be actively engaged in a program designed to boost its own population.[17] The question now became one of maintaining the quality of life for the existing population, and ensuring that the environment was not so heavily degraded that later generations would be deprived of their inheritance. The strategic argument was also less compelling than it had been twenty years earlier; the advent of the nuclear weapons and intercontinental missiles made it difficult to base defense planning on the experience of World War II, and the changing strategic situation in Asia further undermined the notion that security might be found in a larger population. Japan, the enemy of 1941–45, was now a major economic force in the world and the importer of vast quantities of Australian coal and iron ore; China posed no obvious threat, especially after its dramatic opening to the West in 1972. The Vietnam conflict, which had been portrayed in the 1960s as vital to Australia's security interests, was considered by the early 1970s to have been a costly mistake. No other threats were obvious, and in any case the realities of superpower rivalry made it difficult to imagine a situation in which Australia would be required to defend its territory alone against the kind of threat that had emerged in 1942. The old slogan of the late 1940s, "populate or perish", no longer seemed appropriate. At a time when environmental concerns seemed more important than national security, the fear was that overpopulation would in the long term undermine living conditions and place an unbearable strain on natural resources. Although still a sparsely populated country, Australia could not be seen as out of step with the new ideas circulating throughout the Western World.[18]

The policies introduced by the Whitlam government in 1973 marked a recognition of a shift in emphasis from the quantity of the intake to its composition. It had been the Labor Party, guided by Immigration Minister Arthur Calwell, that had launched the postwar immigration drive as a way of rapidly boosting the nation's population. The Labor Party lost office in 1949, and remained in the opposition wilderness until 1972. During those years, national immigration policy was maintained and developed by a series of Liberal–National Party coalition governments and immigration remained one of the relatively few areas where a generally bipartisan approach was sustained. The new Labor administration was much more sympathetic than had been its counterpart in the late 1940s to ethnic diversity within the Australian community, and based its immigration policy on a party platform stressing that there should be no discrimination toward immigrants based on grounds of race, color of skin, or nationality. It was also committed to breaking the link between population growth and immigrant inflow, preferring to place family reunion highest in its list of priorities. Intake targets, which had been as high as 170,000 in 1970/71, dropped to 140,000 in 1972/73 and 50,000 in 1975/76. The onset of the oil crisis in 1973 and the worldwide recession that followed led to a rise in unemployment rates, a fact that made it hard to justify any return to the previously high intakes; as had always been the case, a downturn in the economy raised questions about the value of bringing in new workers to compete for jobs with the native-born. The departure of the Labor Government in 1975 did not lead to any dramatic change of policy, and successive immigration Ministers under the Liberal–National Party administrations of 1975–1982 concentrated on fine tuning the administration of policies that stressed family reunion and the recruitment of immigrants with specific skills or business experience to cover gaps in the labor force. The old approach of attracting large numbers of unskilled laborers was apparently gone forever, and the rising levels of unemployment in the early 1980s dampened any discussion of the traditional link between the size of the immigrant intake and the health of the economy in general. The late 1970s and early 1980s, however, did see the development of a significant and at times disturbing debate about the place of immigration in Australian life, a debate that focused not so much on the volume of immigration, but on its composition, and raised deep-rooted concerns that had shaped Australian attitudes toward immigration policy for more than a century.

NON-EUROPEAN IMMIGRATION: THE OTHER SIDE OF THE COIN

If one major theme in the history of Australian immigration policy until well into the twentieth century has been the concern to build a community based on predominantly British stock, a second major theme can be found in the concern to avoid the inclusion of non-European settlers. In each case, a dramatic reversal of emphasis has occurred within a single generation; the long-standing preference for British settlers gave way in the 1950s in the face of practical considerations: the desired annual inflow of new settlers could not be achieved unless the net was spread wide enough to include large numbers of Central and Southern European migrants. By the 1960s, the Australian community had become far more ethnically mixed than could ever have been anticipated in 1945, and in many respects it had been transformed by the experience of large-scale immigration. At a somewhat later point it also made a second major adjustment in its attitude toward the entry of new settlers—in this case, toward non-European immigrants. In part because of their isolation, Australians traditionally had been suspicious of foreigners, and were slow to accept the presence of European migrant groups whose language and culture seemed in such stark contrast to familiar British patterns. But that suspicion was mild in comparison with the deeply rooted fear of non-European immigration, and the eventual slackening of the constraints that effectively blocked their entry in any numbers was a much more significant and difficult achievement, and one whose long-term implications are still under discussion.

By locating their new penal colony as far as possible from the homeland, the British made it difficult for their Australian colonies to draw additional population from European sources, especially during the first three quarters of the nineteenth century. The Australian continent, however, lay to the south of the large centers of Asian population, and at the western extremity of the island chains of the South Pacific. As resistance built up in the young colonies to the continued transportation of convicts, the British authorities accepted the criticisms of the institution and had discontinued it in the eastern colonies by the 1850s, retaining it only in the case of Western Australia until 1867. The gradual reduction of cheap convict labor created problems for some of the larger landowners in the 1830s and 1840s, and caused some to consider importing coolie labor from India or China, or to draw on the Pacific Islands for a replacement workforce. Relatively small numbers of such laborers were introduced, but the experiments drew criticism from two quarters. The British authorities at home were involved in the complex process of abolishing slavery within the Empire and were hopeful of seeing it abolished generally. The fear that the introduction of a colored labor force into their newer colonies would quickly lead to a system of quasi-slavery alarmed the British and colonial governors were advised to discourage private initiatives of this type. The free white settlers were also generally hostile to such schemes, which they saw as far too close both to the convict system and to slavery, and as such inconsistent with their image of what the emerging colonial societies should be like.[19]

The "Great White Walls" Are Erected

Once the colonies had achieved home rule by the 1850s, colonial public opinion could determine who entered the colonies and under what terms. That the colonial governments, which were elected by a much wider electorate than in Britain, achieved control over immigration policy in the same decade that the gold rushes in eastern Australia drew prospective miners to the country by the tens of thousands proved to be of major long-term significance. Amongst those arrivals during the mid–1850s were large numbers of Cantonese, as many as 18,000 by the end of 1855. They arrived when the first heady phase of alluvial mining was coming to an end, and when disgruntled white miners were likely to find fault with any group that managed to extract even small amounts of gold by reworking old areas and washing the tailings discarded during the first wave. The major gold fields saw the Californian experience replicated; the Chinese became objects of hatred and physical abuse, and the white miners put pressure on the colonial legislatures to impose landing taxes and other measures to limit the further entry of Chinese. On some of the goldfields the authorities reduced the friction by segregating the Chinese into mining villages and appointing Protectors to liaise between the Chinese, the local white communities, and the colonial authorities. At first, attempts to restrict entry were unsuccessful because adjacent colonies allowed the Chinese to enter and to make their way to the Victorian goldfields by land: 15,000, for example, walked from the South Australian port of Robe to the Victorian mines in 1857. Further instances of violence by white miners toward the Chinese led the Victorian government to tighten the entry tax provisions and introduce residence fees in addition.[20]

Although these provisions were eventually repealed, they limited the inflow of Chinese and this, together with the decline of surface mining and the return of many Chinese to their homeland, meant that the issue lost much of its significance by the 1860s. The following decade saw the old animosities resurface, and by the 1880s the now self-governing colonies had joined California, British Columbia, and New Zealand in erecting what the demographer Charles Price has described as "the great white walls," which were designed to protect the European enclaves around the rim of the Pacific.[21] Although directed primarily against the Chinese, the restrictive immigration policies were readily extended to include Pacific Islanders, and eventually to any non-European; race and skin color became basic tests of entry, and both official and public opinion in the Australian colonies became locked into the set of assumptions that would, for another seventy years, underpin what came to be known as the "White Australia" policy. With its roots in the tensions of the gold rush era, and legitimated by the widespread acceptance in the Western world of the doctrine of white superiority, the Australian attitude toward non-European settlers developed a special set of connotations deriving from the local setting. One element was the white Australian attitude toward the Aborigines, a group so culturally distinctive as to be incomprehensible to the incoming white settlers. Few in number, nomadic, and bereft of technology as the European understood the term, the Aborigines had been decimated by contact with white diseases and by the appropriation of their hunting grounds. Only those who were located in the more inhospitable and unattractive areas of the continent were left in anything close to the original tribal organization and lifestyle, while the remnants of those tribes that had inhabited the areas most attractive to white settlers were forced toward the remote inland or allowed to live as fringe dwellers outside rural white communities. The relative ease with which the Aborigines had been supplanted reinforced white notions of superiority and of the inevitable march of Anglo-Saxon civilization; and the apparently primitive nature of what the whites had observed of Aboriginal culture confirmed their view of the link between backwardness and color.

Had white Australians, in either the colonial or national periods, known more of the complex civilizations of Asia, their racial attitudes might have been less self-centered; but again geography militated against close contact. Though located much closer to Asia than to Europe, the Australian settlements necessarily clustered along the eastern and southern edges of the continent where the soils and climate were most likely to accept an adaptation of European agriculture. Located as they were, and producing little that was relevant to Asian markets, most of the Australian settlements were in practice as isolated from contact with Asia as they were from Europe. The fact that so much of Asia was subordinated to one or other of the European empires confirmed both the inferiority and the irrelevance of Asia to Australia, except as a source of large numbers of non-English speaking aliens with strange customs and little that would indicate that they could ever be assimilated into Australian life. In colonial societies so raw and isolated, there was no educated and established elite capable of mediating between foreign cultures and the assumptions of the average working-class colonist, who saw the non-European immigrant as a potential competitor for scarce employment and a tool in the hands of employers anxious to break the solidarity of an emerging labor movement.

Labor unions were to become the most determined and consistent supporters of the exclusion of non-European immigrants, but working class hostility to non-European immigration reflected public opinion in general. Those who did not fear direct competition from Asian labor were driven by other fears: racial hostility to the Chinese was widespread in the nineteenth century and early twentieth century, and the sheer weight of Asian numbers to the north alarmed all who felt exposed by the knowledge that the defense of the vast Australian continent was far beyond the capacity of the white population. In the years before World War II, the threat from Asia was not so much a political or a military one, for only Japan could be considered capable of mounting such a direct challenge. The fear was of inundation, the simple outnumbering of the white population, which could be expected if the "yellow hordes" of Asia were given open entry to the continent, as had been the case for a brief period during the gold rush era. Hence the development of a garrison mentality, a determination to keep Asia at bay while the slow build-up of population drawn from the British Isles gradually brought closer the day when Australia could feel secure against the flood.

THE FEDERAL IMMIGRATION RESTRICTION ACT, 1901

The conviction that Australia must remain a white society was so central an issue at the end of the nineteenth century that the first legislation passed by the new Federal Parliament in 1901 was an Immigration Restriction Act designed to exclude colored immigrants. Later known as the Immigration Act, it remained in force with some modifications until 1959, with generally consistent bipartisan and public support. Its most notorious provision was the use of the dictation test to exclude non-European immigrants ("... any person who when asked to do so by an officer fails to write out at dictation and sign... a passage of fifty words in length in any European language directed by the officer... is a prohibited immigrant"). It was made clear that the test would not be applied to qualified Europeans, although in later years it was used to exclude a few Europeans whose political views were considered too radical. Under Japanese pressure early in the century, the words "European language" were replaced by "any prescribed language," but in practice European languages were always used. Under the initial legislation, the test could be required at any time within one year after arrival; later this was altered to five years, which gave departmental offices more time to trace any ship's deserters who for some reason were not capable of being deported under other sections of the Act. By the late 1940s the dictation test was being used much more for this purpose than for actual prohibition of entry.[22]

The intention behind the inclusion of the dictation test in 1901 was to find a way of enforcing a policy based on race without directly using racial terms, which would cause embarrassment within the Empire or give offense to colored nations. Though it worked effectively in relation to entry, there still remained the question of how to administer the Act in relation to those 47,000 non-European residents in the country at the time the legislation was passed, and whose right to remain was taken for granted. The largest single group—some 30,000 in all—were Chinese, and some had been naturalized by individual colonies prior to Federation and the passage of the 1901 Act. Complications arose when Chinese already in the country wanted to have their families join them, or needed to bring out assistants to help them when they became too old to operate their own business. Others presented problems of definition when they returned to China for extended visits and then needed permission to re-enter. Over the decades a complex set of administrative procedures was developed to meet the legitimate needs of resident Chinese without breaching the overall policy of exclusion. Challenges to the decisions made under these procedures over the years led to court proceedings, which in turn further defined the framework within which the Department of Immigration operated.[23]

The legislation proved more difficult to administer than had been expected, but there could be no doubt as to its general effectiveness. Over the first fifty years of its life, the legislation not only prevented the much-feared flood of non-European (and specifically, Chinese) immigration, but it actually reduced the proportion of non-Europeans within the total population. The "White Australia" policy, as it was generally known, attracted very little criticism or even discussion. The administration of the policy by particular ministers was sometimes regarded as controversial, and Arthur A. Calwell was fiercely criticized in the late 1940s for decisions that had the effect of breaking up families by the deportation of one member for some breach of the policy; but the general principles underlying the policy were widely accepted until well into the 1950s—and are still supported by some sections of the community in the 1980s.

Although both major political parties maintained their support for a restriction on the entry of non-Europeans during the postwar decades when every effort was being made to attract European immigrants, the reasons given went beyond the older reliance on notions of racial superiority. The climate of opinion around the world was changing, and it was clear that political leaders could no longer use racist arguments in international forums as casually as had been the case prior to World War II. In the 1950s the Australian government had to recognize the rise of independent nations in Asia, and to come to terms with the shifts in strategic and economic realities that had begun to transform the Asian region. It became clear that not only had Australia's economic and defensive ties with Britain weakened as the latter withdrew from Asia and turned its attention increasingly toward Europe; Australian observers warned the federal government that foreign policy considerations made it imperative that good relations be developed with populous Asian nations to the north.[24] While it had been possible for Immigration Minister Calwell to state as late as 1949 that he would allow no Japanese to enter the country because of the general anger that the memory of wartime atrocities toward Australian prisoners of war still generated, the signing of a peace treaty with Japan and the rapid development of the Japanese economy made such attitudes unrealistic in the late 1950s.

Despite these pressures, and the knowledge that in many Asian countries, the existence of a "White Australia" policy was the one fact about Australia that was widely publicized, Australian political leaders were reluctant to make radical changes in such a long-established policy. They stressed that there were other than racial considerations at the basis of the policy. The admission of large numbers of Asians would do nothing to alleviate population pressures in the region, it was argued, and the use of a token quota system would be difficult to administer and always subject to pressure for its enlargement. Australia was entitled to try to retain the racial homogeneity that had prevented the racial tensions, so evident in other societies, and produced a peaceful society. The fact that thousands of Asian students had been encouraged to train in Australia and take their skills back to help develop their homeland was cited as evidence of a non-discriminatory outlook.

The New Departures of the 1960s and 1970s

None of these justifications carried much weight in Asia, especially when it was noted that other nations around the Pacific—Canada, the United States, and New Zealand—had managed to find less offensive procedures to control their intake of Asian immigrants. While it was conceded that a number of Asian nations themselves maintained very restrictive immigration policies, it was the use of race as a basis for exclusion that made the Australian case open to criticism. By 1966, the federal government was ready to make a significant departure from its settled policy. Since 1956, resident non-Europeans had been able to apply for naturalization on the same basis as other immigrants; now, under measures announced in March 1966, some especially qualified non-Europeans would be admitted as permanent settlers and allowed to seek naturalization after five years residence.[25] There was no adverse reaction, in part because the opposition Labor Party had begun in the previous year to remove the commitment to the "White Australia" policy from its platform, and also because the concession was a limited one: those who entered would be professionals or technically qualified individuals who were not likely to be numerous and who would not provide competition in the sensitive areas of the labor market. Yet the breach in the "Great White Wall" was a significant one, and its successful accomplishment was to pave the way for the comprehensive reform announced by the incoming Whitlam Labor Government in 1972, committing the nation to an immigration policy that would make no distinctions on the basis of "race, or color of skin or nationality." The "White Australia" policy had been officially buried.

While there was a noticeable increase in the number of non-European settlers following the non-discriminatory policies of the early 1970s, the influx feared by more conservative observers did not eventuate.[26] The emphasis throughout the entire immigration program was on the selection of individuals with qualifications, skills, or experience that would meet an immediate need in the Australian workforce, and this meant that the non-European intake continued to be made up of individuals with special qualifications rather than unskilled laborers. The new emphasis on family reunion affected far more European than non-European settlers, simply because there were fewer non-European residents available to make such requests. In general, the policy changes brought in by the Whitlam Labor Government appear to have caused little comment; an embarrassing policy had been dismantled without social upheaval, and the readiness of the Fraser Liberal–National coalition government to maintain the new approach during the period 1975–1982 suggested that both the major parties sensed that the issue had lost much of its sensitivity for the general public. There was widespread relief among critics of the old policy that the Australian community appeared to have adopted a tolerant and sympathetic attitude to the question of non-European immigration. Given time, it seemed, the old fears and prejudices would wither away, and the nation would be free of an unnecessary handicap in its dealings with other parts of the world. Prospective immigrants could be assured that their applications would be dealt with by a procedure weighted toward indications of their ability to settle in and make a contribution to national life, rather than appearance or place of birth. In a decade when the retention of diverse ethnic identities among the large groups of postwar European immigrants was being accepted as a positive good, the addition of relatively small numbers of non-European immigrants to the mix seemed to present no real difficulties.

The Debates of 1984

In 1983/84, the question of non-European immigration suddenly resurfaced as a controversial issue, and the way in which it was discussed raised doubts about the extent of the level of tolerance within the Australian community. The immediate issue was whether the policies of the Hawke Labor government, which came to power in 1983, were so heavily weighted in favor of non-European immigration that in the long term the racial composition of the Australian population would be profoundly altered. What triggered the debate was concern about the impact of Vietnamese refugee settlement, a development not envisaged when the previous Whitlam Labor government had announced non-discriminatory approach to immigration in 1973. Before it left office in 1975, the Whitlam Labor government had brought in some 500 Vietnamese refugees as part of its response to the growing concern around the world at the problem of refugee resettlement; but the main exodus from Vietnam occurred after Labor had lost office, and the responsibility for deciding on an approach to the problem fell to the Fraser Liberal–National coalition government. Both political parties had taken a sympathetic attitude toward admitting refugees since World War II, but most of these had been Eastern Europeans—Hungarians and Czechs, for example, in the 1950s and 1960s. The Vietnamese presented a particular problem because of the large numbers involved, and because many would not have been eligible for entry under the selection criteria favoring professional qualifications or skills. Moreover, at least some of the refugees had literally arrived at the nation's doorstep, something that had not occurred previously. The spectacle of refugee boats arriving unannounced in the northern port of Darwin after a perilous crossing of the South China and Timor Seas dramatized the refugee crisis in a particularly striking way; but it also provided opportunities for rumours and hostility. Some argued that the boat people were trying to crash their way into the country, refusing to take their place in line and being assessed for entry as thousands of their compatriots were doing in the camps in Malaysia, Thailand, and Hong Kong. There were also suggestions that among the boat people were some wealthy opportunists, or perhaps even criminals, who were using the genuine distress of others as a cover for what was virtually an illegal entry.

Whatever the suspicions of some sections of the community, the overriding humanitarian concerns were compelling, and the Fraser government organized the resettlement of Indo-Chinese refugees on a regular basis. By 1981/82 the intake had risen to just over 13,000, about 9 percent of the total number of settler arrivals. By 1983, some 90,000 had been admitted, the highest per capital intake of any Western nation.[27]

This unexpected consequence of the Vietnam war had produced a situation that politicians and administrators had been careful to avoid: the sudden entry of large numbers of unskilled non-Europeans at a time of rising unemployment levels and economic uncertainty. Indo-Chinese immigrants tended to form very visible communities as they struggled to adapt to a new society, and while their status as refugees attracted initial sympathy, after a time their residential concentration in suburban areas in Sydney and Melbourne brought charges of clannishness and inability to assimilate, and some critics pointed to the additional demands on the welfare system and the competition for scarce jobs.

In March 1984, an address given by a well-known historian, Geoffrey Blainey, triggered a response that revealed that the local resentments directed against Vietnamese immigrants masked a more extensive unease about the volume of Asian immigration in general. Blainey initially questioned the wisdom of an immigration policy that might jeopardize the level of tolerance that had built up within the community by allowing too large an Asian intake in too short a period of time. His concern focused on the report that 40 percent of the intake for the first quarter of 1983/84 was of Asian origin, and he suggested that this reflected an intention on the part of the Hawke government to undermine the traditional Anglo-Saxon dominance in the composition of the population. What followed was a confused debate, strewn with charges of racism on the one hand and favoritism to Asians on the other.[28] Blainey was the subject of student demon-strations, and the unexpected heat of the controversy drew the more vocal par-ticipants into more extreme positions. To a large extent the debate became an argument about the accuracy of the data being cited and the intentions of the government. Given that the Department of Immigration includes in the classi-fication "Asia" such Middle Eastern countries as Israel and Lebanon, the dis-cussion of the pros and cons of Asian immigration invariably became confused. For the general community, Asian meant Vietnamese; very few people had any clear idea of the numbers of Malaysians or Indians included in the intake, and few seemed to realize that aside from the special case of the Vietnamese refugee component, the Asian content of the overall immigration inflow was not large, and that persons of Asian descent constituted only two percent of the total population.

For many observers, the worrying aspect of the debate was that it was occurring at all; many feared that it was not the kind of debate that would focus on firm data and substantive issues, but would rather incite the kind of mindless racial prejudice and antagonism that was felt to be not far below the surface of Aus-tralian society. Yet, after generating extensive media coverage and producing a flurry of books, the controversy died when it failed to take hold at the political level and become an issue at the 1984 federal elections. On some university campuses, anti-Asian graffiti drew attention to the hostility of some students who resented the presence of Asian students at a time when the competition for university admission had become severe. The clandestine nature of this campaign and its rejection by the vast majority of students caused some to suspect that the activity was generated by off-campus fringe groups. In any case, the policy of the Hawke Labor government to recover an increasing proportion of the costs of educating foreign students by raising tuition fees to a large extent undercut the campaign and it rapidly slipped into obscurity.

During 1986 the question of immigration policy retreated as a public issue in the face of the setbacks suffered by the Australian economy, and far more attention was devoted to the declining value of the dollar, the balance of payment problems, and the effect of declining commodity prices on export income and on the general standard of living. The appointment of a low-profile Minister of Immigration and Ethnic Affairs gave critics of government policies little op-portunity to find a foothold, and both major political parties appeared to avoid anything that might reopen the disturbing debates of 1984. The focus of con-troversy moved from immigration to ethnic affairs, with the Hawke Labor gov-ernment risking its standing with ethnic voters by including in its budget-cutting exercise for 1986/87 a number of excisions in programs favored by ethnic groups: English language programs were cut, the television service provided by the Special Broadcasting Service was to be merged with the Australian Broadcasting Corporation, the Institute of Multicultural Affairs was abolished, and other mi-grant services were either reduced or cut as part of the attempt to reduce federal expenditures. The issue of race and immigration did not surface again until the visit of Archbishop Desmond Tutu in January 1987 triggered a reaction from a prominent member of the national veterans organization. In this instance the spectre raised was not Asian but African—a novel development, given the minuscule contact between Australia and Africa over the past two centuries. The suggestion that someone was preparing the ground for a large-scale influx of African refugees from apartheid was sufficient to arouse a small but vociferous group of critics to draw on the familiar complaint that the nation's British traditions, its standard of living, and its social stability would be imperilled if large numbers of black South Africans were given entry by a sympathetic Labor Government. Again, the controversy appeared to have little basis in reality; no large entry of black South Africans had been announced, and only the provision of scholarships for black students had been discussed as a possibility. Ironically, South African immigrants had been arriving for some time; but these were white South Africans, who because of their training, financial resources, or business expertise, could expect to score well in the points system used by the Department of Immigration and Ethnic Affairs.

CONTEMPORARY ISSUES

The extent to which deep rooted fears of non-European immigration are confined to a declining minority or are latent throughout a broad cross-section of the community cannot be assessed; politicians clearly consider the area a potential minefield, and appear determined to maintain what may be a fragile consensus until it has time to harden. Some commentators suspect that sensitivity in this area is confined to an age cohort comprised of those brought up in a culture so committed to a policy of exclusion that they are unable to adjust to the changing values and the political realities of the modern world. The fact that the major social institutions—the media, the political parties, the churches, business organizations, and labor unions appear strongly in favor of racial tolerance suggests that individuals and groups hostile to that view remain outside the mainstream of national opinion. Yet no one knows how closely institutional policies and attitudes are reflected in those of the general population. The fact that a considerable proportion of the population is made up of individuals with recent immigration connections does not provide any sure guarantee of tolerant attitudes. Many immigrant groups come from cultural settings where hostility to other ethnic or social groups is taken for granted, and it is possible that some element of intolerance may be carried on through their descendants. These observers who point to the wider education and expanded outlook of the younger generations of Australians find it hard to imagine a resurgence of the older forms of suspicion and fear; others contend that a highly visible surge in immigration during a period of economic recession puts existing levels of tolerance at risk, especially if it results in striking residential concentration.

The aspect of immigration policy that is more clearly on the open political agenda is the relationship of migrant inflow to the health of the economy and to the social order generally, irrespective of the source of supply. As a small and isolated community, Australia has been more preoccupied than most societies with both the immediate and long-term implications of population growth. The relationship between the physical resources of the continent and the size of the population has long been a matter of debate within the political and scientific community. The tendency to assume that a large land mass must inevitably provide sustenance for a large, prosperous, and powerful nation has over the years brought politicians and planners into conflict with both the natural and social scientists. The latter have had to stress that vast areas of the Australian continent are either hostile to conventional agriculture or rich in mineral resources, which do not require settlement, and that the expectations of boosters and developers must be tempered to the realities of climate, rainfall, and soil quality. There has always been general agreement, however, that current population levels could be increased, so that whenever it became clear that natural increase would not be sufficient even to maintain existing levels over the long term, the case for stimulating the flow of immigration has been compelling. Accordingly, the history of immigration policy in the Australian context has always involved governments making judgments about the state of the economy and the appropriate level of intake, and the outcome of those decisions has been a wave-like pattern of inflow: in prosperous years, both governments and potential immigrants are activated by expectations of growth: in leaner years, governments reduce the annual targets and potential settlers make other arrangements. Australians have come to regard the inflow of immigrants as a normal part of the nation's activities; it is the size of the intake and its composition that are subjects for debate.

The economic recession of the mid–1980s saw a consolidation of the trend established in the 1970s toward modest targets and an emphasis on selectivity. The use of a points system to establish eligibility put a premium on the skills, technical qualifications, facility in the English language, investment capital, and links to relatives already in the country. Family reunion became a most obvious feature of the approach to immigration in the 1980s, for a variety of reasons. Politically, it is attractive to ethnic voters, who value the opportunity to have their relatives rejoin them, and it does not disturb the existing ethnic balance. At the same time, the presence of a family support system weakens the fear that the newcomers will remain unemployed and become a charge on expensive social services. It is the kind of immigration pattern that attracts more approval than criticism, and as such, readily attracts bipartisan support. On the other hand, it raises questions about the hidden social costs that may lie beneath even a planned immigration program; for example, does an emphasis on family reunion increase the proportion of the aged in the community, at a time when the graying of the population appears likely in another generation to put increased loads on social services? Or is an expanded immigration the best way of rapidly increasing the younger age groups needed to provide the productive workforce needed to support the increasing number of elderly citizens?

A review of immigration policy issued by the Department of Immigration and Ethnic Affairs early in 1987 suggested that total population would begin declining within 45 years if immigration were to cease. And while not advocating a return to the 150,000 plus annual intakes of the 1950s, the report did foreshadow a continuation of the upward trend since 1984/85 with a target of 115,000 in 1986/87. At the same time, its profile of the nation's population at the end of 1986 underlined the considerable social impact of the post-World War II immigration program: 21 percent of a population of 15.9 million were foreign born, with more than one third of them British or Irish born, and 100,000 being refugees from Vietnam. The 1986 intake of 12,000 refugees included 6,000 Vietnamese, but it also covered groups from the Middle East, Latin America, East Timor, Sri Lanka, Afghanistan, and Africa. In microcosm, a single year's immigration intake underlines the two major themes underlying the overall trend in immigration policy since 1947—the continued reinforcement of the original British stock, coupled with a progressive variation in the volume and composition of the non-British component. While Australian society has come to accept an orderly inflow of new settlers as part of the normal round of life, it remains nervously uncertain as to just what combination of volume and content best serves the interests of economic growth and social cohesion.

NOTES

1. Don Charlwood; *The Long Farewell* (Ringwood, 1983), Chs. I-III.

2. R. B. Madgwick, *Immigration into Eastern Australia, 1788–1851* (London, 1937; Reprinted, Sydney, 1969), p. 12.

3. Ibid. p. 242.

4. The standard account of the goldrush era is in Geoffrey Blainey, *The Rush That Never Ended* (Melbourne, 1978).

5. R. B. Madgwick, op. cit., p. 246.

6. Trevor Reece, *Australia in the Twentieth Century* (Melbourne, 1964), p. 64.

7. R. T. Appleyard, *British Emigration to Australia* (Canberra, 1964), pp. 29–32.

8. Patrick O'Farrell, *The Irish in Australia* (Kensington, 1987).

9. Appleyard, op. cit., p. 34ff.

10. Arthur A. Calwell, *Immigration: Policy and Progress* (Canberra, 1949), Chs. I, II.

11. Appleyard, op. cit., p. 46ff.

12. Ibid., p. 46.

13. R. T. Appleyard, "Immigration and National Development," in Hew Roberts (ed.), *Australia's Immigration Policy* (Perth, 1972), p. 19.

14. Ibid., p. 18.

15. Charles A. Price, et al., *Australian Immigration: A Bibliography and Digest, 1970*, No. 2 (Canberra, 1971), p. A12.

16. The recommendations of the Galbally Report of 1978 involved higher expenditure on the teaching of English, on ethnic radio, and on grants to specific ethnic groups.

17. Price, op. cit., p. A12, A13. See also, John Wilkes (ed.), *How Many Australians?*

Immigration and Growth (Australian Institute of Political Science, 37th Summer School, Canberra, 1971), and Hew Roberts (ed.), *Australia: Immigration Policy* (Nedlands, 1972).

18. Charles A. Price and Jean I. Martin (eds.), *Australian Immigration: A Bibliography and Digest, 1975*, No. 3 (Canberra, 1976), pp. A4–A13.

19. H. I. London, *Non-White Immigration and the "White Australia" Policy* (Sydney, 1970), Ch. I.

20. Andrew Markus, *Fear and Hatred: Purifying Australia and California, 1850–1891* (Sydney, 1979), Ch. II.

21. Charles A. Price, *The Great White Walls Are Built* (Canberra, 1974).

22. A. C. Palfreeman, *The Administration of the White Australia Policy* (Melbourne, 1967), p. 84.

23. Ibid., Ch. II.

24. H. I. London, op. cit., Part II.

25. Ibid., Ch. II.

26. Frances Milne and Peter Shergold (eds.), *The Great Immigration Debate* (Sydney, 1984), Chs. II, III.

27. Ibid., p. 21.

28. Geoffrey Blainey, *All for Australia* (Sydney, 1984); Andrew Markus and M. C. Ricklefs (eds.), *Surrender Australia? . . . Geoffrey Blainey and Asian Immigration* (Sydney, 1985).

3

British Immigration Policy and Politics

ZIG LAYTON-HENRY

Britain has traditionally been a country of emigration. Since the eighteenth century, considerable numbers of Britons have moved overseas and helped establish and populate the United States and countries of the British Commonwealth and Empire. During the nineteenth century, the majority of migrants went to the United States, but after 1900 most emigrated to Canada, Australia, and other Commonwealth countries. By the end of the turn of the century, migration had become a conscious part of British imperial policy, and it was felt that encouraging emigration from Britain to the Commonwealth would help the economic development of the Dominion territories, strengthen the ties with Britain, and increase the power of the Empire. Land grants and assisted passage were used to encourage people to migrate. After World War I, the self-governing Dominions became more selective in their demands for migrants, requiring skilled industrial workers instead of agricultural workers. There was no halt in the outward flow, however, and between 1919 and 1930 two million people emigrated from the United Kingdom.

The depression between the wars caused a change in the balance of migration and the net flow became an inward one. After World War II, however, emigration resumed at a high level, encouraged particularly by the immigration policies of Australia, which was concerned to increase its population for security reasons and also to maintain its British character. Between 1946 and 1950, 720,260 people left Britain, and most of them were relatively highly skilled.[1] The postwar shortage of labor and the resumption of traditional patterns of migration to the Commonwealth were a source of concern for the Royal Commission on population, which the government established toward the end of the war to assess postwar manpower requirements. Nevertheless, government policy continued to facilitate migration for economic and political reasons. Both the government and

Table 3.1.
Net Gain or Loss by Migration from Great Britain, 1871–1941

1871–1880	−257,000	1911–1920	−857,000
1881–1890	−817,000	1921–1930	−565,000
1891–1900	−122,000	1931–1940	+650,000
1901–1910	−756,000		

Note: Great Britain includes England, Scotland and Wales, but not Ireland.

Source: HMSO, Royal Commission on Population, Cmnd 7695, 1949.

the Royal Commission failed to anticipate that the postwar economic boom would lead to spontaneous immigration from the New Commonwealth. (See Table 3.1.).

Considerable migration has also taken place during the past 150 years within the British Isles, especially from the peripheral countries of the United Kingdom (Ireland, Scotland, and Wales) to England. Ireland in particular was a major exporter of migrants: between 1820 and 1910 nearly five million people left the country, including the large numbers who moved to Britain. In 1861 some 3 percent of the English population was born in Ireland, as was 6.7 percent of the population of Scotland. This migration to Britain was facilitated by Ireland's geographical proximity and by the historical links between England and Ireland, which go back to the twelfth century. In 1801 Britain and Ireland were formally united under one parliament, but the union was dissolved in 1921 with the creation of the Irish Free State. Despite the independence of most of Ireland, however, British governments have always allowed unrestricted movement between the two countries and never treated Irish citizens as aliens. They are accorded full citizenship rights, including voting rights, and are not restricted in any way.

Between 1880 and 1914 a significant migration of Russian Jews to Britain occurred as a result of the Tsarist pogroms. Most of these refugees settled in the East End of London, where they met with considerable hostility. A vigorous campaign to control this immigration was organized and led to the first Aliens Act in 1905. This Act forbade entry to people who could not support themselves and their dependents, to people whose infirmities were likely to make them a charge on the rates, and also to some known criminals. The principle of political asylum was reaffirmed, however, and the Liberal government, elected in 1906, was able to use reports of violence against Jews in Russia to mitigate the effects of the Act, although they did not repeal it.[2]

During and after World War II, some 120,000 Poles who had been members of the Allied force settled in Britain, and for the first time a British government took positive action to assist in the integration of alien residents. A Polish

Resettlement Act was passed in 1947 and a Polish Resettlement Corps was established. The integration of the Polish ex-combatants and their families was achieved remarkably smoothly, despite initial union opposition, partly because they had established an institutional infrastructure during the war, partly due to public sympathy for wartime allies (which facilitated government support), but mainly because the acute labor shortage assisted their rapid absorption into the economy. A number of schemes were devised to encourage European Volunteer Workers to come to Britain, but these were not very successful.[3]

THE BACKGROUND TO NEW COMMONWEALTH IMMIGRATION

Britain has traditionally favored the free movement of capital and labor within the Empire, although by the turn of the century all the self-governing Dominions had acted to control immigration to their territories, largely because of concern over the potential of Indian immigration. Britain alone had no restrictions, a principle reaffirmed by the Nationality Act of 1948. A year later a Conservative Party policy document stated: "There must be freedom of movement among its members within the British Empire and Commonwealth. New opportunities will present themselves not only in the countries overseas, but in the Mother country, and must be open to all citizens."[4] The assumption was, however, that the major population movement would continue to be an outflow from the United Kingdom to the Empire and Commonwealth.

Before World War II there already existed small settlements of "colored" people in such port cities as Liverpool, Cardiff, Manchester, and London's East End. These had been established by colonial seamen during the First World War. The high unemployment during the interwar years provided no incentive for migration to Britain, and those who came were largely migrants unable to establish themselves in the Dominions because of the worldwide recession. The outbreak of war in 1939 dramatically changed this situation and set in train the events that were to lead to the major postwar migration of West Indians and Asians to Britain. During the war, colonial labor was recruited to work in forestry and munitions factories, and in the services. Most notably were the 10,000 West Indians recruited to work as ground crews in the Royal Air Force. Considerable numbers of West Indians, Asians, and Africans served in the Allied forces during the war, as well as in the merchant marine.

After the war, every effort was made to repatriate the colonial labor that had been recruited to work in Britain, but a minority decided to remain; moreover, many who returned to the West Indies quickly came back to Britain to seek work and a higher standard of living. The war had given many West Indians experience of life in Britain, and the continued shortage of labor after the war meant that there were plenty of jobs for those wishing to escape poverty and unemployment. In 1948 the British government set up a working party on "Employment in the United Kingdom of Surplus Colonial Labor" to "enquire into

Table 3.2.
Estimated Net Immigration from New Commonwealth, 1953–1962

	West Indies	India	Pakistan	Others	Total
1953	2,000	-	-	-	2,000
1954	11,000	-	-	-	11,000
1955	27,500	5,800	1,850	7,500	42,650
1956	29,800	5,600	2,050	9.350	46,800
1957	23,000	6,600	5,200	7,600	42,400
1958	15,000	6,200	4,700	3,950	29,850
1959	16,400	2,950	850	1,400	21,600
1960	49,650	5,900	2,500	-350	57,700
1961	66,300	23,750	25,100	21,250	136,400
1962*	31,800	19,050	25,080	18,970	94,900

* First 6 months.

Source: House of Commons, Library Research Paper No. 56, *Commonwealth Immigration to the UK from the 1950s to 1975—A Survey of Statistical Sources.*

the possibilities of employing in the United Kingdom surplus manpower of certain colonial territories in order to assist the manpower situation in this country and to relieve unemployment in these colonial territories."[5] The committee noted the serious unemployment situation in Jamaica and the shortage of labor in the United Kingdom, but was concerned about the discrimination "colored" workers would face and the difficulties of assimilating them. It therefore recommended that no organized large-scale immigration of male colonial workers should be contemplated. However, the deliberations of the committee had already been overtaken by events. The first immigrant ships began to arrive from the West Indies during 1948 and a largely spontaneous movement of people had begun. (See Table 3.2.)

In discussing immigration policy, this chapter will be mainly concerned with the immigration of British subjects from Britain's former colonial territories, in particular the West Indies, India, Pakistan, and Bangladesh. This approach has been chosen because "New Commonwealth" immigration has caused the greatest public concern and has dominated the thinking and actions of policymakers.

Geography and Population

Before World War II, the British population could be considered relatively homogeneous, despite the fact that four "nations" inhabited the British Isles. Virtually all were white, English-speaking, and Protestant—except the Irish, who were Roman Catholic. The independence of the Irish Free State in 1921 partially accommodated the national aspirations of the Irish. There has been considerable intermarriage between the different national groups. For the most part they live harmoniously together, except in Northern Ireland, where a majority composed of the descendants of English and Scottish Protestant settlers is in favor of remaining within the United Kingdom while a minority composed of Catholic Irish would prefer a united Ireland. The campaign being waged by the Irish Republican Army for a united Ireland is almost wholly confined to Northern Ireland.

The United Kingdom is a highly urbanized industrial country with a population of nearly 56 million. It has a high population density: 229 persons per square kilometer. The population is concentrated in England, with 46.5 million inhabitants and 356 persons per square kilometer. The major centers of population are in southeastern England in the Greater London area, the Midlands, South Lancashire, and West Yorkshire. Central Scotland and South Wales are also substantial population centers.

As in other countries, society in Britain has been changing rapidly since the war, with a falling birthrate, longer expectation of life, a higher divorce rate, widening educational opportunities, and a rising standard of living. In 1980 there were 754,000 live births, which outnumbered deaths by 93,000. The birthrate declined from 18.0 live births per thousand in 1966 to a historic low point of 11.8 in 1977, but thereafter rose to 13.5 in 1980. Life expectation is now about 70 years for men and 76 for women. Thus, although the total population has remained stable during the past decade, there have been significant changes in its age and sex structure, including a decline in the proportion of young people under 16 and an increase in elderly people. At present, some 18 percent of the population is over the normal retirement ages of 65 for men and 60 for women.

Migration has also contributed to changes in the British population. Between 1971 and 1980 some 2.25 million people emigrated from Britain and 1.9 million immigrated. Most British emigrants left for North America, Australia, and the European Community, while about one third of all immigrants came from New Commonwealth countries. In 1984 the number of inhabitants of New Commonwealth and Pakistani ethnic origin was estimated at approximately 2.3 million, of whom over 40 percent were British-born.

The establishment of a significant ethnic minority population in Britain was neither planned nor anticipated by policymakers. The Royal Commission that published a report on population needs in 1949 had been concerned with the disadvantages of a falling population, especially as it did not wish to recommend discouraging British emigration to other parts of the Commonwealth. It concluded that "A systematic immigration policy could only be welcomed without reserve if the migrants were of good human stock [presumably European] and not prevented by religion or race from intermarrying with the host population and becoming merged with it."[6] The Commission doubted the capacity of an established society like Britain to absorb immigrants of an alien race and religion. The ability of colonial workers to integrate with and be accepted by the native population was a matter that had concerned the Colonial Office in recruiting such labor during the war but, as it turned out, wartime conditions had facilitated their acceptance and integration. Once New Commonwealth immigration developed after the war, the government proved very reluctant to intervene with a policy of either management or control. On the one hand, the government did not wish to seem to be encouraging such immigration; on the other hand, policies of control would have disrupted relations with Colonial and Commonwealth governments. Immigration control would also have reduced the flow of migrant workers at a time of severe labor shortage.

History and Foreign Policy

The most important factors facilitating the migration of New Commonwealth immigrants to Britain and constraining the freedom of action of British policymakers have been the historical and imperial links between Britain and its colonies in the West Indies and former colonies in South Asia. This imperial relationship meant that Colonial and Commonwealth citizens were British subjects and as such were not subject to any immigration controls. Once their identity and citizenship were established at the port of entry, they were free to enter, settle, and seek employment. As British subjects they had full civic rights and could vote, run for parliament, and serve in the armed forces and public service. The imperial connection seems to have given West Indians in particular a high expectation of the wealth and benevolence of the Mother country and feelings that they would be well received, treated as full and equal citizens, and achieve a high standard of living. Many had good memories or reports of the welcome and treatment that West Indians had received in Britain during the war.

Many postwar migrants, however, were ill-prepared for the harsh conditions experienced by the unskilled workers in an urban industrial society. Indians and Pakistanis appear to have migrated with more realistic expectations limited to gaining jobs, a better standard of living, and better prospects for their children. Asian settlers have thus been less disappointed with poor housing conditions than West Indians and express higher levels of satisfaction with life in Britain.[7]

The historical links between Britain and the sending countries meant that many immigrants had some knowledge of the English language, education, and cultural traditions and history. This was most obviously the case in the West Indies, where language, religion, the education system, culture, and sports owed so much to centuries of British influence. The impact of British culture was much less pervasive in India and Pakistan, although many of the early Asian immigrants had experience in the British armed forces and some knowledge of English.

The importance to British policymakers of a peaceful process of decolonialization as far as this was possible, and of maintaining Britain's position in the world through leadership of a Commonwealth of independent nations increasingly composed of "Third World" countries, was a crucial factor constraining British politicians from introducing immigration controls before 1962. British efforts, for example, at establishing a Federation of the West Indies in the 1950s involved long and complicated negotiations between Britain and the various colonial administrations. British attempts to control immigration would have made these negotiations even less likely to succeed. The West Indian economies were weak, the islands suffered from heavy unemployment, and traditional West Indian migration to the United States had been substantially reduced by the McCarren–Walter Act of 1952. Leading West Indian politicians lobbied strongly against controls whenever the issue was raised in Britain. They argued that controls would be economically disastrous for the islands and would undermine not only Britain's leadership in the Commonwealth but the foundations of the Commonwealth itself.

Colonial and Commonwealth governments were to some extent directly represented in the British cabinet; the ministers of Colonial and Commonwealth Affairs represented their views. There was also sympathy among policymakers for the Colonial and Commonwealth territories since many of Britain's political elite had served in these countries as administrators, politicians, or soldiers, or had relatives who had done so. A final factor influencing British policy was a sense of obligation or guilt toward Commonwealth countries for the legacy of colonial exploitation perpetrated by past British governments. This was most strongly felt by the Left in British politics and can be illustrated by the Trade Union Congress' explanation for New Commonwealth migration: "Congress is of the opinion that these coloured workers are driven from their homeland by poverty and social insecurity which are due mainly to unbalanced economies created by long years of colonial exploitation."[8]

Economy

Britain is a trading nation, exporting a higher proportion of its production of goods and services than any other industrial country of comparable size. It exports some 31 percent of its gross national product. The traditional economic strength of the country was based on manufacturing industry, but this has been declining rapidly relative to the service sector. In 1983, some 35 percent of the working population was engaged in engineering, manufacturing, construction, mining, and related industries. Service industries employed 61 percent. Agriculture engaged only 2 percent of the workforce, a lower proportion than in any other major industrial country.[9] Nevertheless, agriculture is highly efficient and produces more than half of the nation's food. Even so, Britain is one of the world's largest importers of agricultural products and also raw materials and semi-man-ufactured goods. The major exports are aerospace products, electrical equipment, finished textiles, and services such as banking and insurance. Britain has recently become self-sufficient in oil due to production from wells in the North Sea.

New Commonwealth immigrants came to Britain in search of work and a better standard of living. The expansion of the British economy in the 1950s and 1960s created a substantial shortage of labor, particularly in the relatively stagnant sectors of the economy—for example, textiles, metal manufacture, and transport, where low pay, long hours, and shiftwork made the jobs unattractive to indigenous British workers. These industries were unable to compete with the expanding sectors for the limited supply of native labor. In periods of economic expansion, the more prosperous regions with expanding industries quickly de-veloped labor shortages, which were partly filled by immigrant workers who concentrated in the major con-urbations of Greater London, the West Midlands, Manchester, Merseyside, and Yorkshire.

They found work mainly as unskilled or semi-skilled workers. In the most extreme case it was found that 58 percent of Pakistani men were doing unskilled or semi-skilled work, compared with 18 percent of white men, while 8 percent of Pakistanis compared with 40 percent of whites were doing nonmanual jobs. For Indians and West Indians the contrast is less extreme, with 36 percent of Indians and 32 percent of West Indians doing unskilled or semi-skilled manual work. All groups, particularly West Indians (59 percent), are well represented in skilled manual trades, but only Indians (20 percent) and East African Asians (30 percent) are well represented among nonmanual occupations.[10]

New Commonwealth immigrants are strongly over-represented in shipbuild-ing, vehicle manufacture, textiles, the manufacturing industry generally, and also in transport. West Indian women are heavily over-represented in the Health Service where they have traditionally been recruited as both nurses and domestic staff. The Health Service has also recruited significant numbers of New Com-monwealth doctors.

Immigrant workers thus formed a replacement labor force and found work mainly as semi-skilled and unskilled workers. They came in a period of labor shortage made more acute by the continual emigration of Britons to Common-wealth and other countries, which was not discouraged. Once the Poles and European Volunteer Workers had been absorbed, there were no easily available sources of European labor for the British economy (except Ireland) because the faster-growing West European economies were absorbing surplus labor from Southern Europe. It was under these conditions that immigration from the West Indies began in 1948, followed quickly by immigration from India and Pakistan.

One interesting contrast between Britain and other major European countries such as France and Germany was the lack of government planning and involve-ment in immigration policy once the migration developed. Freeman argues that British leaders, unlike the French political elite, failed to recognize the contri-bution of immigration to the national economy and to economic growth.[11] From the very beginning the British government was more concerned with "the problems arising from the immigration into this country of coloured people from British Colonial territories" than with the benefits. These problems related to housing, employment, and law and order; the remedy was seen as restriction and control.

"Colored" immigration thus was not to be welcomed as contributing to national wealth and economic growth, but to be discouraged as far as possible. British policymakers were always very aware of the problems of racial prejudice and discrimination that colored immigrants would face in Britain, as well of the dangers of racial disturbances. They were much more aware of the social and political costs of immigration than of its economic benefits, which explains why Britain moved to a position of instituting legislative controls rather earlier than other West European countries. The perception was that of an already overcrowded island with limited resources facing a potentially limitless stream of immigrants from the Indian subcontinent, rather than that of a dynamic and growing economy being held back by a lack of young, fit workers.

The growth of the British economy in the 1950s and 1960s was slow compared with that of other West European countries, and was punctuated by crises over the balance of payments and the role of the pound sterling, and by worries about inflation. It was also a period of rapid withdrawal from imperial commitments and a realization by the British leaders and people of their declining world status. In such a situation immigration was seen as an added burden—not as a valuable asset.

Trade Unions

British unions have traditionally been suspicious of, and hostile toward, high levels of immigration. In the 1890s the Trade Union Council (TUC) passed several resolutions demanding the control of Jewish immigration. After the Second World War strict conditions were imposed on the employment of European Volunteer Workers before the unions would allow their recruitment. They had to join the appropriate union, be the first to lose their jobs in case of redundancy, and their opportunities for promotion were limited. In practice, these conditions were never enforced because of continued economic expansion and full employment. Even so, in some industries, such as mining, the employment of foreign labor proved impossible because of union opposition.[12]

The reaction of the trade unions to New Commonwealth immigration was surprisingly positive, at least at the national level. The Trade Union Congress in 1955 welcomed the new immigrants to Britain and deplored attempts to erect a color bar against Commonwealth citizens. Clearly, union leaders felt an obligation toward immigrants; they felt that immigrants had been forced to come to Britain due to colonial exploitation and lack of investment in their territories. In addition, opposition to colored immigration might be interpreted as racist. Nevertheless, trade union leaders were not confident about the reaction of their members toward "colored" workers. The Working Party on the Employment of Colonial Labour reported that:

The Leaders of the Trade Union movement generally take the line that while they themselves have no objection in principle to the introduction of coloured workers from British territories, the decision whether or not to go on with a recruiting scheme must in every case be left to the local branch in the area of prospective employment. The local Trade Union Officials usually say that they would help if they could, but that the workers in their particular area are not prepared to accept coloured workers in their place of employment.[13]

Beetham has described the efforts by local branches in the transport industry to exclude black workers.[14] Such resistance was gradually overcome as the problem of labor shortage continued. New Commonwealth workers in Britain have a surprisingly high level of trade union membership, higher than native workers, but in several cases the unions have proved reluctant to defend immigrants' interests, especially when these appear to conflict with the interests of native workers. The major problem the migrants faced was a combination of indifference at the national level and hostility in local union branches where ideological inhibition to racial exclusion was weaker.[15]

Social Welfare

The British social welfare system in 1980 was about 18 percent of GNP, and the largest program was the social security system, designed to ensure a basic standard of living for people in financial need. Medical services are available to all residents irrespective of means through the National Health Service. The local authority social services and voluntary organizations provide advice and help to elderly people, disabled people, and children in need of care. New Commonwealth immigrants, as British subjects, have been entitled upon arrival to the whole range of social welfare services. However, the British Nationality Act of 1981 means that Commonwealth citizens are no longer automatically British citizens as well. Those who are accepted for settlement can receive all the services.

In the housing market, as in employment, immigrants tended to fulfill a replacement role. They were forced to buy or rent cheap, older housing in inner-city areas that were being vacated by native white families moving to new suburban housing estates away from the city centers. They did not qualify, unless homeless, for local authority housing because it required local residential qualifications, often five years' residence, and this excluded new migrants. The outward flow from urban areas to suburbs, dormitory towns, and semi-rural areas has continued, leaving inner-city areas populated by immigrant families and poor, often elderly, whites.[16]

New Commonwealth immigrants have now achieved the residential qualifications necessary for local authority housing, resulting in a large movement of West Indian families into such housing. Nearly 50 percent are now housed this way. Asians have preferred to remain in owner occupation and continue to suffer from overcrowding, although this problem is declining.

The educational system in Britain is comprehensive, although a small but significant private sector also exists. Asian and West Indian children therefore go to the same state schools as native white children. Because of the residential concentration of immigrant families, however, their children tend to go to schools where a majority of the children are also Asian or West Indian.[17]

The presence of substantial ethnic minority populations with their own cultural traditions presents a considerable challenge to the social services. The assumptions underlying the service hitherto provided for a homogeneous population with shared cultural and linguistic codes; these are being undermined. Moreover, distinctive cultural patterns are not being rapidly eroded, as happened with previous immigrants; they are being maintained by such factors as childhood socialization, residential segregation, and also as a result of reaction to the hostility of the majority population.

While in many respects, immigrant families, because of their relative youthfulness, make less demands on the social services than the host population, this is not perceived to be the case by the majority population, who resent the ability of immigrants to receive council accommodation, healthcare and unemployment benefits. Moreover, the cultural distinctiveness of immigrant groups may require ethnically sensitive provision, which draws attention to the welfare benefits they are receiving. This may be strongly resented by parts of the host population, which feels that immigrants should assimilate. Special provision may also be seen as reducing scarce public resources and may thus result in political conflict.[18]

Instruments of Regulation and Control

In the seven years up to 1962 nearly 500,000 New Commonwealth citizens settled in Britain, most of whom were later joined by their wives and other dependents. The 1962 Commonwealth Immigrants Act was introduced to regulate this flow by using a system of employment vouchers to control the number of arrivals for settlement. There were three categories of vouchers: category A for Commonwealth citizens with a specific job to come to; category B issued by British High Commissions overseas to those with such recognized skills or qualifications that were in short supply; and category C for anybody at all on a first-come, first-served basis with priority to those with war service.

Between 1962 and 1965 vouchers were issued liberally in accordance with previous rates of immigration. The importance of the immigration issue in the 1964 general election, however, caused the new Labor government to be determined to stem the flow of New Commonwealth immigrants. In August 1965 the government arbitrarily restricted the number of employment vouchers to 8,500 (of which 1,000 were reserved for Malta). Category C vouchers, for which there was a waiting list of over 400,000, were abolished.

In 1968 additional controls were introduced to reduce the flow of British passport holders of Asian descent from East Africa. The "Kenyanisation" policies of the Kenya government had resulted in increasing redundancies among Asian holders of United Kingdom passports, and the numbers of Kenyan Asians coming to Britain rose from 6,150 in 1965 to 13,600 in 1967. Some 12,823 arrived in the first two months of 1968, by which time a campaign against the movement had been mounted by two rightwing members of Parliament, Duncan Sandys and Enoch Powell.

The government capitulated to this campaign and controls were introduced in the form of the Commonwealth Immigrants Act of 1968. This required all citizens of the United Kingdom and colonies with no substantial connection to the United Kingdom (for example, by birth or descent) to obtain an entry voucher before arriving. This was the first time a distinction was made between patrial and non-patrial citizens of the United Kingdom, and the clear intention of the distinction was to control "colored" immigration from the Commonwealth while allowing white Commonwealth citizens of British descent unrestricted access. At first, 1,500 vouchers were made available per annum for heads of household from East Africa. In 1971, this was raised to 3,000 with an additional 1,500 vouchers for people in special difficulty issued on a once and for all basis. In 1975, the quota was raised to 5,000.

Before the Immigration Act of 1971 came into force, the system of control over the entry of foreign nationals (as opposed to Commonwealth citizens) derived from the Alien Restrictions Acts of 1914 and 1919 and rules drawn up under the Acts to cover admissions, supervision and deportations. Foreign nationals were admitted to Britain to take employment provided they held a work permit issued by the Department of Employment. A permit was issued for a particular job with a particular employer. Employment was limited to a maximum of one year in the first instance, but could be extended on application from the employer. Unlike Commonwealth citizens, foreign nationals were required to register with the police. After a foreign national had been in approved employment for four years he or she could apply to the Home Office for cancellation of the conditions imposed on that employment and length of stay in the United Kingdom, which was normally granted. The foreign national could then stay indefinitely and engage in any kind of employment. Between 1960 and 1968 some 15,000–20,000 people were having their conditions cancelled annually.[19]

The Immigration Act of 1971, still in force today, replaced all previous legislation with one statute that made provisions for control of the admission and stay of Commonwealth citizens and foreign nationals. The Immigration Act recognized a "right of abode" that citizens of the United Kingdom and colonies, and certain Commonwealth citizens, are entitled to because of a close connection with the United Kingdom by birth, descent, or marriage. People who have this right are known as "patrials". They are entirely free from immigration control and may live and work in the United Kingdom without any restrictions. The Act defines patrials as:

1. Citizens of the United Kingdom and Colonies who have citizenship by birth, adoption, registration, or naturalization in the United Kingdom or that have a parent or grandparent who was born in the United Kingdom or has acquired citizenship by adoption, registration or naturalization.

2. Citizens of the United Kingdom and Colonies who have come from overseas, have been accepted for permanent residence, and have resided in the UK for five years.

3. Commonwealth citizens who have a parent born in the United Kingdom.

4. Women who are Commonwealth citizens (including citizens of the United Kingdom and Colonies) and are or have been married to a man in any of these categories.

Everybody entering Britain, including patrials, needs a valid passport or other recognized identity document. In addition, visas are required in the case of foreign nationals or an entry certification in the case of Commonwealth citizens who wish to settle in the United Kingdom; visas are also required from nationals of Eastern Europe, Cuba, and some African and Asian countries.

In September 1986 the government introduced visa restrictions on visitors from Ghana, Nigeria, India, and Bangladesh. This was the first time visas were imposed on people from Commonwealth countries. In addition, visas were required from people travelling from Pakistan. Visas were justified by the government on the grounds that they were necessary to relieve the strain on immigration officials due to an increase of people from these countries claiming to be tourists, visitors, or students but who the government felt were trying to settle in Britain. These five countries were chosen because the pressures to migrate from them were high. The defense of the introduction of visas was made easier by the fact that each of these countries already required visas from British visitors, so the arrangement could be said to be reciprocal and not unfairly discriminatory.

Visitors are admitted for six months (with six months' extension) if they satisfy the immigration officer that they intend to stay for the period stated, can maintain and accommodate themselves and their dependents without working or recourse to public funds, and can meet the costs of their return journey. Overseas students are admitted for the period of their course of study.

Work permits are required for all foreign nationals seeking employment except patrials, nationals of the European community, immigrants of independent means seeking to establish themselves as self-employed businessmen, and young Commonwealth citizens on working holidays. Work permits are available for overseas workers only if they hold recognized professional qualifications or a high degree of skill or experience. For most occupations they are issued only to workers aged 23–54 with a good command of the English language. They are issued for a particular job with a specified employer when there is no suitable worker in the United Kingdom or other EEC country. Work permits are initially issued for twelve months and extensions of stay are granted by the Home Office. After four more years permit holders can apply for the removal of time limit and if granted they are regarded as settled and are free to take any employment with approval. Certain categories of employment are exempt from these restrictions— for example, doctors, ministers of religion, and representatives of overseas firms with no branches or subsidiaries in the United Kingdom.

Wives and children of men settled in the United Kingdom may be admitted subject to the possession of an entry certificate; other elderly dependent relatives may also be admitted, provided their kin have the means to maintain and accommodate them. Husbands of women settled in the United Kingdom will be admitted unless there is reason to believe it is a marriage of convenience.

Refugees are a special category and may be admitted if the only country that they could be sent to is one where they are unwilling to go for fear of persecution. The main example of refugees being admitted since the war are the Hungarians in 1956, Ugandian Asians in 1972, and most recently the Vietnamese boat people. The British government, of course, had special obligations toward the Ugandian Asians, most of whom were British passport holders.

Citizenship of the United Kingdom may be acquired by a Commonwealth citizen through registration and by foreign nationals through naturalization. The conditions for naturalization are five years' residence, good character, a sufficient knowledge of English, and an intention to reside in the United Kingdom. Foreign nationals and citizens of Commonwealth countries of which the Queen is not Head of State must take an oath of allegiance. The granting of naturalization is at the discretion of the Home Secretary. Commonwealth and Irish citizens that were settled in Britain on January 1, 1973, when the Immigration Act of 1971 came into force, have the right to be registered as citizens at any time after completing five years' continuous residence in Britain without satisfying any other requirements. A Commonwealth citizen who is patrial has an absolute right to be registered after five years' residence. A woman who is not a citizen has the right to acquire citizenship by registration if she marries a citizen.

Once a person gains admittance to the United Kingdom he or she is relatively free from internal controls. There are no identity cards or other systems of internal controls and such controls as there are apply only to aliens (excluding the Irish). The Irish Republic forms a Common Travel Area together with Britain, and the two governments cooperate in a joint system of frontier controls. The substantial coastline of the United Kingdom is a possible source of illegal immigrants but does not seem to have been a significant factor thus far. In the late 1960s considerable publicity was given to the arrest of small parties of Asians that were landed on quiet beaches from small boats, but the numbers involved were insignificant.

Evasion of controls has occurred, particularly in the period 1962–1965. The most common form of evasion at present is probably overstaying. The long distance and therefore the cost of travel from the West Indies and Indian subcontinent does not appear to have been a deterrent to migration; communications between Britain and the colonies or former colonies were naturally very good. In fact, communications between Britain and West Indian islands were better than communications between the islands themselves.

THE OUTCOME OF REGULATION AND CONTROL

Recent British governments have found it difficult to limit the inflow of New Commonwealth immigrants as much as they would wish, mainly because there are still significant numbers of dependents, especially in the Indian subcontinent, who have the right to join husbands and fathers settled in Britain. In recent years controversy has focused on the entry of husbands and male fiancés coming from the Indian subcontinent, many of whom are suspected by the government of contracting "marriages of convenience" with the primary intention of securing entry to the UK. Various devices have been used to control this, notably the "Primary Purpose Rule" by which an immigration officer can refuse entry to an immigrant if he considers the marriage or proposed marriage is primarily concerned with securing entry to the UK.

There are also small numbers of East African Asians, now resident in India, who hold UK passports and have the right to come to Britain. In the future as the date for the transfer of Hong Kong to the People's Republic of China draws closer, increasing numbers of Hong Kong Chinese may wish to migrate to the UK.

"Colored" immigration remains a political issue in Britain, despite the strictness of immigration controls and the decline in immigration from the New Commonwealth and Pakistan. Since 1972 such immigration has declined from 68,500 to 22,500 and now constitutes less than half of all immigration to the UK. Total immigration to the UK in 1986 was 46,800, the largest groups coming from Western Europe. (See Table 3.3.)

Despite this decline, the Conservative government feels that the pressure to migrate from the Indian subcontinent remains very high and that continuing tough legislative and administrative measures are needed to keep the numbers as low as possible. Various methods have been used to achieve this. One method has been the strict enforcement of the immigration rules at the ports and the deportation of people who break the conditions of entry. Another method has been the requirement that intending immigrants must obtain entry vouchers at British High Commissions or Embassies in their country of origin. Through the demand for documentary proof of birth, marriage, and identity, prospective immigrants have been made to wait long periods before gaining permission to enter. In August 1985, immigration officials were allowed to admit wives or fiancés for a probationary period to ensure that the marriage was genuine. It has been argued that some prospective immigrants give up the attempt to gain entry due to the delays and bureaucracy and that some children may be disqualified by being over-age by the time the waiting period is over.[20]

The strain and anguish suffered by separated families must be very great.

Table 3.3.
Immigration to the UK from the New Commonwealth and Pakistan, 1962–1986

1962*	16,453	1969	44,503	1976	55,013	1983	27,550
1963	56,071	1970	37,893	1977	44,160	1984	24,800
1964	52,840	1971	44,261	1978	42,940	1985	27,740
1965	53,887	1972	68,519	1979	37,050	1986	22,520
1966	48,104	1973	32,247	1980	33,620		
1967	60,633	1974	42,531	1981	31,370		
1968	60,620	1975	53,265	1982	30,380		

* Second half of the year

Source: HMSO, Control of Immigration Statistics, 1962–86

There have been a number of highly publicized cases where, after a public campaign, Home Office decisions have been reversed. In 1981, for example, a British-born woman of Pakistani origin won her case to bring her three young children to Britain after a six-year campaign. Evidence of parentage, including blood tests, was provided by the television program *World in Action*. In general, however, public opinion appears to be less concerned with the suffering caused by controls than with the enforcement of them, and this is certainly the view of the Thatcher Conservative government.[21] Appeals against the decisions of immigration officers have a low rate of success (20 percent in 1986) and action against illegal entrants has risen sharply. Following the introduction of visas for the four New Commonwealth countries and Pakistan, the government ended the right of Members of Parliament to effect an automatic stop on deportation for people from those countries.

Growing restrictions on New Commonwealth immigrants have progressively undermined the rights that nonpatrial citizens have enjoyed in the past, such as freedom from immigration control, freedom to settle, the right to family life, and the right to pass in and out of Britain without let or hindrance. British citizens of Asian and West Indian descent may have difficulty bringing in dependents due to the need to prove their relationship in order to gain an entry certificate, and they may be anxious about going abroad for fear of problems when they try to re-enter the country. Attempts to reduce "colored" immigration have thus resulted in the refusal of people entitled to come, harsh treatment at the ports of entry, and the long separation of families where dependents are waiting for entry certificates. Some immigrants—for example, East African Asians—have been admitted on temporary visitors' permits so that their entrance does not show up on the numbers accepted for settlement, until they apply for the removal of conditions that reduce their right to work.

Internal control has not been a method much used in Britain in the past, but it may be in the future. Contact with the police may result in colored people being asked to prove their immigrant status. There have been cases of passports being demanded before free hospital treatment was given. In 1980 there were a number of well publicized cases of police raids on hotels and stores to search for illegal immigrants, but these appear to have been isolated cases. Certainly tough immigration policies were an important part of the Conservative administration's electoral promises in 1979, and publicity showing that they were being tough would not be unwelcome to many of the rightwing of the party.

There have been a number of amnesties for illegal immigrants, but they have not been entirely successful. In 1974 the Labor Home Secretary announced an amnesty to overcome the retrospective nature of the 1971 Immigration Act. Yet many immigrants came forward who were overstayers rather than illegal entrants and found they were not covered by the amnesty. A number were deported. Perhaps partly because of this, relatively few people have come forward as a result of amnesties; moreover, the figures do suggest there are relatively few illegal immigrants compared with the numbers of people who break their condition of entry.

At present, the Conservative government has shifted the emphasis of its control from immigration to nationality. The British Nationality Act (1981) defines citizenship so that it relates to close connection with the United Kingdom. The Act removes the imperial obligations of *Civis Britannicus sum* under which all colonial and Commonwealth citizens were British subjects with full rights of citizenship. There are now three types of citizenship: British citizenship, citizenship of the British Dependent Territories, and British Overseas citizenship.

British citizens are people who have a close personal connection with the United Kingdom either because their parents or grandparents were born, adopted, naturalized, or registered as citizens of the United Kingdom or because of their own permanent settlement in the country. As a general rule British citizenship from now on will be transmitted only to the first generation born abroad. Citizenship of the British Dependent Territories is acquired by citizens of the United Kingdom and colonies who have citizenship by reason of their own or their parents' or grandparents' birth, naturalization, or registration in an existing dependency or associated state. They do not have the right to enter and settle in the United Kingdom. British Overseas citizens will not be able to pass on this citizenship to their children, nor will they have the right of abode in any British territory. In reality it is an invitation to those British subjects permanently settled abroad and with no close connection with the United Kingdom to acquire their full citizenship as quickly as possible; since this citizenship cannot be passed on to descendents, some children might be born stateless if their countries of birth refused them citizenship. This residential category—a citizenship without rights—is a clear indication that the Conservative government wishes to divest itself of the remaining obligations related to the imperial status of British subjects. (See Figure 3.1.)

RACE RELATIONS POLICY

Britain has been slow to develop a race relations policy. In the early postwar period special help was given to integrate the Poles, and later special arrangements were made for the Hungarian refugees in 1956, the Ugandan Asians in 1972, and the Vietnamese refugees in 1979–1982. The Mass of New Commonwealth immigrants, however, were largely left to fend for themselves. They had come predominantly of their own accord, and as British subjects had full civic and legal rights; therefore, special measures were not considered appropriate. In addition, there was concern that positive action might lead to popular resentment.

Yet by the early 1960s, when controls were first introduced, it was becoming evident that "colored" immigrants suffered from substantial levels of discrimination, especially in housing and employment. To compensate for its decision to tighten controls, the Labor government passed in 1965 the first Race Relations Act, making discrimination in public places unlawful. This linking of tough controls with positive measures toward ethnic minorities has been a constant theme of successive governments. For example, the election manifesto of Mrs. Thatcher's first government stated that "firm immigration control for the future is essential if we are to achieve good community relations . . . and will remove from those settled, and in many cases, born here, the label of immigrant."[22] Since controls are now widely accepted as being as tough as practicable, the emphasis of government policy is changing toward policies for a multiracial society that contains substantial ethnic minorities suffering particular difficulties. (See Table 3.4.)

The major declared aim of government policy is the integration of ethnic minorities through ensuring that they receive equal opportunities and equal treatment. It is now widely recognized that the integration of New Commonwealth immigrants and their descendents will not result in complete assimilation, as has been the case with past influxes of European migrants.

The new ethnic minorities are keen to preserve their own cultural and religious traditions. The size and geographical concentration of the West Indian and Asian settlements will also help to preserve their distinctive identity, which may be reinforced by their experience of racial prejudice and discrimination. All major political parties, with the partial exception of the far right of the Conservative party, are now committed to the removal of racial disadvantages suffered by ethnic minorities, although there is considerable disagreement as to how this can best be achieved. Many of the left would favor positive discrimination, but this is highly unpopular with public opinion.

The basis of policy to aid integration has been a series of race relations acts aimed at combating racial discrimination. Institutions to enforce the acts and

Figure 3.1
All Acceptances for Settlement: Summary 1975–1985

Number
of persons
(000's)

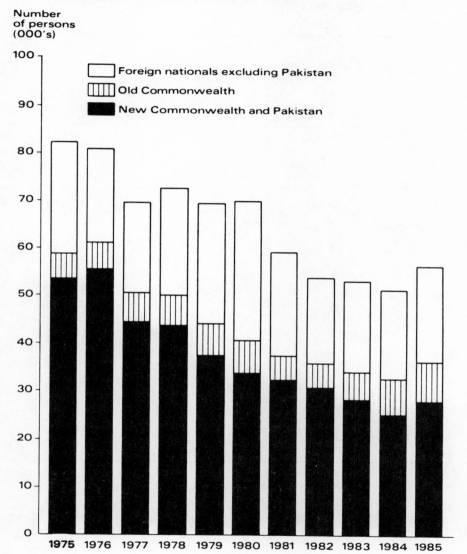

Foreign nationals excluding Pakistan
Old Commonwealth
New Commonwealth and Pakistan

Source: Control of Immigration Statistics, HMSO 1986

Table 3.4:
Population by Ethnic Group, Distinguishing the Population Born in the UK,
Great Britain, 1983–1984

				Thousands
Ethnic Group	1983 LFS		1984 LFS	
	All	Persons Born	All	Persons Born
	Persons	in the UK	Persons	in the UK
White	50,798	48,771	50,895	48,871
West Indian	503	247	529	281
or Guyanese				
Indian	791	263	807	290
Pakistani	355	139	371	151
Bengladeshi	81	26	93	30
Chinese	106	21	109	24
African	91	32	109	35
Arab	69	10	63	5
Mixed	196	148	205	146
Other	109	24	75	19
Not Stated	879	650	829	549
All Ethnic				
Groups	53,979	50,331	54,084	50,400

Source: Labour Force Survey 1983, 1984, HMSO 1986

promote good race relations have been established. The Commission for Racial Equality is a statutory body established by the 1976 Race Relations Act to enforce its provisions, to promote the elimination of racial discrimination, and to foster equality of opportunity and good race relations. It succeeded two earlier bodies, the Race Relations Board and the Community Relations Commission.

Good community relations and racial harmony are avowed goals of government policy but, in spite of the inner-city riots that occurred in 1981 and 1985, the government remains totally opposed to the kind of tough affirmative action policies introduced in the United States in the wake of the urban riots of the late

1960s. This is in spite of continuing evidence that racial discrimination, especially in the labor market, remains at a high level.[23] Positive initiatives to encourage equal opportunity policies have largely been left to the Commission for Racial Equality or to local authorities, some of whom have taken a lead in promoting anti-racist education, housing, and employment policies. This has been very controversial, especially in inner London.

The most critical area is probably police–black relations. There is considerable evidence that relations between young blacks and the police are very bad.[24] Lord Scarman described the 1981 Brixton riots as an outburst of anger and resentment by young blacks against the police.[25] Many of Scarman's recommendations in his report on the riots concerned police procedures, training, and recruitment, but these were not welcomed by the police.[26] In spite of targeted campaigns, the recruitment of officers from the ethnic minorities has been very unsuccessful. In 1986 there were only 882 ethnic minority police officers out of a total police force of 161,855—equivalent to 0.54 percent. The Home Secretary expressed his concern in June 1986, when he said, "It is wrong for any section of society to be excluded or to exclude itself from the policing of the community."[27] But relations between the police and the ethnic minorities are bedeviled by mutual suspicion and distrust. The police in inner-city areas see young blacks as being heavily involved in crime, while young blacks feel they suffer from police harassment. Many black people also feel inadequately protected against racial provocation and attacks by young whites.[28]

INSTRUMENTS OF RACE RELATIONS POLICY

Housing

The allocation of housing in Britain is predominantly a function of private market forces and local authorities, who own about 30 percent of the housing stock. Migrants were initially forced to seek whatever accommodation was available—usually privately rented accommodation in run-down inner-city areas. Accommodation in better residential areas was expensive to buy and difficult to rent because of discrimination and a lack of availability. In the short term, local authority accommodation was unavailable to immigrants, except the homeless, since most local authorities would not accept on their waiting lists people who had not been resident for a period, usually five years. Once on the list, people who had been waiting the longest had priority, depending on need and circumstances.

Since private rents were often high, many immigrants were forced to buy cheap leasehold or freehold property in inner-city areas vacated by white families anxious to move to the more desirable suburban estates being built at a rapid rate in the 1950s and 1960s. These inner-city homes were then often rented to or shared with later arrivals. Homeless people and families are routinely housed by local authorities in their poorest accommodations, in part because low-quality housing is more likely to be available and in part because the homeless have little choice but to accept what is offered. Homelessness is, in other words, not a good way of gaining accommodation.

There is some evidence that the housing situation is changing rapidly, especially for West Indians. In 1978 the National Dwelling and Housing Survey found that the proportion of West Indian households in council housing had risen from 25 percent in 1971 to 45 percent in 1978 and for Asians there was a rise from 4 percent to 10 percent. By 1982, the figure for West Indians had stabilized at 46 percent, but had risen to 19 percent for Asians. Redevelopment of inner-city areas may be a contributing factor, as well as the fulfillment of council requirements by minority families. Owner occupation among West Indians was 41 percent compared to 72 percent among Asians and 59 percent among whites.[29]

One further factor in the housing market is the high concentration of immigrant communities. In a Department of the Environment report it was found that 10 percent of the census enumeration districts housed 70 percent of the black population. In these districts they formed 20 percent of the population. These districts also contained three times as many people living at a density of 1.5 persons per room, which is the statutory definition of overcrowding.[30]

There has been considerable controversy over the concentration of black immigrants and over whether a policy for dispersal in the allocation of housing, as was operated for a time by a Birmingham council, or the busing of immigrant children to schools in other areas to achieve a more racially balanced mix of children, as happened in Ealing, would help integration. It has now been decided that the cost of "forced" dispersal is too high to the minority communities; the policy has now been declared discriminatory and has been ended.

Rex and Tomlinson in their survey of Handsworth found to their surprise that immigrants did not even mount a campaign for equality of access to suburban housing on the new estates. The social development department in Birmingham found that 90 percent of the immigrants interviewed preferred inner-city areas and that there was a marked unwillingness to move to estates located on the fringe of the city. What immigrants did oppose as discriminatory was the dispersal policy itself, in part because it effectively reduced the number of offers of council accommodation that they were likely to receive but also because it involved the forced break-up of black communities.[31]

Employment

New Commonwealth immigrants work in a wide variety of mainly manual occupations and industries and tend to be concentrated in unskilled and semi-skilled jobs. They have traditionally taken jobs rejected by native workers due to low pay, long and unsocial hours, or unpleasant work conditions. New Commonwealth workers are over-represented in shipbuilding, vehicle manufacture, and textiles. In London, West Indians are concentrated in transport and laboring jobs and Pakistanis and Bangladeshis in the clothing trade; over half the workers in the catering industry are also immigrants. In the West Midlands, Asians are concentrated in furnace, forge, foundry, and rolling mills. In the north of England, Asians work mainly in the textile industry. In Yorkshire and Humberside, where 6 percent of the general population work in textiles, 62 percent of Pakistanis do so. This is often permanent nightshift work.[32]

The National Health Service is a major employer of New Commonwealth immigrant workers, and this appears to contribute significantly to the proportions of Indian and East African Asians in professional positions. One third of hospital medical staff and one sixth of doctors in general practice were born overseas. This is also true of 20 percent of student nurses. Smith found that New Commonwealth men had generally little success in penetrating white collar and professional jobs; 40 percent of native whites held such jobs compared with only 8 percent of West Indians, Pakistanis, and Bangladeshis; the proportion of Indians was 20 percent, and East African Asians 30 percent. Many of the immigrants were in lower-paid professional jobs and many of the Indians and Asians are shopkeepers. However, despite the attention given to Asian entrepreneurs, the vast majority of Asians are not businessmen and many that are have markets restricted largely to the supply of their own communities.

Due to their relative youthfulness, a higher proportion of New Commonwealth men are working (91 percent) compared with the general male population (77 percent), although this distinction disappears in the 15–54 age group, where 93 percent of the immigrant males are economically active compared with 91 percent of indigenous males. Among women, 50 percent of the New Commonwealth migrants were working, compared with 43 percent of adult British women. There were considerable discrepancies between different groups of immigrant women, with 74 percent of West Indian women working, 45 percent of Indians, and only 17 percent of Muslim women (Pakistani and Bangladeshi). In the latter case, cultural, religious, and language barriers inhibit employment.[33]

All the major studies show a high level of trade union membership among immigrant workers. Among the men, 61 percent are members of a trade union, compared with 47 percent of native men. Despite high levels of immigrant worker membership, however, and despite union rhetoric in favor of equality of opportunity for black and white workers as well as union resolutions against racism at union conferences, few positive initiatives have been taken on behalf of immigrants. If anything, there has been a reluctance to support industrial action promoted by immigrant members. British unions are also somewhat uncertain about positive action policies, as this might be interpreted as discrimination against white members. Only a handful of black workers have achieved union office and some unions increasingly appear to represent a privileged white aristocracy of labor.

It is illegal for employers to discriminate against job applicants on the grounds of race or skin color, but nevertheless there is considerable evidence that such discrimination takes place. Members of ethnic minorities are particularly vulnerable in periods of recession and the 1980s have seen dramatic levels of unemployment in Britain. Since 1981 unemployment has been around 3 million, or 13 percent of the working population, but unemployment among Asian men has been 20 percent, and among West Indian men 25 percent.[34] Asians and West Indians also tend to suffer longer periods of unemployment. Once unemployed, members of ethnic minorities respond by taking less desirable jobs, which reinforces their position in the lowest sectors of the labor market.

Education

The government and local authorities were slow to respond to the growing number of immigrant children entering the schools in areas of New Commonwealth settlement. The education system was changing from a selective grammar school system to a comprehensive one, but the system was well established and assumed cultural and religious homogeneity. At first the influx of immigrant children was seen as causing problems only when the children were Asian non-English speakers. In the past it had been assumed that foreign children would quickly pick up English in the schools, but the geographical concentration of New Commonwealth immigrants caused white parents in areas of immigrant settlement to protest at the holding back of native children. This caused the Department of Education to recommend, in 1965, that immigrant children should not form more than 30 percent of the pupils in any school.

In the 1960s provision began to be made for additional resources to help with language teaching for immigrant children and modest funds were allocated in the Local Government Act of 1966. In 1976 local educational authorities spent £20 million for additional teachers, liaison officers, interpreters, clerical staff, ancillary school staff, social workers, and educational welfare officers. Some £15 million was contributed by central government. Financial help with school buildings has also been available under the urban aid program that began in 1969 and also from the European Community social fund, but such aid has been very small.

The geographical concentration of the immigrant community has resulted in a considerable amount of segregation of immigrant children. Some authorities for a time resorted to busing to get a better mix of children, but this brought resentment from both immigrant parents whose children suffered long school hours (to include travel) and from white parents. Segregation is often increased in inner-city areas because many of the white families living there are Irish and their children go to parochial Catholic schools.

The presence of immigrant children in the schools has challenged the assumptions and underlying school curricula and has exposed the ethnocentric and even racist bias of courses and textbooks, especially in subjects such as history, English literature, and religious education. Serious research is now being done into multicultural education.

There is increasing evidence that West Indian children are performing badly in terms of academic achievement and, despite a number of inquiries and studies, the reasons for this are unclear. Attention is being given to language problems caused by the use of Jamaican patois or Creole; cultural and consequently behavioral problems that cause West Indian children to be classified as educationally subnormal and dumped into "problem" schools; and problems of family background.[35] In marked contrast to West Indian children, the Asian children appear to perform better academically, despite language problems and deprived family backgrounds. However, both Asian and white children in inner-city areas are disadvantaged because of the low academic achievement expected of children in these areas.

Thus, instead of a national policy on ethnic minority education, there has been only a number of ad hoc expedients. Some of these, such as the establishment of Education Priority Areas and the Center for Information and Advice on Educational Disadvantages, cover ethnic minority children as part of general programs. The Department of Education has established a multi-ethnic inspectorate and a number of local authorities have appointed staff responsible for multi-ethnic education provision.

Inner-City Policy

A further instrument of policy with particular reference to ethnic minorities is the range of programs known as inner-city policies. These programs apply only to all residents, both black and white, who live in inner-city communities; but since these are areas of high minority concentrations, the programs are considered to apply particularly to immigrants. Thus, while the Labor government's white paper on *Inner City Policy in 1977* did not mention race relations, the Minister of the Environment argued that inner-city policy was an important contribution to the fight against racism. This political ambiguity is deliberate; the policy can be defended as universally applicable in the designated areas while, in practice, resources can be steered to areas of racial stress.

A variety of such programs has been initiated, but all have been limited to relatively small resources. The 1974/75 Labor government made more initiatives in this area than previous governments; between 1976 and 1979 approximately £20 million per year was made available to inner-city areas under the Urban Aid program. This has now been substantially increased to improve inner-city investment. Since 1979, the Conservative government has also considered various initiatives to aid the inner cities, but the schemes developed, such as Enterprise Zones and Urban Development Corporations, are extremely limited and not specifically aimed at helping ethnic minorities. The urban riots that occurred in Bristol in 1980 and in London and Liverpool in 1981 resulted in similar small-scale initiatives. In 1987 Mrs. Thatcher reaffirmed her intention of giving high priority to rejuvenating inner-city areas, but a government as committed to public expenditure cuts as the present Conservative government is unlikely to provide the massive investment that these areas need.

Anti-Discrimination Legislation

The Labor government elected in 1964 was concerned, for ideological reasons, to balance its "about face" on immigration controls by positive measures against discrimination. In 1965 the first Race Relations Act was passed outlawing discrimination in public places, but stipulating conciliation procedures rather than criminal sanctions. The Act set up the Race Relations Board and the National Committee for Commonwealth Immigrants.

After considerable evidence of continuing discrimination, especially in employment, the second Race Relations Act was passed in 1968. This Act made it unlawful to discriminate on grounds of color, race, or ethnic or national origins in recruitment, training, promotion, dismissals, and terms and conditions of employment. Complaints were to be referred first to the relevant industrial tribunal; if the complainant was dissatisfied with the decision of the approved industrial tribunal, appeal could be made to the Race Relations Board. The Board would then seek to form an opinion as to whether discrimination had occurred and, if it had, seek conciliation. It was hoped that by these means discrimination would be reduced, not only in the conciliated cases, but also in numerous others where knowledge of the Board's work would have a preventive and educative effect. The Act also outlawed discrimination in housing and the provision of commercial and other services. The publication and display of discriminatory notices or advertisements were also banned. If conciliation efforts by the Board failed, then legal proceedings could be undertaken to secure compliance with the law.

A Parliamentary Select Committee on Race Relations and Immigration was also established in 1968. Since then the Committee has collected considerable evidence on a wide variety of topics concerned with ethnic minorities and has published a large number of reports. One of these reports reviewed the administration of race relations legislation and was influential in determining the content of the 1976 Race Relations Bill that generally strengthened anti-discrimination legislation.

By 1975 both the Race Relations Board and the Community Relations Committee were arguing that existing legislation was insufficient to deal with widespread discrimination, especially in housing and employment. Extensive surveys by Political and Economic Planning confirmed that discrimination in the areas of rented accommodation and employment remained high and that the problems of disadvantage suffered by ethnic minorities also added greatly to their social deprivation. the additional recommendations by the Select Committee caused the Labor Home Secretary, Roy Jenkins, to introduce a strong new race relations bill.

The new bill represented a considerable advance on previous legislation. It extended the definition of discrimination to include not only direct discrimination but also indirect discrimination where unjustifiable practices and procedures that apply to everyone have the effect of putting people of a particular racial group at a disadvantage. It allowed individuals who felt that they had been discriminated against on racial grounds to take their complaint to the County court in all cases except employment, which could be submitted to industrial tribunals. It abolished the Race Relations Board and the Community Relations Commission and established a Commission for Racial Equality (CRE) with greatly increased powers of investigation and enforcement to enable it to make a wider strategic use of the law in the public interest.

In 1980/81 the CRE had a staff of 224 and a budget of £7 million with which it was expected both to promote good race relations practices in the community, especially with employers, local authorities, and other major institutions, and to enforce the Race Relations Act. Not surprisingly, the CRE has failed to live up to the expectations of its liberal supporters. The environment within which it works—a deeply prejudiced society—is hostile to its aims, and without government backing its resources are insufficient to challenge powerful organizations such as building societies, banks, multinational corporations and local authorities. Such backing was lost in 1979 when a Conservative government, unsympathetic to the aims of the CRE, was elected. Attempts to introduce racial monitoring into the Civil Service, to investigate the immigration service after the ''virginity testing'' scandal at Heathrow airport, and to introduce a code of practice for employers, succeeded only after considerable government resistance was overcome.

The Outcome of Race Relations Policy

The aims of race relations policy have been poorly defined and government policy lacks coordination, so that a wide range of government departments, local authorities, and organizations such as the police play important but autonomous roles in dealing with immigrants and especially with ethnic minorities. The Parliamentary Home Affairs Committee was highly critical in its report on racial disadvantage of the passive role of the Home Office, which it felt should play a more positive role in coordinating and assessing the government's policies for combating racial disadvantage and discrimination. But the Minister of State in charge of race and immigration matters rejected the notion that anybody in government should be in charge of monitoring race relations performance in different departments. He told the Committee that he saw the Home Office as exercising only a liaison role—not a leadership role.

Even after fifteen years of aid to local authorities with large ethnic minority populations, no national policy on minority education has emerged. The government often prefers to do good by stealth; thus, for example, the various initiatives on the inner city are general schemes because the government is wary of pursuing policies that may be seen as positively discriminating and therefore electorally unpopular. A number of studies have indicated that there is considerable resentment against the Race Relations Act, which is seen as positive discrimination rather than as protection from unfair discrimination for the minorities.

Much of the initiative regarding race relations policy is in practice left to the major government agency, the Commission for Racial Equality, but so far it has had limited success in promoting fair practices in housing and employment. In spite of its legal powers and powers of enforcement it has met considerable resistance from employers and even some local authorities. It has been subject to considerable political criticism regarding its own management and general competence. However, the all-party Select Committee has recognized the continuing disadvantage and discrimination experienced by the ethnic minorities, and there is some evidence that the government is being forced to give these matters higher priority in order to avoid future outbursts of inner-city rioting.

THE INTERRELATIONSHIP BETWEEN RACE RELATIONS POLICY AND IMMIGRATION REGULATION AND CONTROL

As government policy changed in the 1960s and 1970s toward tighter immigration controls, many politicians felt that greater efforts should be made to promote integration within Britain. In many cases, the policy of control was directly linked with integration because it was frequently argued that controls would reassure people in Britain that their culture and identity was not being "swamped" by large numbers of non-European immigrants; indigenous citizens would be less hostile to immigrants if it was widely appreciated that immigration was strictly controlled. This has always been the basic justification for controlling New Commonwealth immigration. It was also believed that smaller numbers would reduce competition for housing, jobs, and social services so that the visibility of non-white immigrants would be less and resentment against them would be reduced. Integration could then proceed steadily and smoothly. The inherent contradiction between a fundamentally racist immigration policy and a race relations policy within Britain to foster equality and integration has been forcefully exposed by Bernard Levin who wrote in response to Mrs. Thatcher's "swamping" speech[36] that "You cannot by promising to remove the cause of fear and resentment fail to increase both. If you talk and behave as though black men were some kind of virus that must be kept out of the body politic, then it is the shabbiest hypocrisy to preach racial harmony at the same time."[37]

Policymaking and Administration

Immigration policy in Britain is the product of a highly centralized and elitist political system. Policy is determined by the executive, legislated and legitimized by parliament, and administered by the bureaucracy or local authorities. The Civil Service plays an important role in the formulation of policy, especially in advising the key ministers what policy options are practicable. Through consultation with a variety of interested and campaigning pressure groups, the Civil Service also advises the ministers of the likely reaction of such groups and of public opinion to policy initiation. Politicians naturally are also open to lobbying and feel themselves experts on public opinion and pressure groups. The administration of immigration control is a complicated and difficult job and ministers are bound to take serious account of the expert advice of their officials. It is clear that such advice was crucial in the Conservative government's decision to drop both the proposed register of the overseas dependents of immigrants settled in Britain, and a quota for all non-European Community immigrants. These were proposed in the Conservatives' 1979 election manifesto.

One important aspect of the British political system is that the single-member, simple majority electoral system favors the dominance of two major parties who tend to be elected with overall parliamentary majorities despite securing only minority electoral support. As the Conservative and Labor parties support rather different policy positions on most issues, and as they rarely remain in office for more than two elections (Mrs. Thatcher's re-election in 1987 being a recent example), the result is substantial changes in policy as governments change. This has had some influence on race relations and immigration policy, although not as much in practice as might be expected. In the 1960s, when Labor was in office for most of the period, tough immigration controls and moderately positive policies on race relations were favored. In the period 1970–1974, the Conservative Party tightened controls, but despite internal opposition within the party, allowed the Ugandan Asians to come to Britain. After 1974 the Labor government slightly relaxed certain aspects of the immigration rules and introduced the strongest race relations legislation that Britain had ever had, but it failed to repeal the Immigration Act of 1971 as the Labor party had promised. Since the Conservative electoral victory in 1979 the major government initiative has been the British Nationality Act of 1981. The re-election of the Conservatives in 1987 is likely to result in the continuation of existing policies unless particular events force special initiatives. But the government is determined to continue its policy of tough controls and is opposed to special policies for the ethnic minorities which, they argue, increase separation rather than aid integration. This is a high risk strategy given the continuing evidence of discrimination, the high levels of unemployment, particularly among the young, and as a consequence the feelings of rejection experienced by so many of the second generation.

PERCEPTIONS

Immigration has become one of the most important issues in Britain. Both immigration regulation and immigration policy receive extensive coverage in the media and in parliament. The reason for this is the view that "colored" immigration is an issue that the electorate feels very strongly about. Although there is considerable evidence to suggest that the British people are deeply racially prejudiced, some liberal academics have attempted to portray them as generally

tolerant and fairminded—in part, one suspects, from a desire to influence policymakers in a liberal direction.[38]

Lawrence, for example, re-analyzed Rose's *Colour and Citizenship* data for
Nottingham and found that, out of 500 respondents, 65 percent believed that
West Indians took more out of the country than they put in, 61 percent believed
the same of Asians, and 38 percent the same of Greeks; 66 percent considered
British superior to Africans, 58 percent considered them superior to Asians, and
25 percent considered them superior to Americans. Asked whether they thought
color distinction would ever become unimportant in the way people felt about
each other, 8 percent agreed, but 62 percent felt color distinctions would always
be important; 55 percent felt that there should be special immigration regulations
against colored people.[39]

It is clear that politicians and civil servants were concerned about the ac-
ceptability and assimilability of colored immigrants from the beginning of the
migration, but perceived Britain's world role and economic prosperity to be more
important issues. The racial violence of 1958, the increasing evidence in the
opinion polls of public hostility to colored immigration, and an internal campaign
inside the Conservative party led to the 1962 Commonwealth Immigrant Act.
Nevertheless, it was the electoral victory of Peter Griffiths in the General Election
of 1964 that had the most decisive impact on policymaking. After a strong anti-
immigrant campaign, Griffiths captured the Labor constituency of Smethwick,
unseating Patrick Gordon-Walker, the prospective foreign secretary. His achievement was dramatic because he gained a swing to the Conservative party of 7.5
percent in an election where the national swing to the Labor party was 3.2
percent. Dependent on a majority of only five seats, reduced to three when
Gordon-Walker lost another "safe" Labor seat at Leyton in 1965 after the sitting
member had been asked to step down, the Labor government reversed its opposition to the 1962 Act and in 1965 introduced stricter controls.

Public concern over immigration was assuaged by the Labor government's
change of policy, but only temporarily. Enoch Powell and Duncan Sandys successfully campaigned against the influx of Asians from Kenya in 1967/68. Enoch
Powell's "rivers of blood" speech in April 1968 had a dramatic impact and
raised the salience of race and immigration to such a level that it is believed to
have contributed substantially to the Conservative victory in the general election
of 1970. It was no surprise that the Conservative government introduced further
legislation tightening control in 1971. It is clear that public opinion has had a
major impact on policymaking in this area.[40]

Politicians frequently claim that immigration controls have been introduced
and strengthened to ensure that native British do not feel threatened by New
Commonwealth immigrants. The reality is that most people feel that such controls
have come too late to be of very much value. In each of the three national
samples studied by Butler and Stocks in 1963, 1964, and 1966, it was found
that over 80 percent of respondents felt that too many immigrants had already
been let into the country.[41] So, despite politicians' arguments that they are

responding to public disquiet, each tightening of controls can be seen as confirmation of the inadequacy of past policies and the failure of politicians of all the major parties to respond to popular wishes.

What is remarkable is the stability of the findings of opinion polls. As recently as February 1978, the National Opinion Poll found that 86 percent thought that too many immigrants had come to Britain. Majorities exceeding 80 percent were against the admission of parents, brothers, and sisters of those who had settled here.[42] The result of New Commonwealth immigration has been to create a substantial minority of British citizens that are seen by many as intruders and illegitimate competitors for scarce resources. Recent studies of mixed samples in inner-city areas tend to confirm these views.[43] In contrast—and despite high levels of prejudice and discrimination—large numbers of Asians and West Indians claim to be satisfied with their jobs, housing, and circumstances in Britain.[44]

These perceptions of popular prejudice have also been a factor constraining the actions of employers, trade union leaders, and the police, but since the prejudices are so widely disseminated among the population, it is clear that they are shared by many of the elite as well.

One argument used by politicians, especially Conservative politicians, has been that to ignore rightwing populist demands for an end to colored immigration would result in growth and support for the National Front and other far-right groups. This was a clear implication of Mrs. Thatcher's "swamping" speech in January 1978, and it was noticeable that in the general election of 1979 the electoral support for the National Front collapsed and appeared to go to the Conservatives. Mrs. Thatcher's attempt to win back these voters to the Conservatives appeared to have been successful. One major problem has been that every concession to the far right has been received as confirmation of the justice of their case and thus led to increased demands.

As has already been emphasized, Commonwealth citizens (including those from the New Commonwealth) have full civic rights by virtue of their status as British subjects. They are able to vote in local and national elections, stand for political office, and serve in the armed forces and the public and diplomatic service. In the early period of immigration their numbers were small, many failed to register on the electoral rolls, and participation in British politics was low. Many remained more interested in the politics of their countries of origin, and branches of the major Indian, Pakistani, and Caribbean parties were established in Britain. After 1958, when immigration became a political issue of some significance, it was the impact on the white electorate that was crucially important. This remains true today, although during the 1970s it gradually became clear that because of their geographical concentration and increasing numbers, immigrant electors were able to play a significant role in a small but growing number of constituencies in both local and national elections. By the late 1970s significant numbers of Asians and West Indians were being elected to local councils, predominantly but not exclusively as Labor councillors. In some areas large numbers of Asians appeared to be joining constituency Labor parties and exerting some influence in the election of local council candidates. All election studies of the voting behavior of New Commonwealth voters show incredibly high levels of support for the Labor party and little support for any other party. Independent minority candidates have not done well. Asian voters have the highest rates of participation, followed by native whites; West Indians have relatively low rates of turnout. In the general election of 1987 four black Members of Parliament were elected, all as Labor party candidates. These successes are of tremendous symbolic importance for the black communities and represent a considerable political breakthrough for black Britons.

THE MAKING OF IMMIGRATION POLICY

The determinants of immigration policy are political. British politicians have adopted highly exclusionary policies toward "colored" immigrants in response to public opinion. Wide powers have been delegated by parliament to immigration officers at the ports of entry and to officials in British High Commissions and Embassies abroad, and these officials carry out the policy of the government. Their decisions are subject to a system of adjudication, with tribunals that hear appeals. Applicants can also appeal to the courts and to sympathetic politicians for assistance. The Home Office is the department of state with responsibility for immigration and one of the ministers at the Home Office is given special responsibility for race relations and immigration matters. He will normally review the decisions that come to the Home Office for final appeal. Final responsibility rests with the Home Secretary and the government. Because immigration and race relations are so politically sensitive, the Home Secretary devotes considerable time to this part of his work.

Since the first control bill was passed in 1962, considerable parliamentary time has been devoted to race and immigration matters. The first bill was highly controversial and the government was forced to make a number of concessions, one of which was that legislation would lapse if not reviewed by parliament. Between 1963 and 1970 there were thus annual debates on immigration policy as the legislation came up for renewal. This ceased with the enactment of the 1971 Immigration Act. In the 1970s the activities of the far right, especially the National Front, kept immigration to the fore as a political issue, even though controls were very tight. In the general election campaign of 1979 the Conservatives promised to strengthen controls even further and in the general elections of 1983 and 1987 have continued to make similar promises.

The Administration of Immigration Control

Immigration control is organized in the sending countries by the need to gain entry certification and at the ports of entry by the need to satisfy immigration control officers of the right to enter. The Foreign Service controls immigration by issuing of entry certificates, visas and passports to British citizens and applicants overseas. The Home Office controls immigration at the ports of entry and decides on applications to change the condition of entry, applications for naturalization, and the deportation of criminals, illegal immigrants, and those who have violated immigration control. There is a government-funded agency, the United Kingdom Immigration Advisory Service,which helps prospective immigrants with appeals against administrative decisions, but many applicants prefer the Joint Council for the Welfare of Immigrants, an independent body that helps prospective immigrants with immigration problems and also campaigns for more liberal immigration policies. The only special arrangements made for particular national groups have concerned political refugees.

Critics of government policy feel that it is becoming increasingly harsh. More people are being refused entry into Britain and more people are being detained at detention centers while their appeals against refusal of entry are considered. The policy is clearly discriminatory: Asians are 50–60 times more likely to be refused entry compared with travellers from Canada and Australia. Moreover, internal controls are increasing, with the growth of police raids on places where illegal immigrants are thought to be employed and an increase in deportations.

CONCLUSION

In the postwar period, the debate focused on "colored" immigration, while immigration as such has not been an issue. In the future, it may become one, if there is an expansion of migrants within the European Community, now that Spain and Portugal have been admitted to membership. White immigration, whether of kith or kin (former British settlers overseas) or aliens, has not been an issue, while the immigration of relatively small numbers of colored people is an important political issue. British governments have been hampered in their efforts to control colored immigration by the colonial legacy, the lack of precise definition of citizenship, and the lack of internal controls whose imposition would be highly controversial. Even legislation defining British citizenship tightly and restrictively, which has now been introduced,is politically controversial because of the large numbers of Britons settled abroad who wish to keep dual nationality and maintain their right of entry and abode in the United Kingdom. Millions of Britons have such relatives abroad, especially in the United States and the "Old Commonwealth" countries such as Canada and Australia.

The major failures of British immigration and race relations policy concern the lack of government action. Successive British governments have failed to give priority and resources to ensuring the successful settlement and integration of New Commonwealth immigrants, or even to developing a policy on immigration before 1962, when the remedy adopted was control. Once settlement has occurred on a substantial scale, positive policies were again needed to ensure equal rights and opportunities. Little has been done, and it has been half-hearted and sporadic. The major problem facing future British governments will be to ensure that second and third generations of black Britons are not alienated from their country of birth but feel full and equal citizens.

NOTES

1. J. Cheetham, "Immigration," in A. H. Halsey (ed.), *Trends in British Society Since 1900* (London; Macmillan, 1962).

2. J. A. Garrad, *The English and Immigration* (Oxford University Press, 1971).

3. J. Tannahill, *European Volunteer Workers in Britain* (Manchester University Press, 1958).

4. *The Right Road for Britain* (Conservative and Unionist Central Office, 1949).

5. Ministry of Labour; *Report of the Working Party on the Employment in the United Kingdom of Surplus Colonial Labour* (Ministry of Labour Papers, 26/226/7503, Public Records Office, 1948).

6. *Royal Commission on Population*, Cmnd 7695 (London: HMSO, 1949), pp. 226–7.

7. J. Rex and S. Tomlinson, *Colonial Immigrants in a British City* (London: Routledge Kegan-Paul, 1979).

8. Trade Union Congress, *Annual Report* (London: 1955).

9. Office of Population Censuses and Surveys, *Labour Force Survey 1983 and 1984* (London: HMSO, 1986).

10. D. Smith, *Racial Disadvantage in Britain* (Harmondsworth: Penguin Books, 1977); and C. Brown, *Black and White Britain* (London: Heinemann Educational Books, 1984).

11. G. P. Freeman, *Immigrant Labour and Racial Conflict in Industrial Societies* (Princeton University Press, 1979).

12. J. A. Garrard, op. cit.

13. Ministry of Labour, *Report of the Working Party on the Employment in the United Kingdom of Surplus Labour*, op. cit.

14. D. Beetham, *Transport and Turbans: A Comparative Study in Local Politics* (Oxford University Press, 1970).

15. R. Miles and A. Phizacklea, *Labour and Racism* (London: Routledge Kegan-Paul, 1980).

16. P. Ratcliffe, *Racism and Reaction: A Profile of Handsworth* (London: Routledge Kegan-Paul, 1981).

17. J. Rex and S. Tomlinson, op. cit.

18. R. Billard, "Ethnic Minorities and the Social Services," in V. S. Khan (Ed.), *Minority Families in Britain* (Macmillan, 1979).

19. Central Office of Information, *Immigration to Britain: Notes on the Regulations and Procedures*, Reference Pamphlet No. 164 (London: HMSO, 1981).

20. R. Moore and T. Wallace, *Slamming the Door: The Administration of Immigration Control* (London: Martin Robertson, 1975).

21. Conservative and Unionist Central Office, *The Campaign Guide 1987*, pp. 397–401.

22. Conservative and Unionist Central Office, *The Conservative Manifesto 1979*.

23. *Racial Disadvantage: Fifth Report from the Home Affairs Committee, 1980/81*, House of Commons 424–1 (London: HMSO, 1981); and C. Brown, *Black and White Britain* (Heinemann, 1984).

24. D. Smith and J. Gray, *Police and People in London* (Aldershot: Gower, 1985).

25. Lord Scarman, *The Brixton Disorders April 10th–12th 1981: Report of an Inquiry*, Cmnd 8427 (London: HMSO, 1981).

26. Z. Layton-Henry, *The Politics of Race in Britain* (London: Allen and Unwin, 1984), pp. 160–165.

27. Conservative and Unionist Central Office, *Campaign Guide 1987*, op. cit.

28. J. Benyon, "Spiral of Decline: Race and Policing," in Z. Layton-Henry and P. Rich, *Race, Government and Politics in Britain* (London: Macmillan, 1986).

29. C. Brown, *Black and White Britain*, op. cit.

30. Department of the Environment, *Census Indicators of Urban Deprivation* (London: 1976).

31. J. Rex and S. Tomlinson, op. cit.

32. D. Smith, *Racial Disadvantage in Britain*, op. cit.

33. Ibid.

34. C. Brown, *Black and White Britain*, op. cit.

35. *West Indian Children in Our Schools, Interim Report of the Committee of Inquiry into the Education of Children from Minority Groups*, Cmnd 8273 (London: HMSO, 1981); and Department of Education and Science, *Education for All* (London: HMSO, 1985).

36. *Verbatim Report of an Interview with Gordon Burns*, World in Action, Grenada Television, January 30, 1978. Mrs. Thatcher was interviewed on the subject of immigration. During the interview she said: "People are really rather afraid that this country might be rather swamped by people with a different culture." She promised that the Conservatives would bring an end to immigration as Britain had experienced it in the postwar years. Her proposals appeared to command considerable popular support.

37. *The Times*, February 14, 1978.

38. E. J. B. Rose, et al., *Colour and Citizenship* (Oxford: Oxford University Press, 1974).

39. D. Lawrence, "Prejudice, Politics and Race," *New Community* 7, no. 1 (1978/79), pp. 44–55.

40. D. Studlar, "Policy Voting in Britain: The Coloured Immigration Issue in the 1964, 1966 and 1970 General Elections," *American Political Science Review* 72 (1978), pp. 46–72.

41. D. Butler and D. Stokes, *Political Change in Britain* (London: Macmillan, 1969).

42. D. Lawrence, *Prejudice, Politics and Race*, op. cit.

43. R. Miles and A. Phizacklea, *Labour and Racism*, op. cit.

44. J. Rex and S. Tomlinson, op. cit.

4

German Immigration Policy and Politics

MARILYN HOSKIN AND
ROY C. FITZGERALD

To many who study immigration, the inclusion of Germany in a comparative analysis is something of an anomaly. Historically, immigration into Germany has been permitted only in response to national economic needs and has been marred by periods of government-sanctioned forced labor. Officially, all recent and current policy statements begin with the disclaimer that the Federal Republic "is not an immigration nation." Buttressing this claim is the conclusion of most scholars that both government and popular orientation to politics is more committed to principles of pragmatic problem solving than to the lofty humanistic goals usually associated with immigration in Western democracies.

Despite these factors, German policymakers face questions similar or identical to those at issue in classical immigration nations. There are currently over four million noncitizens in the Federal Republic, most of whom have been there for more than ten years. Although recruitment of foreign workers was halted in 1973, the fact that a significant number of their family members have joined them has combined with a higher birthrate among foreigners to produce a growing proportion of non-Germans in the overall population. In addition, the number of foreigners seeking refugee status and political asylum has increased dramatically in each of the last four years. As a result Germany like other relatively prosperous nations, is struggling to define policy appropriate to its own needs as well as to those of potential new arrivals and those already in residence.

In representing an intriguing variation on traditional immigration experience and analysis, the German case may be especially instructive in its reflection of the pressures increasingly faced by other nations. As such, it is important to understand both the origin of such a qualified immigration policy and its socioeconomic and political consequences. Our analysis is structured to allow us to pinpoint when and how key features of German immigration policy developed, and how they are maintained or challenged under current pressures to rethink and rationalize immigration policy generally. We begin by presenting a brief historical overview of immigration and its variations in modern Germany, then proceed to detail the policy that evolved out of this experience. At the heart of our analysis is an investigation of popular sentiment toward immigrants, undertaken on the assumption that governments devise policies only within a range of limits defined as acceptable by their constituents. Finally we offer some tentative conclusions about the prospects and limits of future absorption of foreigners into Germany compared with other nations considered here.

AN HISTORICAL OVERVIEW

Early Brushes with Immigration

One of the intriguing aspects of the contemporary immigration issue in Germany is its lack of clear historical guidelines. Hartmut Esser and Hermann Korte, for example, begin their essay on the topic by stating unequivocally that ''in many respects the present situation in Germany in regard to immigration and immigrants is unprecedented'' (1985:165). The German situation may have few comparative parallels as well. Unlike the United States and Canada, open spaces and the lure of a new world were never associated with Germany; unlike Britain and France, no colonial tradition placed whole areas of the Third World in favored positions for entry into its society. Losing two world wars cost Germany territory as well as any image as an appealing place to which one might want to emigrate, during periods when other nations were experiencing large influxes of immigrants (Reimann and Reimann, 1979). At least in comparison with other Western states, Germany seems to have lacked elements that facilitated earlier waves of immigration.

At least as important as these comparative factors, however, has been the way German governments have historically defined the conditions under which foreigners might live and work there. As most scholars who write in the area note, Germany prior to 1890 was largely a nation of emigration, losing population mainly to the Americas and Australia. When industrialization created a major need for labor after 1890 (first in the agrarian sector and later in the industrial centers), the Reich government compromised its own hostility to its neighbors to encourage large numbers of Poles to enter, first as seasonal labor and later as a more or less permanent urban work force (Esser and Korte, 1985). It is important to note, however, that the tension that most nations experience as they admit to the need but not the desirability of foreign labor, appears to have been especially grating for Germany and its neighbors. In particular, centuries of shifting borders and national hostilities likely produced an especially virulent distaste for those proximate foreigners available for low-level employment (Dahrendorf, 1967). In this instance, the German government reinforced such an attitude, first by limiting the entry of foreigners to the agricultural season, then when their labor became integral to industry, attempting to force their assimilation into German culture by prohibiting the teaching and use of the Polish language. The initial experience with immigrants was thus characterized more by reluctance and restrictions (which some scholars found serious enough to label xenophobia) than by any plan to welcome their economic or cultural contribution to the host society (Reimann and Reimann, 1979).

After this initial period (roughly extending between 1890 and the onset of World War I), the German experience included two wars in which it made extensive use of forced labor. Such policies voiced the official lines that foreign workers were there only to serve the Reich and that they would not be suitable for eventual assimilation as German *Volk*. Under such circumstances neither immigrants nor hosts could find the relationship hospitable. It is thus not surprising that no new or imaginative policies (or, for that matter, new interest in migrating to Germany) were developed in the chaotic period between wars. As late as the postwar years after 1945, therefore, Germany had no extended period in which it had to deal with what other nations handled as traditional immigration demands—those in which people from less prosperous or promising societies sought entry in order to better their individual or family lot.

Serious Immigration and Serious Immigrants

As we noted earlier, the end of World War II forced Germany to accept not only a loss of territory but also the responsibility for Germans desiring to return from areas formerly part of the Reich (including some 12 million Germans living in East Prussia, Silesia, Poland, Hungary, Yugoslavia, Rumania, and the Sudetenland). Thus the postwar growth that began in the late 1940s was fueled quite well by the labor of refugees and Germans adjusting to the new economy (Reimann and Reimann, 1979). It was not until the recovery was well underway that the building of the Berlin wall in 1961 cut off the supply of workers from the East and dramatized the need for more labor than West Germany had at its disposal. By then, a model agreement for facilitating the movement into Germany of Italians who were seeking work had been concluded with the government in Rome.To expedite the arrival of even larger numbers of foreigners in need of employment, similar binational arrangements were formalized with Southern European and North African nations and with Turkey.

These agreements formed the basis for the large influx of foreign workers that occurred between 1961 and 1973. During this period German firms, aided by the government, established recruiting offices in Italy, Spain, Yugoslavia, Greece, Turkey, and North Africa, and arranged for the work and residence permits initially granted for short periods (usually one or two years) in order to allow for frequent assessment of the need for such labor. As a matter of fact, the expectations stated in the early arrangements were that foreign workers would spend a relatively short period of time in Germany and then be replaced by others on a short-term, rotating basis (Mehrlaender, 1980). As a practical matter, rotation made little sense for business and industries where experience and continuity contribute greater efficiency and productivity, and the "revolving door" principle was never really enforced.

Despite recessions in 1967 and 1972/73, which saw some unemployed foreigners returning to their homelands, the total number of foreigners (including family members) continued to increase. It is fair to say that by 1973, the assumption that foreigners could and would be easily moved in and out of the nation had to be abandoned. As the oil-inspired recession of 1973 continued to dampen the German "economic miracle," the government decided to ban further recruitment, and the flow of new workers was effectively stopped. It was ironic, if entirely predictable, that the end of sponsored in-migration brought an actual increase in the foreign population, since many stayed rather than be cut off from German employment in the future, and others hastened to send for their families before any additional restrictions might be established. The end of the problem of immigration policy as *regulation of the flow of arrivals* thus ushered in the real beginning of the problem of immigration policy as *reconciling non-nationals into the host society*.

However brief Germany's period of conscious recruitment of foreigners, therefore, it set the stage for the real immigration policy issues that the Federal Republic currently faces. The number of long-term resident foreign workers is itself significant (almost 2 million as of 1985). Moreover, their integral place in the economy is widely recognized, as their steady employment in the lower rungs of many industries keeps these industries running at full capacity. Finally, several analysts have noted that the employment of foreign workers became a continuous substitute for German labor, allowing expansion of their educational horizons as well as a kind of "collective mobility" for Germans (Rist, 1978; Esser and Korte, 1985; Miller, 1981). At issue is not really the current foreign workers' jobs but how their children will be educated, employed, and ultimately accepted into the social and political fabric of German society. Since these questions derive directly from the immediate circumstances and expectations of the 1961–1973 immigration periods, we devote the next section to detailing the important features of immigration policy and law, which was established then and which has changed relatively little in the years since 1973.

OFFICIAL POLICY TOWARD NON-GERMANS

Assumptions

The single most important characteristic of German policy toward noncitizens is its continuing commitment to the premises of the 1961–1973 recruitment program. As Esser and Korte note, the 1965 Aliens Act, which still constitutes the basis of regulation for foreigners, was "intended to make immigrant labor in the Federal Republic of Germany a maneuverable resource, easily controlled and regulated, for the solving of economic problems (primarily those of manpower shortages)'' (1985:170). At that time, however, there was substantial consensus among sending nations as well as Germans that economic benefits would accrue to both host (reliable labor supplies, direct and immediate growth) and sending nations (immediate unemployment relief, transfers of capital, and the eventual return of skilled and experienced nationals) (Nikolinakos, 1976). Under such circumstances it had to be relatively easy to insist that German economic considerations would be the basis for all policy toward foreign workers.

That the policy was also shortsighted in its self interest has not lessened the resolve of governments since 1961 to maintain economic conditions as the basis for continuing policy. As we noted earlier, all official government documents, including the Federal Ministry of the Interior's *Record of Policy and Laws Related to Foreigners in the Federal Republic of Germany* (1985), specifically claim that the Federal Republic is not an immigration nation. Esser and Korte maintain that the reality of foreign worker permanency is still denied by policymakers:

Neither the instruments nor the aims of immigrant policy are based on permanent immigration or on a special minority status for foreigners. They are merely intended to tackle such specific problems as better job training and to prevent conflicts resulting from, among other things, the cultural marginality of the second generation. (1985:195–96)

The empirical corollary to this non-immigration assumption is the policy position that Germany has reached its population capacity. As the Interior Ministry document cited above states:

The absorptive capacity of the Federal Republic has been exhausted at around 4.4 million foreigners (corresponding to a proportion of 7.3% of the population); in some areas with a proportion of over 20%, it is exceeded. Especially important is the difficult state of the labor market, the intractable problem of providing living room, and problems of integration, especially that of young foreigners. (1985:4)

The final assumption of policy that we note is that despite all the disclaimers, denials, and caveats just described, most of those who deal with this issue do admit to the difference between taking in significant numbers of new immigrants and paying heed to the needs of those who are already there. It is possible that the recognition exists only because Germans fear the socioeconomic costs of an uneducated, unintegrated generation born to the first wave of guestworkers. Nonetheless, the commitment to addressing the social welfare of foreign workers and their families is one major objective built into official policy (Esser and Korte, 1985; Conradt, 1982).

If there is inconsistency in these assumptions, it is one that has plagued policy more generally ever since the recruitment of guestworkers was initiated. Indeed, it is a contradiction which, as we noted earlier, has cropped up whenever nations experienced the tension of needing foreigners but not really wanting them. What will be more interesting, therefore, is not the existence of the tension but how it is handled, and especially how it is guided by the dictates and support of public policy. It is to that question that we turn next .

Formal Policy: Foreign Resident Rights and Restrictions

As we noted earlier, basic provisions governing noncitizens are essentially those detailed in the Aliens Act of 1965. All foreigners must obtain residence permits, renewable for periods of 2–5 years, then changed to a right to residence after eight years if the foreigner has become "part of the economic and social life of the Federal Republic." Work permits are applied for separately. Initially, they were tied to employment guarantees, but by 1985, 85 percent of the work permits were in the unrestricted category, meaning that their holders had at least five years' uninterrupted work experience, were married to a German citizen, or had asylum status. At least technically, initial work permits are difficult to get for those who are poorly educated or new to Germany, and the law gives clear preference to nationals who compete for jobs with foreigners. Realistically, however, such foreigners (usually guestworkers' children or spouses) can obtain the permit if they complete any one of a number of language or educational programs (*Record*, 1985:17–19). In 1984/85, only 5 percent of the applications for new or continuing work permits were rejected. Apparently policymakers have concluded that since Germans almost never want the jobs that poorly qualified foreigners might get, facilitating their employment with work permits makes better sense than guaranteeing their unemployment by denying them.

Foreigners are also entitled to a broad array of social benefits. At the time of the initial massive recruitment programs, German unions, fearful that imported labor could and would undercut domestic jobs and salaries, insisted that virtually all of the substantial wage and fringe components of union contracts be applied to guestworkers as well. As a result, unemployment, health, and retirement insurance, as well as support for children are provided to virtually all workers. In short, once foreigners manage to get a work permit and work, their benefits are standardized. As David Conradt has observed, since they are covered by all of these programs, they do not constitute a "subculture of poverty in the Federal Republic" (Conradt, 1982:70).

One area in which a kind of subculture exists by design is that of political rights. Although foreigners technically are protected in their basic freedom of expression and organization, that freedom is certainly qualified by the fact that they are not guaranteed the permanent right to remain in Germany to enjoy it. There have been very few instances in which the right to organize has been seen as dangerous to the interest of the Federal Republic (and hence reason to revoke the residency right of the foreigners involved), and the government has even noted officially that the isolated incidents that might be labelled politically extreme have been those involving issues of homeland politics (*Record*, 1985:29). Certainly the right to strike has been exercised, but not frequently or violently (Miller, 1981: Freeman,1979).

The real test of long-term rights is naturalization to German citizenship, and the patterns here do not suggest that foreigners are moving toward eventual full political parity with citizens. During a heavy year only 40,000 foreigners are naturalized, a figure that has prompted Lisolette Funcke, Commissioner for Foreign Residents, to conclude that the requirements are too difficult and the encouragement of government officials inadequate (*Deutsche Nachrichten*, September 1986). Indeed, the official line articulated in the Interior Ministry's *Record* states:

Naturalization should not be an instrument for the promotion of integration, but rather should stand at the end of a successful integration process. The Federal Republic does not intend to facilitate naturalization. (*Record*:32)

Interestingly, the attitude toward children is not identical:

A special situation, to be sure, exists for those who were born here and grew up here. Their life is in Germany and they are aliens to their country. The public interest is in naturalization, since no state wants a large group with no loyalty. The Federal Republic is of the view that the naturalization of foreigners from the second and third generations should be promoted through easing the process. (*Record*:32)

That the same policy statement takes a different position on citizenship for children can hardly be reassuring to their less favored parents and, one should surmise, might well have the effect of discouraging the children from separating themselves from their elders in this fashion. It is also relevant to note that to date the process has not been eased for the younger generation.

Over all, the rights of foreign workers appear to be fairly well protected certainly in comparison to those of illegal aliens in other states and even in comparison to legals in certain nations. Nonetheless, the reluctance to push a naturalization program, especially for long-term residents, must take away from the real benefits that foreigners do enjoy. Even before addressing the question of social integration, therefore,we should probably note the ring of truth in Esser and Korte's conclusion that:

On the whole, the legal regulations on immigration have created a lasting insecurity concerning future life in the Federal Republic of Germany, and this in turn affects the everyday life of immigrant families. (1985:189)

Formal Policy: Socioeconomic Integration

It is only when we step beyond the realm of policy defining legal rights that the real variations in government positions and programs become evident. The Interior Ministry's 1985 statement on foreign residents begins by noting that policy is based on three principles: (1) integration of foreigners and their families who have been in Germany for a long time; (2) the limitation of further future entry of foreigners; and (3) assistance to foreigners who desire to return to their homeland (*Record,* 1985:1). We leave for later discussion the question of the problem that asylum-seekers present for the second and third principles, and the potential contradiction posed by the third principle and consider first what has been involved in defining and implementing official policy on integration of foreign workers and their families.

It is most important to note that "social and economic integration" were clearly not part of the labor recruitment problems of 1961–73. As we noted earlier, initial expectations naively included rotation of labor and, in effect, no permanent relocation. Even as it became clear that German businessmen wanted their guestworkers to stay for longer periods and as their families began to join them, there was still at least the hope that by continuing their status as "guest-workers," Germany need accept no major responsibility for integration.

Rist (1978) and Esser and Korte (1985) point out that it was not until 1975 that the federal government began to establish genuine integration programs (language and vocational training) geared to easing social and work life. Despite a continual stream of recommendations for such programs from the various European Social and Human Rights Commissions, from the mid–1960s on, most German states initiated only small-scale educational requirements or alternatives for foreign children and their parents. Rist details the broad variation among states, ranging from mandatory German instruction to optional participation in educational programs run out of the homeland consulates. Not surprisingly, the educational programs for foreign children has been very limited. One report claimed that even in the early 1980s, 25 percent of foreign children were not attending school regularly, and the rate of completion of any of the basic or vocational curricula is far below that of German children (Rist, 1978; MacRae, 1980; Wilpert, 1980; Mehrlaender, 1981).

Current policies that the Federal Republic refers to as "integration" are almost completely those that run various types of language or vocational training programs. The "German for Foreign Workers" language courses, which have been offered since 1974, have enrolled some 280,000 participants, but Esser and Korte maintain that their success has been marginal. Programs for young or adolescents who have not completed a schooling track include language and job-training short-courses, which can be used to obtain work permits, and they have officially attracted about 20,000 students. A short course in German for house-wives drew 12,000 participants in 1984.

"Integration" programs described here might easily be seen as short-term responses to real and potential economic and social problems. First evident during the recessions of 1967 and 1973, unemployment among foreign workers has run higher than that among nationals, and since the late 1970s there has been a dramatic increase in the number of foreign workers on welfare. Moreover, some evidence and more public perception point to increasing criminal rates among foreigners, especially those without jobs and clear loyalties in the Federal Republic (Conradt, 1982).

It is important to note, however, that policy responses to what have been seen as basic structural social problems have been relatively narrow. Although adult foreigners surely benefit from practical language and cultural programs, their children's need for basic education is absolutely central to their ultimate integration. To be sure, it is also expensive. Yet this critical area of policy has been largely delegated to state governments, where it has been addressed primarily as but one part of an overall commitment. That commitment, in turn, can best be characterized as general, lacking in operational detail, and, as we noted earlier, frequently in conflict with other goals.

A chronology of policy best illustrates this point. The first official federal commission on this issue was established in 1976 with a broad mandate to study and propose comprehensive policy with respect to

the balancing of the social and humanitarian claims of foreigners living in the Federal Republic, the interests of their countries of origin, and the social and economic interests of the Federal Republic of Germany. (quoted in Mehrlaender, 1980:156)

Even with such a broad charge, the commission shied away from major policy recommendations, suggesting only minor modifications in existing law (German instruction for children, shortening the waiting period for residence permits). Another commission endorsed expanded integration programs in 1979, and in 1980 the Cabinet agreed that a *"future* priority of immigration policy should be the social integration of second and third generations" (Esser and Korte, 1985:180; emphasis added). At the same time, the Cabinet also endorsed stronger foreigner ties to their homelands and a continuation of the ban on new recruitment.

The official position on homeland ties is an interesting example of a very clear program in a generally vague overall policy. In 1983 the government sponsored a program of *Rueckkehrfoerderung* (assisted return) in which any foreigner who agreed to leave Germany permanently was assisted with (1) a cash payment of 10,500 German marks, plus 1500 for each returning child; and (2) the refund of all insurance and retirement benefits that the worker had paid into the German social security fund. No coercion was employed, and over 250,000 foreigners chose to leave under these conditions. Clearly, some government policies are more specific and backed by resources than others, and at least this one, dedicated to integration's opposite, was decisively formulated and implemented by the administration.

What emerges from this somewhat unsystematic discussion of social and economic integration policy is a portrait of unsystematic policy. The only generally firm official commitment is that which continues the ban on new inmigration; one of the few concise commitments has been that of assisted return. On the broader general goal of social integration, less visible progress and less visible policy programs have been the norm. Perhaps best evidence of the hypothesis that the Federal Republic's commitment to integration of its de facto immigrants is found in the Interior Ministry's elaboration of its goals for foreigners. It begins by noting that since a majority of foreigners in Germany have been there for more than ten years, "there is no alternative to integration" (*Record*, 1985:6). Such a grudging acceptance of integration, however, is followed by an official interpretation of the term that underscores its limited and pragmatic rather than humanistic tenor:

This [integration] does not mean *assimilation*, but rather the participation of foreigners in our society's life as much as possible without damage to their own cultural ties, and above all the appropriate insertion of foreign youths into the work force. (*Record*, 1985:6)

Asylum as Special Immigration Policy

In a very real sense asylum presents the most difficult immigration problem for German policymakers. Although discriminatory treatment of foreigners and minorities has certainly not been unique to Germany historically, no Western nation bears the legacy of twentieth century persecution as dramatically as does the heir to the Third Reich. Those who developed the German Basic Law were careful to specify the new government's commitment to those seeking refuge from persecution elsewhere, assuring all who requested entry a full review of their application for status as political refugees (*Record*, 1985).

In addition, it is clear in retrospect that the guestworker programs were bound to open new channels of information and encouragement for other foreigners seeking entry. However inferior their status relative to German citizens might be, guestworkers enjoyed legal protection and a minimum standard of living that far surpassed that of foreigners seeking to escape from areas plagued by internal strife, border wars, and all the conditions of Third World poverty. As a result, the number of foreigners asking for refugee admission has skyrocketed in the past decade: for 1984 the numbers jumped by 79 percent over the previous year; for 1985 it increased 109 percent; and the 1986 figure was greater by 90 percent. The majority have been from the Middle East (including Lebanon, Iran, Turkey, India, Afghanistan, Pakistan) and Poland. By 1986, many new applicants had relatives who were at some more advanced stage of the review process (*Record*, 1985).

The dilemma for German policymakers is that their history and their overtures to refugees run counter to their commitment to resist any new immigration. Aside from the burdens of implementing the review and assistance process, the real cost is that there is no easy way to contain the flow short of looking dangerously insensitive to the world's persecuted. As other studies indicate, the line between political and economic repression is too fine to draw without the appearance of using any criteria to close the gate. For Germany, that appearance may be the most severe disadvantage which it will experience as it attempts to enforce a ban on immigration by banning those claiming to be bona fide refugees. However much such a policy fits with Conradt's depiction of Germans as lacking either a "strong tradition of civil liberties or a culturally ingrained sympathy for the underdog." It is not a policy that will do much for Germany's image as a responsible democracy (Conradt, 1982:64).

Policymaking on Foreign Worker Issues

Most works on politics in Germany note that the prime movers in the policy process are the major parties and their respective leaderships. Obviously, each party has constituencies pressuring for favored policies, but some relatively clear programmatic distinctions among parties serve to organize political debate and ultimate policy resolution on most issues (Conradt, 1982; Edinger, 1977).

On issues that affect foreigners, however, the process has not been so clear. We noted in an earlier investigation that political parties have been unusually cautious in defining specific or long-term positions (Hoskin, 1984). In truth, both major parties are internally split on this policy issue. The Social Democrats are ideologically supportive of policies that benefit the working classes but face opposition from their German members who feel most threatened by foreign labor. For the Christian Democrats the problem is reversed, since they have no real empathy for guestworkers but recognize the central role they have assumed in the Germany economy. Faced with the contradictory pressures, both have opted to devise short-term, pragmatic solutions to immediate problems rather than confront the question of long-term policy. The government documents which we have quoted extensively reflect this ambivalence. As Reimann and Reimann note, governments controlled by each party have preferred "a policy of indecisiveness, postponing a real solution to the dilemma" (1979:76).

That description, in fact, may actually overstate their attentiveness to the problem. In the American Institute for Contemporary German Studies' 1986 election-year volume on *West German Political Parties,* the self-portraits by each of the parties include virtually no mention of policy toward foreigners in the Federal Republic. Curiously, only the Free Democrats—usually a party of business—list the treatment of minorities as a serious issue, and even they limit themselves to a general statement supporting undefined integration programs.

In the absence of clearly defined party positions, two policy anomalies have developed. One has been alluded to throughout this discussion, as an inconsistent overall policy toward foreigners. In place of a policy at least framed by a consensual idea of what Germany's needs and obligations are with respect to its noncitizens, the current "policy" is, as Daniel Kubat observes, "at base a patchwork sum of separate group demands" (1979:36). Virtually every policy area, from refugee resettlement to education to housing, is addressed on an ad hoc, least-damage basis.

The corollary to this overall pattern is the variation in the policymaking *process* that prevails for these issues. Unlike other issues where major interest groups have unqualified and intensely-held positions, long-term immigration brings out consistent positions only from less central groups. Conradt argues that the German churches, charitable organizations, and labor unions, by insisting on human programs, have done more to address the needs of foreigners than the government (1982:71–72). Following up on this theme, Esser and Korte accord a definitely tertiary role to traditionally influential organizations:

The greatest influence on immigration policy is exerted by "socially concerned groups," which mainly include the Deutsche Gewerkschaftsbund, the Bund Deutsche Arbeitgeber, the Protest and Catholic Churches, welfare organizations, and the political parties. (1985:176)

Finally, it is worth noting that despite the concern that officials voice over the increasing difficulty of dealing with immigration-type issues, responsibility for their resolution is widely dispersed among different agencies at the federal level and between federal and state functions. As we indicated earlier, one approach that seems to have been favored by the government is the use of commissions. Although they may be highly visible at the time of their report, they enjoy neither permanence nor enforcement power, and some observers are cynical enough to conclude that the government employs them precisely for their inherent limitation to act. Even after twenty years of experience with foreigners, there exists no central ministry or agency charged with coordinating federal and state regulations and programs relevant to the 4.4 million people affected.

What conclusions can be drawn from this overview of current immigration policy? The most obvious is that it is far from resolution, either in direction or as to specific programs. In addition, we should note that by not having firm commitment to one position or another, the government and perhaps even the parties have abdicated potential leadership roles in shaping how foreigners will fit into German society in the future. If these conclusions are correct, we should pursue the question of their fit into the society from another perspective—that of the society's perception of foreigners' place. In fact, we might have argued that even *with* a firm official policy, public sentiments would be critical in determining the degree to which such policy would succeed. In either case, the logic of examining public opinion on issues of immigration and integration is strong, and we proceed to a rather detailed analysis in the following section.

PUBLIC OPINION TOWARD FOREIGNERS

The Role of Public Opinion

Irrespective of the particular context, a nation's political culture is probably the single most important determinant of the extent and success of its immigration policies. As we noted earlier, Germany's history has included limited and mostly negative experiences with immigration (Esser and Korte, 1985). Moreover, many scholars have linked the phenomenon to the particularly intense nationalism evident throughout the nineteenth and twentieth centuries (Craig, 1978; Holborn, 1970). In the period since 1945, research has been most consensual in documenting a pragmatic, unemotional public opinion, which lends itself more to goals of social and economic efficiency than to those of humanitarian outreach (Almond and Verba, 1963: Conradt, 1982; Edinger, 1977).

Given these traditions, it is not surprising that a recurring question posed by analysts of postwar Germany has been how well it would do in developing liberal democratic norms. For our purpose this question is central. Foreigners constitute and will continue to constitute a sizable proportion of the labor force, and they are crucial to some sectors of the economy. Perhaps more important, they require and will continue to require state services, particularly in education and retirement benefits. How tolerant and supportive German citizens are in recognizing these guestworkers' roles and needs may well be the major factor in their ability to adjust and eventually fit in to the host society.

A brief review of research on this question indicates that it is not yet resolved. An early perspective is Ralf Dahrendorf's seminal inquiry into *Society and Democracy in Germany* (1967). In this analysis he derives a general standard for democratic development, including (1) a public commitment to pluralism and the tolerance that requires; (2) a sense of public virtue among citizens; and (3) support for institutions that are "open for ever new solutions" (1967:13–14,16,330–332). His assessment is that the liberal achievement of public sentiment in the early 1960s was cautious but negative, and he specifically cites German attitudes toward foreign workers in reaching that conclusion. Most of the popular literature has been critical as well, ranging from ideologically-based journalistic accounts to Gunther Wallraff's account of the life and experience of Turkish guestworkers in his best-selling *Ganz Unten* (1985). Finally, the limited evidence from empirical studies suggests that opinion is at best lukewarm (reluctantly accepting guestworkers but not embracing their full integration), and at worst ready to send them home rather than support their long-term naturalization (Hoskin, 1984, 1985; Conradt, 1982).

Still, some analysts are more optimistic. The authors of *Germany Transformed* (1981) carefully document an increase in support for democratic institutions between 1953 and 1976, and opinion polls have shown a similar increase in sympathy for the plight of foreigners (Noelle-Neumann, 1981). As we noted above, the major churches, welfare organizations, and unions have supported equitable pay and better social programs. And, some would argue, the sheer passage of time makes foreigners less foreign within the host society and more likely to be accepted into its life.

Our purpose here is to assess the most recent evidence on public opinion toward guestworkers and compare it where possible to earlier patterns. We rely primarily on data from the National Social Survey Cumulative file (1980–1984),[1] whose questions include a battery of items on guestworkers. Although the timespan is relatively short, it does include years of economic stagnation and one

Table 4.1.
Public Opinion Toward Guestworkers Among Germans (percentage agreement)

Attitudinal Statement:*	Totally Agree		Mostly Agree		Somewhat Agree		Not Sure/No Opinion		Somewhat Disagree		Mostly Disagree		Totally Disagree	
	1980	1984	1980	1984	1980	1984	1980	1984	1980	1984	1980	1984	1980	1984
1. Should adjust life-styles	30	29	15	13	21	19	14	15	8	9	5	7	8	8
2. When jobs tight, send home	26	20	12	9	15	13	14	16	10	12	8	11	16	19
3. No political activities	36	29	9	9	12	9	13	12	10	10	9	10	18	20
4. Marry among their own	24	18	11	8	11	8	14	13	9	9	8	10	25	33

* Full text of the questions:
   1. Guestworkers should adjust their lifestyles to the German lifestyle.
   2. When jobs are tight, guestworkers should be sent home.
   3. Guestworkers should be forbidden all political activities.
   4. Guestworkers should choose from among their own people.

in which the official program of assisted return was devised and implemented. Even the four-year comparison can provide us with some indication of both aggregate change and possible changes in the factors that facilitate positive or negative attitudes toward foreigners.

General Patterns

The 1980 and 1984 surveys included identical questions in which respondents specified their relative agreement or disagreement with statements about four aspects of guestworker life in Germany: adaptation of their lifestyles, political activity, intergroup marriage, and economic dispensability (deportation) in a tight job market. Exact wording is found in Table 4.1, above.

We noted in a research report on the 1980 survey that the overall pattern of response to these items found a majority of Germans favoring restrictions on the rights and social integration of foreign workers. Adding the 1984 data allows us to note both overall and specific shifts. First, throughout the detailed table are small but consistent changes away from the positions restricting guestworkers. The number of points changing varies from none to eight, but in no category is there an increase in the *negative* opinion. Moreover, the largest increase in responses favorable to guestworkers occurs in the extreme categories at both ends of the range rather than the middle, where changes of category might have made the shifts appear less pronounced.

A second point of interest in this overall table is its perspective on the question of interpretation raised with the 1980 data. We asked in the earlier analysis if the sizable majority preferring that foreigners adjust their lifestyles to German society might be advocating integration rather than simple hostility to the varying lifestyles they represent. In that instance we concluded that the preponderantly negative patterns in the other questions lead us to interpret that breakdown as part of an overall negative sentiment. With the 1984 data, however, the possibility of treating that item differently makes more sense. A majority still favor foreign worker adjustment of lifestyle, but when that breakdown is coupled with the significant change in attitudes that oppose their having to marry only within their own groups, it appears plausible that an increasing number of Germans see the desirability of foreigners becoming part of German society. Although it is not exactly best evidence of support for cultural pluralism, it also is a measurable improvement on the pattern of relatively clear hostility toward the guestworker that we have seen in other evidence.

The final general observation is a simple additive one. For the 1980 data we constructed an overall scale of hostility/receptivity toward guestworkers by summing responses to the four questions and collapsing the resulting 4–28 total range into three categories of roughly equal numbers of respondents in each (scores of 4–14 were coded as a receptive category, 15–21 into the neutral or mixed group, and 22–28 in the category labelled hostile). Using the same summing and collapsing rules in 1984 produced a notably different percentage breakdown among respondents: the receptive or liberal category grew from 31 to 39 percent of the sample, the hostile category dropped from 33 to 26 percent, and the neutral category stayed much the same (36–35 percent). This change is buttressed by the increase in strength of correlations among the four items (see Table 4.2 below), and the fact that all four load positively on a single dimension in a principal components factor analysis. The overall and particular shifts between the two surveys reflect an increased constraint among respondents on foreigner issues, loosely interpreted as a recognition that empathy with one aspect of guestworker existence should be accompanied by empathy for other aspects of their lives. The overall shift noted above, then, becomes more notable when the combined responses and codes differentiate interpretable categories with quite significant changes for this period. In general, we may report a steady and consistent shift toward attitudes that are more accepting of foreigners.

Table 4.2.
Matrix of Pearson Product Moment Correlations for Guestworker Issue Questions

Variable	Lifestyle	Repatriation	Political Activities	Intermarriage	Scale
Lifestyle	1.00	.36	.38	.34	.66
Repatriation		1.00	.50	.46	.77
Political Activities			1.00	.49	.80
Intermarriage				1.00	.77
Scale					1.00

Hard Times and Opinion Toward Foreigners

By almost any measure we might employ the 1980–1984 period was one of economic strain in Germany. Real economic growth was virtually nonexistent; unemployment ranged around 9–11 percent of the work force; and perhaps worst of all, there was little evidence of either industry-level upturns or shifts to new sources of economic growth. In this general context it is remarkable that opinion toward foreigns improved. What we need to ask, however, is if the improvement in opinion occurred in groups that were largely unaffected by the sluggish economy. If that is the case, we might well expect the foreign worker issue to become more volatile if those whose jobs are most threatened see their countrymen sympathizing with their competition.

For this question another detailed category-by-category presentation is in order (see Table 4.3, below). One definition of Germans most at risk from the job competition of foreigners is those who are or have recently been out of work. It is clear from the table, however, that that category expressed greater receptivity toward guestworkers in 1984 than it did in 1980. To be sure, the group blessed by continued employment exhibited a much greater increase (from 32 to 43 percent). Nonetheless, it is significant to note that even in a period of high unemployment, those without jobs do not appear to make a direct link between their status and the availability of large numbers of foreign workers. It is possible that they do not see themselves and foreigners competing for the *same* jobs, but they still do not express apparent hostility toward those groups.

Carrying this line of reasoning a little further, it is possible that those who are out of work are less job-competitive with foreign workers than those who

Table 4.3.
Economic Sources of Opinion Toward Guestworkers, 1980–1984

Opinion Toward Guestworkers	UNEMPLOYED IN LAST DECADE:			
	Yes		No	
	1980	1984	1980	1984
Receptive	42	46	32	43
Neutral	31	34	39	35
Hostile	27	20	29	22
n=	156	181	1242	1131
p	<.05		<.05	

are currently employed in the lower ranks of the labor force. That is, unskilled and even semi-skilled workers are objectively that most threatened by a foreign labor force, which is employed almost completely in this type of skill category. In fact, in the 1980 study we found the highest levels of hostility among such groups. In Table 4.4, we note that the highest levels of hostility in 1984 were recorded among these groups, but still, in comparison with 1980, the negative proportion declined. Among the skilled workers, the growth in receptivity is greater, and the increase in supportiveness among the self-employed and white collar occupations is remarkable. Nonetheless, it is worth noting that occupational hostility does exist, at the level most proximate to that which the guestworkers occupy. That finding is consistent with the reports of class-based resentments found in earlier studies (Freeman, 1979; Labonte, 1975; Gaugler, et al., 1978) and reported in Wallraff's account of guestworker life (1985).

As our data indicate, those in the lower occupational strata are hardly promoters of the good lives of foreigners. Our data also suggest, however, that their attitudes are not linked directly to economic conditions; their hostility decreased during a period of relatively severe recession. What we may be observing is an expression of general hostility, perhaps even one couched in the terms of job competition, but not really rooted in it. They may be the last group to mute their belligerence toward foreigners as the lower occupations traditionally have been elsewhere, but our data indicate some movement in that direction.

Table 4.4.
Occupational Status and Opinion Toward Guestworkers

Opinion Toward Guestworkers	Unskilled, Semi-skilled 1980 1984		Skilled 1980 1984		Self-Employed 1980 1984		White Collar, Civil Service 1980 1984	
	OCCUPATIONAL STATUS							
Receptive	22	24	26	34	27	42	39	51
Neutral	35	37	43	35	36	32	38	35
Hostile	43	39	32	31	38	26	23	15

n=
1980 2925
1984 1320

P
1980 <.05
1984 <.05

Predictors of Good Will

Referring back once again to the analysis of the 1980 survey, we note that one major conclusion of that study was that hostility toward guestworkers was broadly based and not clearly linked to ideological, partisan, or basic demographic factors. The only identifiable sources of support for foreigners were small, often directed primarily to other issues, and just as often opposed to the kind of organization that is most effective in influencing policy: those groups included a minor party (the Greens), the best educated (those with at least an *Abitur* background), those with frequent contact with foreigners, and those whose political priorities ranked procedural democratic goals above traditional goals of order and economic stability (postmaterialists).[2]

In no case did one of these groups include more than 10–12 percent of the public. It is not surprising that our prognosis for the spread of popular support for guestworker rights was cautious but pessimistic, arguing that those groups were "defined by what might be called the 'greater opportunities' syndrome of the post–1960s period" (Hoskin, 1984:207), and that such a syndrome was largely dependent on prosperity for its continued appeal.

Clearly, prosperity has not characterized the period under investigation here, yet overall support for guestworkers has increased. What we now want to ask is whether these groups have, despite the economic downturn, increased their

Table 4.5.
Change in Composition of German Republic, Along Selected Variables

	1980	1984
A. EDUCATION		
none of these	2	1
Volks-Haupt	62	59
Mittle/Real	22	22
Fachhochschule	4	4
Abitur	10	15
B. PARTY PREFERENCE		
CDU	38	42
SPD	41	38
FDP	11	5
GREENS	6	10
C. NUMBER OF CONTACTS WITH GUESTWORKERS		
3	0	1
2	9	9
1	27	31
0	62	59
D. VALUE ORIENTATION		
Materialist	37	29
Mixed	49	49
Post Materialist	13	22

proportions in the population and continued or increased their commitment to the integration of foreigners in Germany. Both questions are easily addressed in the data available here.

A simple examination of the distribution of respondents among the categories listed above reveals that despite an absence of prosperity, some growth of favored groups has taken place. Table 4.5 notes the changes. A major increase (from 10 to 15 percent) occurred in the proportion of the sample with an *Abitur* educational achievement (the highly selective college-preparatory track); the percentage of those favoring the Green Party increased from 6 to 10 percent. Contacts with foreign workers increased marginally. Most dramatic, however, is the increase in self-defined postmaterialists, from 13 percent in 1980 to 22 percent in 1984. Such an increase is consistent with the interpretation offered

by the concept's creator, Ronald Inglehart, that education, generational replacement, and continued *relative* affluence necessarily enhance the appeal of this
value orientation in industrialized societies (Inglehart, 1977; 1987). It also adds
to a growing body of data indicating that commitment to postmaterial values is
apparently not seriously undercut by nondramatic economic trends. In any case,
the sheer growth is an impressive reason to inquire further into the ways in which
this and other sources of receptivity to foreign workers relate to the overall shift
in opinion.

Table 4.6 provided mean scores on the overall scale measuring combined
responses to the four questions on guestworker rights and treatment, for all
categories of the variables listed above, for 1980 and 1984. Several patterns are
worthy of note. First, across all variables and all groups there is a lowering of
mean scores, indicating a more receptive orientation toward foreigners. That is
consistent with our later observation that receptivity had apparently increased
even among groups most threatened by the presence of foreigners. Second, the
highest levels of good will are still found among those groups with an explicitly
liberal/democratic purpose in life. Although the raw differences are not large,
the scores among those favoring the Greens and those committed to postmaterialist views indicate that they are still the most likely supporters of more favorable
policy for foreign residents.

The case of the postmaterialists is worth a slightly closer look, since we argued
in the earlier study that they—by virtue of their disproportionately high representation in positions of political and economic power—might bear a special
responsibility for leadership on this type of issue. As we noted above, those with
postmaterialist values are a much larger proportion of the sample in 1984 (22
percent) than they were in 1980 (13 percent). Unlike other categories we have
used throughout this paper, however, the percentage of postmaterialists who are
in the receptive category in their opinion toward guestworkers remained constant
between 1980 and 1984 (71 percent). A slightly higher percentage of materialists
were receptive in 1984 (20 percent) than in 1980 (17 percent). In short, although
postmaterialists remain the most visible and strong defenders of foreigners in
Germany, their level of support did not increase over the four-year period.

Finally, what might not be immediately evident is the fact that with the
lowering of the scores on the foreigner-support scale across the board (reflecting
higher support levels), the task facing those most supportive of foreigners—that
of persuading others to accept them into German society—should be easier in
1984 than it was even in 1980. If the overall decline in resistance to foreigners
marks any kind of acceptance of their continued presence and especially if it
marks a threshold of acceptance, the enthusiasm of an ever larger band of political
activists should be able to make an impact on those responsible for policy. As
a footnote, it should be noted that the law of generational replacement would
seem to be working toward this end as well, since the most hostile category in
1980 and almost the most hostile in 1984 was the age group over 55; the younger
cohorts in each year are strikingly more receptive.[3]

What emerges from this analysis of public opinion is a portrait quite different

Table 4.6.
Mean Integration/Nonintegration Scores Among German Groups

	1980		1984	
	MEAN SCORE	n	MEAN SCORE	n
A. PARTY PREFERENCE				
CDU	19.2	(922)	18.1	(961)
SPD	17.4	(1014)	16.7	(876)
FDP	16.8	(258)	15.6	(107)
GREENS	13.4	(136)	11.3	(230)
B. VALUE ORIENTATION				
Materialist	21.2	(1093)	19.6	(854)
Mixed	18.6	(1444)	17.0	(1455)
Post Materialist	13.1	(387)	11.6	(658)
C. EDUCATION				
Grundschule	19.3	(1885)	18.3	(1734)
Real	16.6	(640)	15.5	(656)
Fach	15.2	(98)	13.1	(109)
Abitur	12.0	(296)	12.0	(428)
D. NUMBER OF CONTACTS WITH GUESTWORKERS				
none	19.0	(1837)	17.6	(1687)
1	17.6	(806)	15.6	(917)
2	16.1	(260)	14.6	(281)
3	13.6	(20)	11.4	(35)
E. AGE				
18 to 35	15.4	(910)	13.8	(962)
36 to 55	18.9	(1044)	16.6	(1018)
56 +	22.3	(968)	19.2	(987)

from the one we sketched as likely in our introduction to the section. To be sure, there are still predictable bastions of hostility toward foreigners, primarily among the unskilled and semi-skilled labor categories. And, the overall pattern of opinion certainly does not define a haven for immigrants. Nonetheless, it does reveal an improving climate of opinion toward foreigners, or at least a climate in which their rights are accorded higher levels of acceptance. Perhaps more important, the improvement has occurred under conditions that are usually seen as producing negative opinion—even backlash—against immigrants. Such a pattern provides us with an intriguing set of formal and informal policy determinants, which we may consider in our assessment of the overall policy options available in West Germany. With this array of factors we turn to such an assessment.

CONCLUSIONS

We began this chapter by noting that Germany was an unusual focus for a comparative immigration analysis, if only because its history and current position on this policy would seem to deny that there is much to study there. Indeed, much of our analysis of historical and recent governmental policies has documented themes of tentativeness, reluctance, and inconsistency. Such descriptives are visible in all aspects of immigration, from the admission of refugees to the employment rights of relatives of currently employed foreigners to the question of whether to educate children for a German future or possibly one linked to their homeland. It is not surprising that the overall image—indeed, even the specific details—of the German commitment is largely one of half-hearted and grudging necessity.

That image is hardly countered by clarity in the decision-making process. Political parties have abdicated their traditional leadership role, and less obvious groups have assumed central positions in pressing for official policy and implementing unofficial programs. Even where strict new rules might be developed to confront an unanticipated influx that was *not* a result of shortsighted prior policies (e.g., the dramatic increase in asylum-seekers), conventional policymaking appears to be unable to meet the demand for decisive, and clear objective rules.

Given these circumstances, the chances for public acceptance of foreigners would appear to be small. Yet our analysis indicates that public support for the rights of these groups in German society is increasing, even in a period when the economy was stalled and demands for social services were on the rise. Moreover, not only was there an overall increase in public acceptance or sympathy, the increase occurred even among those groups harmed or threatened by the economic hard times. To be sure, the increase was greater among traditionally liberal and affluent groups, but its existence over the entire spectrum of political and economic categories is surely indicative of an improvement in the general climate for immigrants.

How can we explain this apparent public acceptance of foreigners in the absence of government encouragement—indeed, in the absence of clear government policy? To answer this question it is necessary to step back from the German case, with its peculiar and specific set of official denials of immigration sponsorship, and view the process from a broader comparative perspective. A simple reference to other papers and published research tells us that immigration is almost never a popular phenomenon. Even those nations founded on immigrants have witnessed successive waves of protest and resentment by those who, having gained entry, would like to close the door to others. Even when economic conditions are improved by the arrival of immigrants willing to take the lowest-paying jobs in the economy, at least those in the next-to-lowest positions harbor real prejudice, and those in more remote economic strata fret about the ''foreignization'' of some sectors of society. In short, even when sanctioned by government or important groups, immigration rarely if ever evokes visible public enthusiasm and support.

The necessary corollary to this ubiquitous phenomenon is that governing parties and governments may have a structural need to be able to change policy directions with some speed and, more generally, to be vague in their actual positions. In this respect they are almost like a mirror image of their constituents: they cannot confess to *liking* the influx of immigrants, even if they can often see an *advantage* to their arrival or a real *cost* to trying to shut them out. Once foreigners have arrived, moreover, it is usually easier to make room for them and accept their differences than try to force their departure—especially when history informs us that most such foreigners will sooner or later take on our values and habits.

What we are arguing, in short, is that public opinion and official policy are really two sides of the same coin on this seemingly volatile issue. Which side is examined first is largely irrelevant to the fact that the other will sooner or later be turned over and seen as similar. After all, the question of whether the positions of governmental leaders shape public opinion or are shaped by it is as old, pervasive and unanswerable as politics itself. And, at least in democratic societies, that is as it should be.

That government does not have clear statements of policy goals and the mechanics necessary to implement them is not, in this view, as distasteful as a situation in which government goals are totally out of step with public sentiment on an issue. In the German case, had the initially clear government goals discussed here been accompanied by obvious policy mechanisms, foreign labor might well have been rotated out of the country in the 1970s. The German case allows us to examine in some detail what has happened in the absence of clear policy. Public opinion has, gradually, made strides toward an acceptance of foreigners in the society, which ultimately should allow the government to sponsor vigorous programs of naturalization. That it has not done so prior to this time is perhaps dismaying and perhaps reflective of governments that have been unwilling to take bold but necessary steps. On the other hand, it may also be reflective of a painfully slow but eventually less conflictual process through which foreigners are assimilated into societies that initially appear to be especially unsuited to their integration.

NOTES

1. The 1980 and 1984 surveys reported here included interviews with almost 3,000 respondents in each year. Data preparation completed by the ZUMA organization in Mannheim.

2. Post-materialists are defined as those respondents who rank two democratic procedural goals (free expression and mass participation) above more tangible goals of law and order and stable prices. The concept and measure were developed and elaborated by Ronald Inglehart in his basic work, *The Silent Revolution* (1977) and in numerous articles since then. Those respondents who mix goals in their first two priorities are coded as "mixed" in their value orientations; those ranking the two tangible goals first and second in priority are labelled "materialists."

3. It should be noted that we examined a number of other plausible predictors as well (including population density, percentage of the workforce held by foreigners, and *land*), but found no contribution to outlook among these demographic factors. The single best predictor in both years was value orientation.

5

Israeli Immigration Policy and Politics

BAT-AMI ZUCKER

The purpose of this chapter is to focus attention on one of Israel's existential problems: who is a citizen in the recently established state of Israel. It is not a new subject; others have written on it already, using legal, social, and political approaches. The orientation of this chapter is to examine this question from its ideological perspective; namely, the ideology behind the definition of an Israeli citizen who is also Jewish—in that the state of Israel was created for the Jewish people and Jews form the majority of its population. Israel's nationality policy with regard to its non-Jewish citizens, however, will be dealt with below.

One may ask why should ideology be relevant to the question of nationality when in order to acquire, for example, U.S. citizenship, one does not necessarily invoke American culture, national anthem, or a certain religion. In Israel, this chapter will attempt to show, as a direct result of the uniqueness of the Jewish state, the situation is completely different. Whereas U.S. nationality may lead to an American identity, in the State of Israel it is Jewishness that conditions automatic Israeli nationality. Jewishness, as both religion and nationhood, had therefore to be legally defined so that the necessary ordinances and procedures concerning nationality could be enacted. Since, however, Israel is a secular, democratic state with a majority of nonobservant Jews, the attempts to legally interpret "Jewishness" have led to ideological and legal controversy, often threatening the stability of coalition governments composed of religious as well as secular ministers.

Although it was eventually decided in 1970 to incorporate the traditional religious definition of a Jew in an Amendment to the laws of immigration and nationality, the question of "Who is a Jew" has been and still is the focus of ideological polemic and serious social tension, continually affecting Israel's nationality policy. The controversy is viewed here through the analysis of the relevant Israeli laws, decisions of the Supreme Court, and conflicting opinions prevailing in Israeli society at large.

I would like to express my gratitude to the Archives of the Knesset in Jerusalem for granting me permission to use unpublished files and to the Tel-Aviv Bar Association for most helpful assistance. Finally, special thanks to my mentor, colleague and friend, Professor A. Saltman, who took time to comment and to provide me with necessary suggestions and criticism.

ISRAEL'S NATIONALITY POLICY

Israel's nationality policy is set out in two basic laws specifically emphasizing the raison d'etre of the State as "the ingathering of the Exiles" (1, *Laws of the State of Israel* [hereafter LSI]:3. See also Justice Landau, in *Rufeisen v. Minister of the Interior,* 1962:16; *Piskei-Din* 2428:2447 [hereafter PD]). Since the State of Israel has been established to create a homeland and shelter to the Jewish people who wish to cast their lot with the new state, the policy of "open door to Jewish immigrants is one of its fundamental principles" (Akzin: 181).

Accordingly, the Law of Return, 5710–1950, and the Nationality Law, 5712–1952 (4, LSI:114; 6, LSI:50) grant preference and automatic nationality to Jews wishing to acquire Israeli citizenship. Such preference demonstrates the character of the state of Israel as a Jewish state and the fundamental values upon which it is based. The special nature of Israel to which the scattered Jewish people will return also forms the basis for the declaratory provision of another statute, the World Zionist Organization–Jewish Agency (Status) Law, 5713–1952 (1, LSI:3):

The State of Israel regards itself as the creation of the entire Jewish people, and its gates are open, in accordance with its laws, to every Jew wishing to immigrate to it . . . The mission of gathering in the exiles is the central task of the State of Israel. (1, LSI:3, Sections 1, 5)

As far as the legal framework is concerned, however, individuals within the state enjoy equal rights and are subject to equal duties regardless of ethnic or religious differences. Together with the Nationality Law, which ensures equal status to all citizens, the Declaration of the Establishment of the State of Israel of May 14, 1948, guarantees that:

The State of Israel. . . . will ensure complete equality of social and political rights to all its inhabitants irrespective of religion, race or sex; it will guarantee freedom of religion, conscience, language, education and culture; it will safeguard the Holy places of all religions, and it will be faithful to the principles of the Charter of the United Nations. (1, LSI:3)

A distinction should be drawn between the right to Return and the right to nationality. The Law of Return enacted by the Knesset (Israel Legislature) on July 5, 1950, granted to all Jews everywhere the legal right to immigrate and settle in Israel but did not "deal with nationality at all" (Justice Landau, *Salem Manashe v. Chairman and Members of the Rabbinical Court of Jerusalem*, 1951, 5, PD 714, at p. 720). In fact, for a period of about two years before the Nationality Law was promulgated, the right to return "was a right unto itself" (Rubinstein:160). Thus, despite the connection between immigration under the Law of Return and the grant of Israeli nationality under the Nationality Law, there does exist an independent status of immigrant under the Law of Return, irrespective of nationality. Such an immigrant may not necessarily acquire Israeli citizenship; yet, his position as an *oleh* (Jewish immigrant) is more privileged than that of any other person granted permission to settle permanently in Israel. It is also his status as *oleh* under the Law of Return and not his Israeli nationality that determines such matters as customs concessions and tax exemptions (LSI, 1968:22; LSI: 43). Citizenship in Israel is acquired only by virtue of the Nationality Law, which provides six ways of obtaining nationality, only one of which—by Return—is almost unrestricted (Nationality Law, Section 2[a]), to be effective from the day of arrival in Israel. In conjunction with the Law of Return, the Nationality Law provides Israeli citizenship automatically for Jewish immigrants, unless they formally renounce the grant.

Although separate and independent, the Law of Return and the Nationality Law share equally in providing the constitutional and practical framework of Israel's nationality policy, and were so envisaged by their legislators. Presenting the Bills jointly to the Knesset for their first reading on July 3, 1950, then-Prime Minister David Ben-Gurion declared that both "are connected by a mutual bond and share a common conceptual origin, deriving from the historical uniqueness of the State of Israel." These laws, explained the prime minister, "comprise the central mission of our State to fulfill the vision of the redemption of Israel . . . by the ingathering of the exiles";

it is not the State that grants the Jew from abroad the right to settle in the State. Rather, this right is inherent in him by the very fact that he is a Jew. . . . The right to return preceded the State of Israel and it is this right that built the State.

These laws, he concluded, present the "Bill of Rights, the Charter" which is guaranteed to all the Jews in the State of Israel (*Divrei Ha'Knesset* [Knesset Records], 6, 1950:2035–37). On announcing the unanimous passage of the Law of Return on July 5, 1950, chairman of the Knesset Nir declared that "the Law of Return symbolizes the fulfillment of two thousand years of Jewish hopes" (ibid.).

When comparing the number of immigrants arriving in the state of Israel in the first decade of its establishment (1948–1958) with the massive waves of immigrants to the United States, Israel would hardly fit into the picture. When one recalls, however, that the Jewish population of the country in May 1948 consisted of 650,000, and that a decade later, due to immigration during that time, it almost tripled—then Israel can certainly be considered a major immigrant nation. It should be noted, moreover, that the uniqueness of Israel as an immigrant country lies in its obligation to absorb refugees. In that respect, there may be a similarity with the early history of the United States. Yet such comparison leaves one only at the surface of a much deeper phenomenon.

The uniqueness of Israel has been characterized by two dominant events in 20th century Jewish history: the Holocaust and the establishment of the state of Israel. The disproportion in the dimension of the immigrant process in Israel after the Holocaust is clearly the result of the state of emergency in which Jewish refugees in Europe found themselves. Their survival was literally at stake. There was an immediate need to find a quick solution by providing them with asylum. There was no time to deal with or even prepare for the enormous problems such a massive immigration caused. The demographic, social, cultural, and economic questions had to be postponed for later years. The major task was to absorb Jewish refugees: to collect them at the ports, to provide them with food, lodging, and employment and to help them to adjust to the new country.

The following figure and tables illustrate the waves of immigrants to Israel for the time periods demarcated. Figure 5.1 presents graphically the total influx of immigrants to Israel for the years 1919 to 1970, dramatically showing the relatively massive immigration of the 1948–1951 period. The tables show immigration data for the period 1948 to 1951, and for 1948 to 1959.

THE LAW OF RETURN: *"HOK HA" SHVUT*

Shvut—the Hebrew name chosen for this law of immigration—indicates the somewhat mystical and messianic connotation applied to the term in Jewish liturgy. The term in Hebrew implies two meanings: to come back, and to be free from bondage. "There is no better name to express the close connection between the Jewish people and the land of Israel," stated J. Lamm on behalf of the Constitution, Legislation, and Juridical Committee when presenting the Bill to the Knesset on July 5, 1950 (*Divrei Ha'Knesset,* 6, 1950:2094). Indeed, the Law of Return, which has been described as the most Jewish law of the state, is also one of Israel's basic laws stating clearly that the state of Israel belongs to the entire Jewish people. "Every Jew," proclaims section 1 of the Law, "has the right to come to this country as an *oleh* (immigrant)." The terms "immigrant" and "immigration" do not express the unique meaning applied to the words *oleh* and *aliyah* in Hebrew. The terms in Hebrew imply the Jewish and Zionist philosophy that regards the return of the Jews to Israel as an act of self-fulfillment and ascent (see Rubinstein:160–161).

The uniqueness of the law's approach to immigration is demonstrated when, for example, it is compared with immigration legislation of the United States. Under the Immigration Reform and Control Act (IRCA) of 1986 the U.S. government imposes complete control on the number and qualifications of persons who wish to settle in the country. In contrast, the Law of Return prescribes one

Figure 5.1.
Immigration of Jews to Israel, 1919–1970

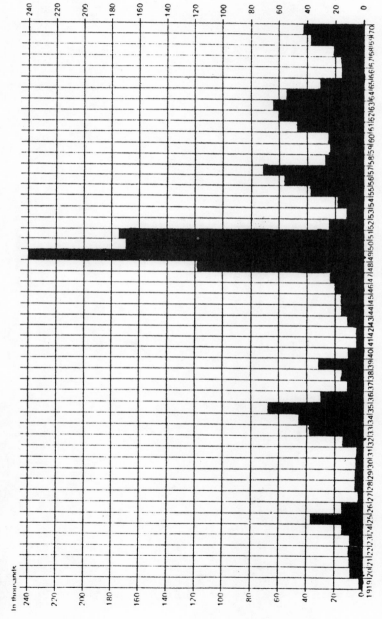

Source: Encyclopeadia Judaica. Vol. 9 (Keter Publishing House: Jerusalem, 1971): 473.

Table 5.1.

Mass Immigration, May 1948–December 1951

All Countries	684,201		
Eastern Europe		**Africa**	
Rumania	118,940	Morocco	30,750
Poland	103,732	Tunisia	13,139
Bulgaria	37,231	Algeria	1,523
Czechoslovakia	18,217	Libya	30,482
Hungary	13,631	South Africa	584
Yugoslavia	7,595	Ethiopia	83
Soviet Union (Lithuania, Latvia)	4,698	Egypt	16,508
		Other Countries	108
Total	304,044	Total	93,177
Western Europe		**Western Hemisphere**	
Germany	8,856	United States	1,909
France	4,008	Canada	233
Austria	2,994	Argentina	1,134
Greece	2,005	Brazil	442
Britain	2,143	Other Latin American Countries	870
Italy	1,415		
Belgium	1,108	Total	4,588
Netherlands	1,102		
Spain	412	Australia	171
Sweden	429	Unregistered	19,993
Switzerland	386		
Other European Countries	147	**Asia**	
		Iraq	121,512
Total	25,005	Turkey	34,213
		Iran	24,804
		Aden	3,155
		India	2,337
		China	2,167
		Cyprus	136
		Yemen	45,199
		Other Countries	3,700
		Total	237,223

Source: Encyclopaedia Judaica. Vol. 9 (Keter Publishing House: Jerusalem, 1971): 535.

Table 5.2:
Jewish Immigration, by Origin, for Selected Periods, 1919–1959

Jewish Immigrants By Area, 1919-1956			
	1956:	1948-56:	1919-48:
All Countries	56,234	734,525	452,158
Asia	3,310	256,593	40,767
Africa	45,138	198,536	4,033
Europe	7,048	352,995	377,487
America/Oceania	735	7,229	7,579
Not Stated	3	19,172	22,283

Percentages:

	America/Oceania:	Europe:	Africa:	Asia:
1919/48	1.8	87.8	0.9	9.5
1948/59	46.0		54.0	

Absolute Numbers:

	Unknown:	America/Oceania:	Europe:	Africa:	Asia:	Total:
1919/48	22,283	7,579	377,487	4,033	40,776	452,158
1948/59	19,424	425,564		500,273		945,261

Source: Adapted from: *Statistical Abstracts*, No. 11 (Jerusalem, 1959/60, pp. 34, 70).

law for all Jews by offering an open invitation to every Jew to come and settle in Israel. Not only is the state unable to restrict the number of Jewish immigrants, it is obligated under the Law of Return to accept, apart from a few exceptions that will be discussed below, all those who answer the invitation including the old, the poor, and the disabled. (See, by contrast, the basic exclusionary provisions of the U.S.'s IRCA of 1986, in *C.Q.Weekly*, October 18, 1986:2595– 98.) Equally, section 4 of the Law of Return states that "every Jew who has immigrated into [the] country before the coming into force of this Law, and every Jew who was born in this country, whether before or after the coming into force of this Law, shall be deemed to be a person who has come to this country as an *oleh* under this Law" (Law of Return, 1950, section 4). In other words, in the eyes of the Law it is not the new immigrant who is considered as though he was a native-born Israeli but rather the Jew, born in Israel and settled before the enactments of the Law, who is deemed to be an *oleh*. Such an approach reflects an attitude aiming to equate both *oleh* and native-born Jew, by granting them one status. But perhaps the most striking difference, when compared to the United States, lies in the obligation to grant an immigration visa or certificate to every Jew who expressed his wish to immigrate. Even when it can be undeniably proved that it has never been the immigrant's intention to settle in Israel, but that he intends to exercise his right of Return to facilitate his settling elsewhere, the Minister of the Interior has no authority to deny, except in three cases discussed below, or revoke an *oleh* visa unless it has been obtained by supplying false information.[1] In the case of *Golan vs. Minister of Interior* (HC 81/62, *Barbara Golan v. Minister of Interior*, 3, 16 PD 1969), the petitioner was granted an *oleh* visa but later sought to have it nullified. The Court held that "the Minister of the Interior has no general authority to revoke such visa or certificate; he was limited to cases in which an *oleh* visa was acquired by false pretenses (Ibid.:1972).

The rights granted to an *oleh* under the Law of Return were limited to Jewish immigrants alone. Under the original Law the *oleh*'s family, had it not been Jewish, was not entitled to the same rights. Non-Jewish family members could, however, immigrate and acquire citizenship under different statutes (Entry into Israel Law, 1952: the Nationality Law, 1952). Only in 1970 an Amendment to include family members of a Jewish immigrant within the operation of the Law of Return and the automatic grant of nationality was enacted. Section 4A (a) of the Law of Return (Amendment no. 2, 24 LSI:28), 1970, provided for the extension of all the rights of an *oleh*—such as tax benefits, housing, and other privileges provided to new Jewish immigrants—to his or her spouse, children, and grandchildren. All these rights are granted through the new Amendment to the non-Jewish members even though the Jew from whom their right derives may have died before exercising his right to immigrate to Israel or may not have immigrated together with them, with the sole exception being to "a person who has been a Jew and has voluntarily changed his religion." Moreover, since the Law has been couched in the present tense it is open to retroactive construction in favor of immigrants already settled in Israel. This Amendment was motivated by the legislature's desire to maintain family integrity. The fact that this important extension of the Law of Return did not cause much public controversy may indicate that there prevailed a wide consensus to pursue the human need of family integrity and to avoid any discrimination between the Jewish and non-Jewish members of the same family (Ben-Meir, MK, in DHK, 57, 1970: 1119).

Despite the all-embracing nature of the Law of Return, the Minister of the Interior may refuse to grant an *oleh* visa when he is "satisfied that the applicant (1) is engaged in an activity directly against the Jewish people: or (2) is likely to endanger public health or the security of the State, or (3) is a person with a criminal past, likely to endanger the public welfare" (*Divrei Ha'Knesset*, 15, 1954:816). The first two exceptions were intended to prevent immigration of people who are engaged in activity against the Jewish people, and those who might endanger public welfare or state security. It should be noted that the present tense is deliberately used in the first qualification to emphasize present activity as to differentiate it from activity in the past. "It refers," explained Ben-Zion Dannenberg, MK on behalf of the majority of the Constitution, Legislation, and Juridical Committee, "to a person who has committed or is now engaged in an act against the Jewish people, and its effects are still apparent" (*Divrei Ha'Knesset*, 6, 1950:2102). Thus a person who had, for example, collaborated with the Nazis during the Second World War could not, under this section, be refused an *oleh* visa unless the Minister was satisfied that the applicant was still likely to endanger public welfare (Gouldman, 1970:33). The second qualification refers to those likely to endanger public health; however, if applying for an *oleh* certificate while in Israel, he "should not be regarded as endangering public health on the account of an illness contracted after his arrival in Israel" (Law of Return, Section 3(b)).

The suggested exceptions caused much controversy in the Knesset and were not easily adopted. The main objection referred to the violation of the "natural right of every Jew to return to his homeland" (J.BarYehuda, MK, in *Divrei Ha'Knesset* 6, 1950:2041). Only members of the Israeli Communist Party objected to the qualification concerning "the security of the State" (Divrei Ha'Knesset 6; 1950:2101). "No government," argued Benjamin Mintz, MK, "no minister and no Jew had a right to deny another Jew his historical and most basic right of immigrating to Israel" (Ibid.:2047). And Jacob Gil, MK, declared that even if a Jew was ill abroad, "We should bring him into Israel, heal him or isolate him if he endangers public health" (Ibid.:2044). In his reply on July 5, 1950, Prime Minister David Ben-Gurion strongly defended the exceptions:

This Law is in fact the Charter of Zionism. . . . Every Jew has a right to Return to Israel . . . but this is not a metaphysical right. We are building an *Eretz-Segula* [an especially virtuous state] for the Jewish people, not a prison or an asylum. . . . A Jew immigrating to Israel comes to participate in building a homeland, in developing Jewish culture and strength and not to be imprisoned as a person endangering the public health. (*Divrei Ha'Knesset* 6, 1950:2099)

In fact, no instance is known whereby use has been made of the Minister's power when the security of the state is endangered, nor has an act against the Jewish people ever been alleged. On the other hand, there were cases where an *oleh* visa was refused for reasons of health, including cases of insanity. Yet, as a rule, Israeli policy has always been to pursue full implementation of the concept of Return.

Bitter and even more ardent was the opposition raised in the Knesset when the third exception was introduced in 1954. The qualification aiming to prevent the immigration of Jews "with a criminal past likely to endanger public welfare" (Law of Return (Amendment), 5714–1954, section 2(b)(3)), was necessary, explained the minister of the Interior, "to keep away criminals who use the right of Return to escape the arms of the law of their domicile"(*Divrei Ha'Knesset*

15, 1954:816). Similar to the objections heard with regard to the original exceptions to the 1950 Law, the members of the Knesset who opposed the 1954 Amendment emphasized the violations of a natural right. "The Law of Return," argued Zerach Warhaftig, MK, "declared that a Jew returns to Israel by right. We have no authority to deny him this right. We rather accept criminals than violate this great principle" (Ibid.:823–24). "If we accept the Amendment," stated H. Rubin, MK, "there will be no difference between the Law of Return and immigration legislation of other countries" (Ibid.:831). Despite the considerable opposition, however, the Amendment was enacted and later discussed in several well-known court decisions.

The difficulties connected with the newly adopted exception to the Law of Return were both ideological and judicial. As for the ideology involved, the restriction attempted to reconcile two conflicting principles: the gates of Israel open to every Jew wishing to settle on the land, as against the reluctance of a state to serve as a refuge for criminals. This conflict was well presented by Justice Sussman in the case of *Marion Lee Gold v. Minister of the Interior*:

I do not think that a Jew should be deprived of his right to immigrate to this country by reasons of any offense. . . . The gravity of the act which is liable to proscribe the right of immigration must be weighed against the importance of the right which is taken away from the person. It is not enough for it to be a trifling matter. (HC 94/62, *Marion Lee Gold vs. Minister of Interior*, 3, 16 PD 1846:1857)

On the other hand, even if the right to immigrate to Israel is the rule and the restriction prescribed by section 2(6) the exception alone, "the duty of the Minister of the Interior to close the door to criminals is no less important" (Ibid.). The Court, therefore, had to decide on the future character of the state: will Israel be an asylum for criminals?

In the Court's view there was no conflict between the principles of open gates to all Jews and the restriction laid on Jewish criminals:

The State of Israel . . . was established in order to be open to Jewish immigrants and for the ingathering of the exiles. It was not established to serve as a focal point for the settlement of all those who had contravened the laws of the countries of their domicile and were therefore desirous to escape the arm of the law, even though they are Jews. (Ibid.:1885)

The same approach was confirmed nine year later. In the case of *Lansky vs. Minister of the Interior* (HC 422/71, *Lansky vs. Minister of Interior* 2, 26 PD:337), the question arose with regard to an American Jew who had been convicted by a U.S. Court of certain misdemeanors concerning gambling, for which he had been sentenced. While in Israel, on a tourist visa, he applied for an immigrant's certificate. His application was rejected owing to information received connecting him with organized crime in the United States.

The Lansky case gives rise to some thoughts. Is a conviction for misdemeanor connected with gambling an adequate reason for refusing immigrant status? As for his connection with organized crime, he was never charged with an offense, much less convicted. Yet the Court, sitting as the High Court of Justice, confirmed the authority of the Minister of the Interior to deny Lansky immigrant status in order "to prevent the gathering in Israel of persons though Jewish, who had violated the law somewhere else" (Ibid.:339). Nevertheless, despite a strong desire in Israel to function as a law-abiding country, "one has to bear in mind," stated Justice Sussman in another case, "the nature of the Law of Return. It is undesirable to define the expression 'with a criminal past' in exact terms, but rather it ought to be independently defined in each case" (*Gold vs. Minister of Interior,* op. cit.:1856).

In addition to the difficulties that arose in regard to the seemingly ideological conflict behind sections 1 and 2(b)(3) of the Law of Return, the vague expressions of the exception gave rise to several legal questions. As the Law neither defined "a criminal past" nor provided objective tests for determining an applicable likelihood "to endanger public welfare," it remained, under the Law, for the Minister of the Interior to decide whether the two conditions prescribed in section 2(b)(3), namely, a criminal past and likelihood to endanger public welfare, should be invoked. The Minister's discretion, however, did not solve the legal problems. The questions—who is a person with a criminal past, were the two conditions cumulative, need there be a conviction at all, or whether one conviction was sufficient evidence for the administrative act—were only later decided by the Court.

In three leading cases,[2] the Court agreed that "a person with a criminal past" was not synonymous with a "a man with a previous conviction" (*Gold vs. Minister of the Interior*:1855). It all depended on the type of offense committed. Some offenses, such as traffic violations, do not necessarily indicate a criminal past (Justice Cohen, Ibid.:1850). On the other hand, "a person possessing a criminal past for the purposes of the Law of Return is one who has committed criminal offenses, and one such offense alone may be sufficient for this purpose" (Justice Sussman, Ibid.:1853). The commission of "an act of murder," ruled the Court, "is sufficient to infer the existence of a criminal past, even if such a person has only committed one murder."[3] The gravity of the offense is, therefore, the criterion to be used when deciding to label a person with "a criminal past" in regard to the exception under the Law of Return. For that matter the same principle applies where a person with no previous criminal record is charged with the commission of a serious offence but flees to Israel before he can be brought to trial (HC 125/80, *Angel and Prizeman vs. Minister of Interior*, 4, 34 PD:328). To put it in Justice Sussman's words: "Does not the murderer who flees judgment endanger public order in Israel exactly as the murderer who is convicted?" (Justice Sussman in *Gold vs. Minister of Interior*:1855).

A conviction, therefore, is not a condition precedent to prove a criminal past of a person. The Minister of Interior is authorized to invoke this exception under the Law of Return if he is convinced that the person in question is likely to endanger public order. In such a case, ruled the Court in a later case, the test of substantive evidence, as used by the administrative bodies, prevails (*Lansky vs. Minister of Interior*:359).

To sum up, in these leading cases the Court established the rule that each offense must be independently weighed and evaluated. It also confirmed the authority of the Minister of the Interior to deprive a person of the right of Return even if he had no criminal record. It is a power vested in the Minister of Interior to deny the status of an immigrant when he is satisfied, on the strength of evidence in his possession, that the applicant has a criminal past that is likely to endanger the public welfare. It should be noted, however, that another important procedure was established. The Court, using its reviewing powers, ensured that the basic right of Return would not be prejudiced until the minister had made proper use of his powers (Ibid.: 354–55,339). Furthermore, a person who has been denied an *oleh* certificate and faces deportation is entitled to seek relief from the Court. He can not be expelled from Israel until the Court has been given the full opportunity to examine the lawfulness of each act of deportation (Regulation 21, Entry into Israel Regulations, 3734–1974, *Kovetz-Tikunim* [hereafter TK] 3201 of 5734–1974: 1517; see also, Rubinstein:169–70).

The Law of Return, although dealing exclusively with the natural right of every Jew to immigrate to Israel, has nonetheless determined Israel's nationality policy by being fully incorporated in the Nationality Law, 1952, under section 2(a). It is this section that grants the National Law its ideological importance, by providing a unique Jewish identity to Israel's nationality policy. It is to a discussion of that Law we next turn our attention.

THE NATIONALITY LAW

In contrast to the speedy enactment of the Law of Return, which took a mere two days (*Divrei Ha'Knesset,* 6, 1950:2049), it took two years of continuous debate in the Knesset and its committees to finally adopt the Nationality Law on April 1, 1952. The main opposition to the proposed Bill focused on two issues: the issue of double nationality permitted under the Law to Jewish immigrants only, and the nationality policy toward non-Jewish residents who seek to acquire Israeli citizenship. In both these issues a preference was given to Jews. We should remember, however, that this preference demonstrated the unique character of the state as a Jewish state, and its fundamental principle to serve as a national home for Jews everywhere. Such a principle does not violate the rights of non-Jewish nationals in the State of Israel. The Minister of the Interior, M. Shapira, on introducing the Bill in July 1950, stated that "the Law guarantees equal rights to all Israeli nationals"(*Divrei Ha'Knesset* 6, 1950:2038). "The Nationality Law," he argued in answer to accusations of discrimination raised by Arab Knesset members, "does not deprive Arabs of any right; on the contrary the Law grants equal legal status to all state citizens. Once the Israeli nationality is acquired, there is no discrimination whatsoever between Arab citizens and Jewish citizens in the State of Israel'' (Ibid.:2134). Yet, although the Law indeed provides equal legal status once they become nationals, it nonetheless grants unconditioned automatic nationality to Jews alone, and thus facilitates their road to Israeli citizenship.

Such preference to Jews under the Law follows a fundamental principle prescribing the acquisition of Israel nationality according to the ''law of kinship''— *jus sanguinis*. Under this principle, nationality is transferred from parents to children without any reference to the place of birth.[4] Israel as a country absorbing immigrants should perhaps have adopted the ''law of the land''—*jus soli*—in order to quickly create a common denominator for all its residents; however, because of its unique character as a Jewish state it prefers the ''law of kinship,'' and only to a limited extent recognizes the ''law of the land.'' It will be seen below that this preference for *jus sanguinis* has created legal difficulties, public controversy, bitter disagreement, and has even caused political crises.

Despite considerable opposition the Nationality Law was adopted on April 1, 1952, leaving all matters of Israel nationality to be regulated exclusively by the Law (see section 1, second sentence). The Nationality Law provided six ways to acquire Israel nationality: by Return, by residence in Israel, by birth, by birth and residence (section 4A added by Amendment only in 1968), by naturalization, and by grant.

Nationality by Return

The scope of nationality by Return is extremely wide and forms the most basic provisions of the Law. Section 2(a) states: ''Every *oleh* under the Law of Return shall become an Israel national.'' In regard to Jewish immigrants the Nationality Law does not stipulate any conditions, not even a minimum period of residence. Moreover, an *oleh* acquires Israel nationality irrespective of one or more other nationalities he possesses (see Bar-Ya´acob:Chap.14; Gouldman:551). Section 2(b) prescribes five classes of persons who acquire automatic nationality by Return. Two classes concern native-born Jews, born in the country before or after the establishment of Israel; another two are Jewish immigrants to the country before or after the establishment of Israel (Gouldman, 1970:15, 42–44). The fifth class is especially outstanding when compared with such legislation in other countries. Section 2(e) of the Law, as amended in 1971, authorizes the Minister of the Interior to grant Israeli nationality to a person who has expressed his desire to settle in Israel and is entitled to receive an *oleh* visa ''by virtue of Return even before his *aliya*.''[5]

This provision was mainly intended for Russian Jews who have renounced their Soviet nationality and see themselves as Israeli citizens, but who were prevented from immigrating by the Soviet authorities (see note to Amendment 3, *Hatza´aot Hok*, no. 935 of 5731:192).

All the provisions mentioned above demonstrate the ideology behind the Law.

There is no differentiation between Jews born in Israel and Jewish immigrants. All Jews acquire their nationality automatically from the right of Return and not as a right of birth. Still, there are six cases in which automatic nationality should not apply. The first concerns a person who has severed his ties with Israel before the enactment of the Law (Nationality Law, 1952, section (c)(1). The sixth case concerns a Jew "born in Israel to a diplomatic or consular representative of a foreign state" (as amended, 1980, 34 LSI,254). The other four concern immigrants who hold foreign nationality and do not wish to become Israel citizens. Their cases require a positive act in the form of a written declaration by the immigrant that "he does not want to become an Israel national."[6]

The declarations under the above provisions were often made to enable the *oleh* to keep his foreign nationality. It was feared by the legislators that the acquisition of Israeli nationality would adversely affect the immigrant's other nationality and keep potential immigrants from coming into Israel (*Divrei Ha'Knesset,* 6, 1950:2038–39; and 10, 1951:430).

In the debates concerning the adoption of the Law, opposition was raised in the Knesset in regard to "double nationality," permitted under the Law to immigrants who hold foreign nationality. "Such a position," argued Israel Bar-Yahuda, MK, "will enable thousands of Israeli citizens to hold a different passport in each pocket" (*Divrei Ha'Knesset,* 10, 1951:412). "It is a matter of double loyalty, " stated another, "that might cause serious problems to a person possessing two nationalities" (J. Baker, MK, in Ibid., 6, 1950:2042). The Law, eventually adopted in 1952, permitted double nationality (section 14(a),(b)). The motivation for such a provision, explained Z. Warhaftig, MK, defending the Bill, was to "encourage immigration. If keeping one's foreign nationality helps to diminish the immigrant's doubts about settling in Israel—we might as well allow it" (*Divrei Ha'Knesset* 6, 1950:2043).

The same motivation was responsible for the adoption of the original section 2(c), (2), (3) of the Law, which enables an immigrant with a foreign nationality to opt out of Israeli nationality by a declaration made on or before the day of immigration (Nationality Law, 1952, Section 2(c)(2)). Time proved, however, that the decision the *oleh* had to make in haste was sometimes regretted (see, for instance, the case of H.C. 128/60, *Feigngoim vs. Minister of the Interior,* 2, 14PK:966). In order to help the *oleh* over his initial difficulties the provision, as amended in 1968 and in 1980, gave an *oleh* a three month period of grace during which he might decide to waive Israeli nationality. It should be noted, though, that the acquisition of nationality by Return is not deferred for a period of three months. The *oleh* who does not opt out within that period is viewed as a national from the day of his immigration. Once, however, the right to opt out is exercised, section 2(c)(2) is deemed—retroactively—never to have applied at all.[7] The right of renunciation also applies to a minor of foreign nationality born outside Israel who has been included in his parents' declaration, and to a minor who came to Israel without his parents. In the latter case, a written declaration by the parents should state that they "do not want him to become an Israel national," provided they themselves are not Israel nationals (Section 2(c)(3)(4) as replaced by the Nationality [amendment no.4] Law, 1980).

Nationality by Residence

Similar to the automatic grant of nationality to Jews by Return, sections 3, 3A, and 3B (the latter two of which were added by amendment in 1980) of the Nationality Law provided for nationality to be granted to non-Jewish permanent residents in Israel. In contrast to the easy procedure to be followed by Jews seeking Israeli nationality, however, non-Jewish residents are required to comply with more stringent conditions. These conditions were included in the Law to ensure that nationality would not be given to Arab residents who left Israel during the War of Independence, had illegally returned to their villages, and might use Israeli nationality to endanger Israel's safety (HC 155/51, *Khaldi vs. Minister of the Interior*, 6 PD 52; HC 24/52, *Chakim vs. Minister of the Interior*, 6 PD 638).

In the debates concerning section 3, Arab representatives and Knesset members of the Israeli Communist Party rejected the provision on the grounds of racial discrimination (*Divrei Ha'Knesset* 11, 1952:1682–87). "This section," argued E. Perry, MK of the Left Labor Party, "might deprive 90 percent of the Arab residents of their citizenship" (Ibid.:1682). The section was adopted despite the opposition. The great majority of Israeli Arabs and their descendents have, in fact, become Israeli nationals under this very section (Amnon Rubinstein, "Israel Nationality," *Tel Aviv University Studies in Law* 2, 1976:171).

The termination of the British Mandate in Palestine and the establishment of the State of Israel on May 14, 1948, created a somehow peculiar situation for the non-Jewish minority residing in Israel. Whereas the Jewish inhabitants acquire legal status under the recognized principle of kinship (*jus sanguinis*; Ibid.:11), Arab residents were not provided with any legal status. The immediate predecessor of the Israel nationality—Palestine citizenship (regulated in 1925 under the Palestine Citizenship Order, 3 *Laws of Palestine*:2640)—had, according to the ruling of the Israeli Supreme Court, ceased to exist with the disappearance of Palestine as a political entity. To put it in the words of Justice Landau: "Palestine citizenship was revoked and vanished from the world with the establishment of the State of Israel."[8]

Prior to the enactment of the Nationality Law in 1952, there prevailed, therefore, a situation in which Arab residents, who had been Palestinian citizens immediately prior to the establishment of Israel, as well as their yet unborn children, were left with no nationality at all. This legal vacuum was filled by the passing of the Nationality Law in 1952, and the creation of indigenous Israeli nationality. Nationality by residence was devised as a means of granting Israeli nationality to the non-Jewish population, with effect from the day of the establishment of Israel. Such nationality was regulated by section 3 of the original

Law and by sections 3A and 3B of the 1980 Amended Law (Amendment No. 4).

A person of this category must have been a Palestinian citizen prior to the establishment of the State, must have been registered as an inhabitant of Israel, and must have resided there "from the day of the establishment of the State to the day of the coming into force of this Law, or entered Israel legally during the period" (Nationality Law, 1952, Section 3 (a)). If he was born after the establishment of Israel, and in the day of coming into force of the Law he was an Israeli resident, and one of his parents was from an Israeli national by residence, he became an Israeli national from the date of his birth (section 3(b)).

The requirements set out in section 3 are absolute and if not fully complied with, the Court is not empowered to intervene. Yet, effective intervention may be achieved by the Court using a flexible and more liberal interpretation. The Court, indeed, adopted such an approach, which was motivated by its desire not to deprive a non-Jewish resident of nationality— "one's most important and valued possession"—for trivial reasons (HC 328/60, *Nagíb Mussa vs. Minister of the Interior*, 1, 16 PD:69). The same approach was later reflected in the 1980 Amendment, which extended nationality by residence by adding more eligible categories of persons. Sections 3A and 3B granted nationality by residence to persons who were born before the establishment of Israel (i.e., prior to 1948), but who resided and registered only in 1952, and to their children, provided they had not been nationals of enemy countries.

Nationality by Birth

Section 4 of the Law grants nationality by birth to a person born in or outside Israel "while his father or mother was an Israel national" (replaced by Amendment 4, 1980). For the purposes of this section, the place of birth or residence of the parents and/or children is irrelevant. The determining factor to nationality by birth is the national status of the parents (thus section 4 follows the principle of *jus sanguinis*). In other words, a person is granted nationality, by birth only if one of his parents holds Israeli nationality, being acquired by Return, residence, or naturalization (section 4(a)(2)). Israel nationality is, therefore, transferred from parents to children by birth, *ad infinitum*. Taking into consideration (1) that Israeli nationality is given to Jews and non-Jews alike in perpetuity, even with regard to a family that has severed all links with Israel and (2) that Israeli nationality is only lost in extreme circumstances (discussed below), the sometimes absurd implications can perhaps be assessed. Jews of such a category, even second generation nationals born abroad, are subject to recruitment into the Israel Defence Forces.[9] In regard to non-Jews, absurdity can reach even greater length, when nationality by birth applies to Arabs who emigrated from the country as a result of their opposition to the very existence of Israel, and yet under this section find themselves Israeli nationals.

Nationality by birth, therefore, may answer for the fundamental "principle of kinship'' dominating Israel's nationality policy: the fact, however, that nationality by birth is granted automatically with no relation whatsoever to residence in Israel has in practice caused undesirable effects.

Nationality by Birth and Residence in Israel

In contrast with the other methods discussed above, where acquisition of nationality operates automatically, nationality by birth and residence required the submission of an application on the part of the would-be-national. Section 4A of the 1968 Amended Law (Amendment No. 2), was designed to remedy shortcomings in the original law, which had in fact left many residents stateless. The section provides the right to nationality to a person of full age (that is, 18 years old), born in Israel after the establishment of the state, who has never been a national of any country, and who has resided in Israel for five years prior to the submission of the application.

Although not expressly stated in the Law, this method was meant for non-Jews only. Jews born in Israel after the enactment of the Nationality Law in 1952 automatically became nationals by Return with no possibility of rejecting it. Nationality by birth and residence, furthermore, could only be available to a person who has never been a national of any country. This method—very much the same as nationality by birth and residence—answers problems in regard to the non-Jewish minority in Israel. All three methods were motivated by the sole aim of equating the national status of Israeli Arabs to that of the Jewish majority.

Nationality by Naturalization

When compared with the requisitions for naturalization in other countries, the prerequisites for naturalization included in section 5 of the Nationality Law are not particularly harsh. When contrasted with the methods to obtain Israeli nationality discussed above, however, three distinctions may be drawn. Only in the case of naturalization must a loyalty declaration be made. This declaration expresses the desire of the applicant to take upon himself the obligation of loyalty to his new state (section 5 (c)). Naturalization thus means a binding decision on the part of the individual to throw his lot with the state of Israel. Yet in contrast with the United States, for example, this declaration of allegiance does not contain any doctrinal or ideological requirement or disqualification. Such a voluntary act on the part of the individual must, under the law, be reflected in the formal renunciation of the applicant's former nationality. Unlike the nationality by Return, which is granted to Jews with or without foreign nationality, a person applying for naturalization—Jewish and non-Jewish alike—must end all his former national ties to prove his sincerity (section 5(a)(6)). The third difference applies to the Minister of the Interior's overall discretion to grant or withhold nationality by naturalization even when the prescribed conditions for naturalization have been complied with. [10] The Minister's decision, however, is not as autocratic as it might at first sight appear. An aggrieved applicant, in fact, is free to appeal to the court and in case of an arbitrary dismissal "the court will order the Minister of the Interior to grant a certificate of naturalization in the manner prescribed by law" (HC 328/60, *Nag'ib Mussa vs. Minister of the Interior*, 1, 16 PD:69).

Nationality by Grant

This method was originally devised as a special form of naturalization for minors who were residents but whose parents were either dead or unknown, or were not residing in Israel (Nationality Law, 1952, section 9). The 1980 Amendment extended the Minister of Interior's powers, by empowering him to grant nationality to a person whose nationality has been terminated while a minor, provided he applies for nationality between the ages of 18 and 22 (Amendment 2, 1968). [11]

Taken together, the ways to acquire nationality reflect the two basic principles guaranteed in the "Declaration of the Establishment of the State of Israel, " namely, the "ingathering of the exiles" and the "complete equality of social and political rights to all . . . inhabitants." It might perhaps be alleged that the Nationality Law was over-doctrinaire; yet when evaluated with the Amendments enacted by the Knesset and through judicial interpretation, its contribution to the unification of the people of Israel is no doubt impressive. The Nationality Law, with a view to placing all nationals on equal footing, has provided original solutions to the somewhat unique problems facing the state of Israel. As the only Jewish state in the world, its gates were to be kept open to all Jews. As a country with strong democratic convictions, though surrounded by hostile Arab countries, Israel has made great efforts to confer equal rights on its non-Jewish minority. Once Israeli nationality is obtained, there are no different classes of nationals. It is granted in perpetuity and may be lost, to Jews and non-Jews alike, only under extreme and serious circumstances.

Loss of Nationality

The annulment of Israeli nationality operates in three cases in which certain acts have been committed against the state. The first refers to a person who has left the country illegally for an enemy state or has acquired its nationality. The second and third may apply when "an act constituting a breach of allegiance to the State" has been committed or when Israeli nationality has been acquired under false pretenses (Nationality Law, Amendment 4, 1980, section 11(b)(c)). Whereas the first case is absolute, the other two are left to the discretion of the Minister of the Interior. [12] Although not expressly stated in the Law, it seems the same limitations on the Minister's administrative powers could be invoked by appealing to the courts. The Minister's expressed consent is also needed in regard to a voluntary renunciation made by a person of full age and his/her minor child, provided all of them are not Israeli residents (section 10 of the Nationality Law, Amendment 4, 1980). The Minister, furthermore, may under special circumstances even refuse to terminate Israel nationality of such a minor (Ibid., section 20(g)).

Section 10 A is of special interest. It is typical of Israel's approach to encourage unlimited immigration by providing for more than one nationality. The section, added to the Law only in 1980, empowers the Minister of the Interior to consent to a declaration of renunciation made by an Israeli national residing in Israel when such declaration is made in order to protect a second nationality. The section is outstanding in its approach since to permit double nationality is one thing, but it is quite a different matter to consent to a renunciation of Israeli nationality so that the other nationality would be preserved.

THE UNIQUE CHARACTER OF ISRAEL'S NATIONALITY POLICY

The question immediately arising after examining the various ways of acquiring nationality is that of a definition. A definition of nationality as a politico-legal relationship between a state and its citizens, creating rights and duties for both, equates Israeli nationality more or less with that of other countries. Israeli nationality, however, implies more. For a Jew, Israeli nationality means also belonging to a people. As such it reflects religious, traditional, historical, social, and cultural ties—all factors that have created an ideology and outlook peculiar to the Jewish people and the Jewish state.

Two factors are basic in any comprehensive study of the matter: the concept of Return, and the ties that link Jews everywhere with the land of Israel. Just as the notion of Israel as a Jewish state is inextricably bound up with the return of Jews to the land of Israel, so Israel Nationality Law—as a reflection of the prevailing national ideology—cannot be comprehended until this concept of Return and the nature of the special ties between the Jews and Israel have been fully grasped.

Nationality in Israel, as stated above, does not stop with legal provisions; it embraces tradition, religion, and a long history of common culture and fate. The establishment of the state of Israel did not create a new nation; it only gave modern geographical and political definitions to a very ancient people returning to its homeland after almost nineteen centuries of wandering. David Ben-Gurion expressed this link between the Jews and the land of Israel as follows:

The State of Israel was established merely two years ago, but its roots are grounded in the far past and it is nourished by ancient springs. . . . On the fourteenth of May, 1948, a new state was not founded *ex nihilo*. . . . It must be clear that the renewal of the State of Israel is not a beginning, but a continuation of days long ago. (*Divrei Ha'Knesset*, 6, 1950:2035–36)

A denial of such a link between the Jews and the land of Israel, argued Justice Agranat in 1965 (HC 1/65 *Yerder vs. Chairman Central Committee for the Sixth Knesset*, 3, 19 PD:265), "means the total negation of the long history of the Jewish people and its yearnings" (Ibid.:385). The same approach was elaborated by the Court in an earlier case:

It is necessary to mention the Declaration of the Establishment of the State of Israel which opens with the description of the historic and traditional attachment of the Jewish people to the land of Israel to indicate that the Jewish people has never ceased to pray and hope for their return to that land, and for the restoration in it of their political freedom. (Justice Landau, in HC 72/62 *Rufeisen vs. Minister of the Interior*, 4, 16 PD:2428 at 2447)

Since a definition of Israeli nationality includes "Jewishness" as one of its most fundamental principles, it calls for a definition of the Jewish people. Are Jews a religious group or a nation? The question, first raised during the French Revolution, has since been the focus of controversy. "It appears to me," wrote Isaiah Berlin to David Ben-Gurion in 1959, "that the status of the Jew is unique and anomalous, composed of national, cultural, and religious strands inextricably intertwined" (*Divrei Ha'Knesset* 57, 1970:1140). "In fact," argued one of Israel's better known jurists, B. Akzin, while describing the consensus prevailing among Israeli scholars, "the peculiar interrelationship between Judaism as a religious denomination and the Jewish nationality in the ethnic sense . . . [is] so close indeed that any attempt to draw a line of demarcation between them becomes highly speculative."[13]

Israel is not a people like other peoples. . . . It is the only people in the world that from the beginning has been at once a religion and a nationality. . . . this basic unity of nationality and religion has kept the Jewish people in the Diaspora. Without it there is no possibility to comprehend this historic fact which is Israel. (Buber, 1961:130,132)

The fact that religion and nationhood are inseparable in Judaism has naturally affected Israel nationality policy, especially when amidst public controversy and a controversial Court decision (HC 58/68, *Shalit vs. Minister of the Interior*, (2)23 PD:477), the Law of Return (as amended by Amendment 2, 5730–1970; 24 LSI 28) defined "Jew" in accordance with Jewish religious law. Thus, the secular state of Israel was obliged to adopt religious laws rooted in the *Halacha*— the Jewish laws. Although there is no established religion in the ordinary sense in Israel and Jewish religious law does not enjoy preferential treatment under Israeli law,[14] in fact because religion is so fundamental in Judaism, it plays a decisive role in Israel society. The problem involves the issue of state and religion. In Israel, "the most ancient of religions and the most ancient of peoples is faced by an unprecedented Church and State problem . . . of a peculiar kind" (Talmon:30). In Judaism national aspirations took on religious forms and vice versa. As long as Jewish national aspirations were not realized the question of sovereign secular power was less acute. Once the State of Israel emerged the confrontation was inevitable

The problem concerning the limits a religious heritage may set upon a sovereign secular state or, more simply, what status and place should religion occupy in Israeli law, has been agitating public opinion since the establishment of Israel. It led to hectic debates in the Knesset, was reflected in legal decisions, and even provoked several government crises. The subject involves difficulties—legal, extra-legal, political, social, and emotional—resulting many times from religious pressures. A constitution, establishing the right balance between lay and religious powers, might perhaps have helped to clear away any clouds. As it is, Israel lacks a written constitution. The only instrument that prescribes any general principle is the Declaration of the Establishment of the State of Israel, which is not legally binding and certainly carries no constitutional authority.[15] While specifically stating that Israel is a Jewish state, the Declaration nonetheless guarantees freedom of religion and conscience to all Israel inhabitants. It should be stressed that following that part of the Declaration that was recognized by the Courts as "the credo and vision of the people" which must "guide every public authority in Israel"—freedom of religion should not be violated (*Ziv vs. Gubernick*:72,HC 262/2, *Perets vs. Kfar Sharyahu Local Council*, 3, 16PD:2101). "Our State," declared Justice Landau referring to freedom of conscience, "is based upon freedom of conscience and therefore no Jew may be compelled to declare himself an adherent of the doctrines of the Jewish faith when he does not believe and accept the Jewish law" (HC 72/62, *Rufeisen vs. Minister of the Interior*, 4, 16 PD 2428 at 2446). But on the other hand, as a Jewish state Israel should preserve a Jewish public visage. The Declaration, deliberately avoiding reference to the status of religion in the state, left this basic problem unsettled (Rubinstein, 1973:105).

The legal status of religion in Israel is therefore ambiguous. On the one hand, from a statutory point of view, Israeli law is secular, deriving its authority from the Knesset. Only in the sphere of personal status do the religions of Israel have an exclusive standing (HC 359/66, *Gitiye vs. The Chief of Rabbinate and Jerusalem Religious Council*, 1, 23 PD:290). On the other hand, this is only the formal position, since the Knesset, exposed to the very same pressures as the government, has in fact incorporated Jewish law into its secular legislation (such as the Amended Law of Return). The fact that religious and nonreligious Jews alike view Israel as a Jewish state complicates the problem even more. It is difficult to achieve the right balance between deep-rooted religious beliefs and secular powers in a state where religion and nationality together form Israeli identity.[16] "A Jewish state is unimaginable without embodying historic patterns of immemorial antiquity which have prescribed the identity of the Jewish people and constituted its distinct historic personality" (Talmon:31).

The uniqueness of the state of Israel lies, no doubt, in its Jewish character—in its inseparable ties with religion, tradition, history, and culture—that have linked the Jewish people with the land of Israel. "Jewish Israel nationals are first Jewish," stated the historian Gershom Scholem; "the State of Israel is the place for the ingathering of the Jewish people . . . it will rise with [its] identification with the Jewish people and will fall when denying our Jewishness" (Scholem:143–44). It is this identification of "Israeliness" with "Jewishness" that has most affected Israel's nationality policy, by creating a unique and unprecedented form of a "national."

WHO IS A JEW? THE PROBLEM OF JEWISH IDENTITY IN ISRAEL

Jewish Israel nationality reflects a deeprooted bond with both the traditional heritage of the Jewish people and the land of Israel. The factor that singles out such nationality is to be found not so much in the interrelationship of the individual and the state but rather in the Jewish component of the Jewish Israeli national. Whereas citizenship in general expresses the formal legal mutual undertaking between a person and his state, it is more complex in the case of a Jewish Israeli citizen. With him it is Jewishness that provides the legal claim for citizenship.

Nationality by Return constitutes the basic factor of Israel Nationality Law. As such, it has incorporated the Law of Return and provided for automatic citizenship to every Jew who desires to settle in the State of Israel (Nationality Law, 1952, section 2, 6 LSI:50). It is, therefore, critical for purposes of both laws (and of others, such as marriage and divorce laws) to define who is a Jew eligible for automatic admission and citizenship.

The question, "Who is a Jew?" which might seem to be one solely of a legal/judicial context, proved in Israel to be one that "cut to the heart of one's Jewish identity and self-perception" (Liebman, 1985). "Our examination thereof and its ideological constituents," stated Justice Silberg in a cause célèbre of 1968, "call for the most profound and penetrating self-scrutiny of our existence as a people, our essence as a nation and our Zionist-political task in the renaissance of this country" (HC 58/68, *Shalit vs. Minister of the Interior*, 2, 23 PD:477 at 492; see also Felix and Elman:48). Indeed, the question surpasses the legal complications and involves the issue of the identity of an Israeli citizen who is Jewish. Since religion and nationality (herein understood in its ethnic connotation[17]) are inseparable in Jewish identity, a definition of a Jew must reflect both. A statutory definition, however, would compel the legislators to decide whether to incorporate the traditional religious Jewish law, which recognizes as a Jew only "one born of a Jewish mother" (Mishnah, *Kiddushim*, 66b and 68b; Maimonides, *Hilchot Issure Bi'ah*, xii,7 and xv, 4; *Shulhan Aruch: Even Ha-Ezer*, 8,5), or to include persons who consider themselves Jewish although not answering to the requirements of the Jewish law. In either case, controversy would no doubt ensue. That was the main reason for the deliberate omission of a definition of the term "Jew" in the original Law of Return, 1950. A proposal to add "according to the Law of Moses" to the word Jew was rejected by the Constitution, Legislation, and Juridical Committee while debating the bill. Its Chairman, Nir, stated that the government felt it would be better to leave the matter undefined.[18]

Prime Minister Ben-Gurion, eager to increase immigration, sought a broad definition of Jewishness to include people who considered themselves Jewish and who were willing to accept the responsibility of Jewish self-identification. As Israel serves as the center for the ingathering of exiles, and as the integration of all immigrants into one nation is one of Israel's most vital tasks, "every effort must be made . . . to root out as far as possible every thing that makes for separation and alienation" (Ben-Gurion letter, in *Congress Weekly*, January 5, 1959, 25:8). This approach was strongly opposed by religious leaders, who held that the *halacha* was to be implicitly observed. The seemingly simple question of "who is a Jew?" under Israeli law has thus proved to be one of the most difficult to answer. It has reflected the perplexity of a secular society which could not escape its traditional heritage without violating its identity.

Three cases may illustrate the problem and its sometimes ironic implication. Rina Eitani was born in Germany to a Protestant mother and a Jewish father. During World War II her mother chose to follow her father to a concentration camp, where he was murdered by the Nazis. After the war, Rina managed to enter Palestine as an illegal immigrant. She stayed in a Kibbutz and served with distinction in the Israeli army, married an Israeli Jew by a Jewish religious ceremony, and gave birth to two children, who were raised as Jews. She was active in politics and was eventually elected to the council of her hometown. Being involved in political–religious disputes over the issue of religious schools, she was accused by her political opponents of not being a Jewess. After an inquiry, the Ministry of the Interior held that Mrs. Eitani was not Jewish, that she had obtained her citizenship under the Law of Return under false pretenses, and that she should therefore surrender her passport. The Ministry offered her the alternative of either undergoing a formal conversion to Judaism or of applying for naturalization—both of which she rejected. After three emergency Cabinet sessions and two stormy debates in the Knesset (*Divrei Ha'Knesset* 42, 1965:1057–59), a compromise was achieved. In March of 1965 the Minister of the Interior ruled that Mrs. Eitani's passport was valid since she had acted in good faith. On her part, she agreed to undergo a formal Orthodox conversion to Judaism (see Abramov:3–13). Although decided outside the courts, the case caused bitter resentment, especially among nonreligious Israelis who felt Mrs. Eitani had done more than her share in proving identification with the Jewish people and the state of Israel. The fact that in Germany she had been persecuted as a half-Jewess but in Israel she was not recognized as Jewish added to the general uneasiness (*Divrei Ha'Knesset*, 42, 1965:1058; see also, Kraines:37).

Whereas the Eitani case stirred up resentment, it was the earlier case of Brother Daniel that brought the issue into the open, revealing the complexity of and the perplexity over the issue in Israel (HC 72/62, *Rufeisen vs. Minister of the Interior*, 4, 16 PD:2428). Oswald Rufeisen (Brother Daniel) was born in Poland in 1922 of Jewish parents and became an ardent member of the Zionist Youth movement.

He was active against the Nazis in Poland during the Second World War, found refuge in a convent, was converted to Christianity and in 1945 joined the Carmelite Order under the name of Brother Daniel. In 1948, he petitioned the Polish government to permit him to go to Israel but obtained permission only in 1958, after waiving his Polish nationality. On arrival in Israel, he entered a monastery and requested Israeli citizenship under the Law of Return and the Nationality Law. When the Minister of the Interior rejected this request,[19] Rufeisen petitioned the High Court of Justice for an order *nisi* against the Minister. The Court was divided in its opinion, the majority holding the petitioner's request should be dismissed.[20]

The issue before the Court was the meaning of the term "Jew" in the Law of Return. Two main questions arose: the first, which test should be applied to the term "Jew"—religious, halachic or secular; the second, did the term "Jew" include an apostate Jew, who continued to regard himself as a Jew in his ethnic affiliation. To put it bluntly, could Judaism be divided and separately denied as religion and nationality, while retaining the ethnic connotation?

The situation was all too bizarre. Here was Brother Daniel—a member of the Order of Our Lady on Mount Carmel, in brown habit and sandals, invoking Rabbinical Law to prove his Jewishness and stating: "My religion is Catholic, but my ethnic group is and always will be Jewish. . . . if I am not Jewish what am I?" (*Selected Judgments*:26–27). There was the Attorney General, appealing to the Common Law canons of interpretation of statutes to prove that the halacha should not be applied. The paradox, to add more color to the matter, was that, in fact, Brother Daniel's claim had standing in the Jewish religious law which recognized as a Jew one born of a Jewish mother. Brother Daniel was no doubt born of Jewish parents. If a religious criterion had been applied to the term "Jew" in the Law of Return, Brother Daniel would have met the requirements.[21] The majority opinion, however, held that the Law of Return was a secular law and the term "Jew" within it to have a "secular meaning, as it is usually understood in common parlance . . . by the ordinary simple Jew" (*Rufeisen vs. Minister of the Interior,* at page 2437). Such a formula precludes a Jew who has converted to another religion from being considered a "Jew" under the Law of Return. "A Jew who has become a Christian is not deemed a Jew. . . . 'Jew' and 'Christian' are contradictory terms . . . " (Ibid.:2438–39).

The Rufeisen case, in spite of its importance in the application of a secular test to the term "Jew" in the Law of Return, did not in fact provide a legally binding definition. The decision to apply an objective secular test—"in common parlance"—and as used at the present time by the people left much to be interpreted (see Cohen, at 2443; *Selected Judgments*:18). The dilemma continued to vex Israeli society.[22] What the Court did, however, was to confirm the indivisibility of nationality (nationhood) and religion in Judaism. The Rufeisen case acknowledged that to be a Jew in Israel, even under a secular criterion, meant the acceptance of both religion and nationality as basic principles of identity. "A Jew who, by changing his religion, cuts himself from the national past of his people,'' stated Justice Landau in his concurring opinion, ''ceases thereby to be a Jew in the national sense to which the Law of Return gives expression. . . . The meaning of the Law of Return cannot be severed from the sources of the past from which its contents are derived, and in these sources nationalism and religion are inseparately interwoven'' (*Rufeisen vs. Minister of the Interior*:2447;*Selected Judgments*:22).

In spite of the Court's decisive ruling in the Rufeisen case the question, whether Jewish *le'om* (nationality/ethnic group) can be maintained independent of Jewish religion, arose again six years later in connection with an entry to the Population Registry Law, 1965 (HC 58/68, *Benjamin Shalit and Others vs. Minister of the Interior and Another*, 2, 23 PD:477). This Law provided for thirteen entries, among them ''religion'' and ''nationality'' (*le'om*), to be listed on the identity card each had to carry, and recorded in the Population Registry. Although aiming mainly to supply statistical data, and without being legally binding, the registration caused resentment among those who sought to register their children as Jewish by nationality, but who were prevented from doing so because the children did not meet religious standards qualifying them as Jews. The matter was discussed in the *Shalit* case—one of the most difficult cases to come before the High Court of Justice—argued for the first time in its history before nine out of ten judges.[23] The petitioner, Benjamin Shalit, a Jew born in Israel serving as a major in the Israeli navy, applied to the Population Registration clerk to have his children registered as Jews by nationality. He declared that it was his intention to continue living in Israel with his family, and to educate his children as Israelis and Jews in culture and spirit. But the clerk, following directives issued by the Minister of the Interior in January 1960, refused to register them as Jews since their mother was not Jewish. Shalit alleged that this refusal derived from religious, and therefore improper motives. He contended that the Law was to be interpreted by secular criteria. By such standards, he argued, a child born in Israel to a father who is Jewish, an Israeli national, and an officer serving in the Israel Defence Army, brought up and educated in Israel—ought to be registered as belonging to the Jewish ethnic group.

The Minister of the Interior, while agreeing that the Population Registry Law was not a religious law, insisted however that even according to a secular test a person born of a non-Jewish mother was not to be considered a Jew. The accepted rule was based on the principle of maternal descent. The Rufeisen doctrine might limit this rule so as to exclude a Catholic monk from recognition as a Jew even though he was born of a Jewish mother. It could not, however, extend the rule so as to confer Jewish status on a child of a non-Jewish mother. To depart from the principle of maternal descent which had been accepted by the Jewish people from time immemorial, even in a secular law, would only result in confusion and uncertainty (Kraines:48).

The issue was not new. Ten years earlier, on October 27, 1958, facing a Cabinet crisis, the then Prime Minister David Ben-Gurion had addressed a query to forty-five prominent Jewish scholars, religious leaders, and legal philosophers throughout the world, asking their opinion on the question of registration of children born in Israel of mixed marriages whose parents wished to register them as Jews.[24] The purpose of the letter, explained the Prime Minister, was to formulate registration rules "in keeping with the accepted tradition among all circles of Jewry . . . and with the special conditions of Israel (*Israel Digest*:p. 11). The letter pointed out that although the laws of the State of Israel forbade discrimination on grounds of differences in color, race, and sex, it was necessary to register people by nationality (*le'om*), since it established the basis for the right of every Jew to immigrate to Israel, by virtue of being a Jew. It was also necessary to register people by religion because matters of personal status are under the sole authority of the various religious courts: Jewish, Moslem, and Christian (Ibid.:36).

The answers were illuminating (see *Divrei Ha'Knesset*, 56, 1970:724). While it was expected that spokesmen of Jewish Orthodoxy would abide rigidly by the ruling of *halacha*, it was not a little surprising that many of the non-Orthodox scholars supported the Orthodox position, and only a small minority of the respondents recommended any deviation from the traditional religious definition of a Jew (Litvin and Hoenig:297–303). Accordingly, on January 1, 1960, the Minister of the Interior issued new directives defining "who is a Jew" for the purpose of registration of "*le'om*" and "religion" in the Population Registry. Under the new instructions, no person could be considered a Jew in nationality (*le'om*) in Israel unless he was born of a Jewish mother or converted to Judaism (*Divrei Ha'Knesset* 56, 1970, p. 723). The legal validity of these directives was put on trial in the Shalit case.

Although the majority opinion of the Court invalidated the 1960 directives and ordered the registration of Shalit's children as "being of Jewish nationality and without religion" as petitioned, it was the minority opinion that in the long run established the rule.[25] In contrast to the majority judges who restricted themselves to the scope of the registration officer's authority, stating that "the entire object of the Population Registry Law [was] to provide registration and statistical needs" and not to formulate criteria for determination of one's Jewishness, the President of the Court dissenting with three more judges (Silberg, Kister, and Landau) recognized the historic significance and relevance of the terms "Jews" and "*le'om*" for the purposes of the registration of Jews.[26] In the opinion of Justices Silberg and Kister, Jewish nationality cannot be entirely severed from its religious foundations: "The term 'Jew' is indivisible. Belonging to the Jewish people cannot be separated from belonging to the Jewish religion" (*Shalit vs. Minister of the Interior*:115). Only religion unites the Jewish people, and the religious–halachic criterion has and still is the only criterion for determining the national identity of a person as a Jew (Ibid.:493, 500–501). "If the whole Jewish nation had wanted to abandon its tie with religion/heritage [*Torah*]," argued Justice Kister, "new criteria would have to be prescribed for such a Jewish people. . . . Down to the present, I know of no new criteria which could fit the whole Jewish people" (Ibid.:547). Justice Silberg went further, concluding that "the search after a new test of our national identity constitutes in fact a complete denial of the continued existence of the Jewish people. . . . The culture of the past is first and foremost our definitive national identity laid down at least 2400 years ago" (Ibid.:503).

Whereas Shalit himself was satisfied with the Court's ruling to register his children as "Jewish by nationality," the judgment created a storm, especially in religious circles.[27] Far from settling the issue, this decision exacerbated it further, even threatening the stability of the Coalition Government. Following a threat to resign from the government made by the National Religious Party unless the decision be rescinded, the Cabinet in January 1970 initiated an Amendment to the Law of Return that effectively reversed the Court's decision.

In spite of the bitter and hectic debate in the Knesset during which both the Court's decision and the proposed Bill were attacked (*Divrei Ha'Knesset* 56,1970:726–27), and spectacular performances of protest by Knesset members (see Kraines:54–55), Amendment 2 to the Law of Return, was adopted on March 10, 1970 (24 LSI:28). The enactment, "being a direct result of the Court's decision in the *Shalit* case" (*Divrei Ha'Knesset*, 56, 1970:723), incorporated a "most material principle of the Jewish law" (see Alon: 41), by supplying for the first time a statutory definition of the term "Jew" in accordance with the *halacha*. Thus, the decision in the *Shalit* case ruling on the issue of registration and not directly connected with the Law of Return was, however, taken as a guide to the way in which the term "Jew" should be interpreted in both laws.

The main feature of the amended Law was the definition of the term "Jew" as "a person who was born of a Jewish mother or has converted to Judaism, and who is not a member of another religion" (Law of Return, 1970 section 4B). By applying the same definition for the purposes of registering a person's Jewish nationality (*le'om*) in the Amended Population Registry Law (section 3 A (a)(b)), the new Law yielded to a large extent to the religious law test, rejecting the secular contention that Jewish religion and nationality (*le'om*) are separable. In regard to conversion, however, it ignored the religious law since it neither specified the nature of the required conversion nor named the authority to control it. In contrast to the government intention to leave the term vague, enabling every form of conversion, so as to allay the anxiety of American Jewish Conservative or Reform congregations, some Knesset members argued for a statutory definition placing Orthodox procedure as the only recognized conversion. (*Divrei Ha'Knesset*, 1970:781, 1137). Yet, a proposal to add to the words "converted to Judaism—in accordance with the *halacha*" was rejected both in the Constitution, Legislation and Juridical Committee and in the Knesset, on the second reading of the Bill (*Divrei Ha'Knesset*, 56, 1970:1137, 1143, 1170). As it is, the issue has since been the subject of debates among legal scholars.[28] Moreover, every government since 1970 has been approached by the religious parties to enact that only conversion to Judaism carried out in accordance with the *halacha* be valid.[29]

The three leading cases discussed here—Eitani, Brother Daniel, and the Shalit children—and the 1970 Amended Law of Return indicate the uncertainty and social perplexity over the issue of "Who is a Jew?" in Israel. The cases, though different in motivation, development, and results, express a single, common idea. All three parties concerned felt and considered themselves to be Jewish by ethnic affiliation but were not acknowledged as such because their religion was not Jewish. Whereas Rini Eitani, whose case was decided outside the Courts, and the Shalit children did not meet with the Jewish religious requirements, Brother Daniel was definitely born of a Jewish mother; yet, since "Jew" and "Christian" are contradictory terms, the Court in the Brother Daniel case— while holding to a secular test for the term "Jew"—ruled that "a Jew who has become a Christian is not deemed a Jew" (*Rufeisen vs. Minister of the Interior*:2438:39). In spite of the Court's decision to adopt a secular criterion in the cases of Brother Daniel and Shalit, the 1970 Amended Law of Return, reversing the *Shalit* decision, adopted a halachic definition to be used in secular law— such as the Law of Return, the Nationality Law, and the Population Registry Law—thus providing statutory authority to the indivisibility of nationality (*le'om*) and religion in Jewish Israeli identity. The 1970 Amendment, however, has not supplied a definite and complete answer to the question "Who is a Jew?" If the government, when initiating the Amendment, proclaimed that the Law would put an end to the controversy, it certainly did not accomplish its aims.[30]. The issue continues to occupy the Israeli public, the Knesset, and the Courts, posing what Oscar Kraines calls "an eternal impossibility . . . an impossible dilemma . . . " (Kraines, 86, 94).

CONCLUSION

Since its foundation the State of Israel has been troubled by the question of its own identity as a Jewish State. It was evident from the start that this state has a destiny to follow; namely, to provide a homeland for the scattered Jews. The mission, as the State of Israel understood it, was to gather in this people— which had stubbornly maintained its uniqueness for centuries by observing one religion and sharing one tradition, heritage, history, and fate—under one political entity, a Jewish State. The expression "Jewish State" indicates both the nature and mission of the state of Israel (see Frenkel:99–100). It has never been intended to be a multi- or dual-ethnic state, but a one-nation state, where Jewish nationals form its dominant element, fulfilling the national destiny of the Jewish people.

Keeping to the main task of *Kibbutz-Galuyot*, the "ingathering of the Exiles" solemnly declared in its Declaration of Independence, the State of Israel indeed opened its gates for every Jew returning to settle in the land of his forefathers. It is therefore no surprise that the Knesset, acting on behalf of this fundamental principle, gave preference to Jews wishing to immigrate and to acquire citizenship. In fact, what marks Israel's national policy is that Jewishness stands as the legitimate and ultimate claim for automatic citizenship (Nationality Law, 1952, section 2(a)(b); 6 LSI:50). When translated into legal terminology, however, the seemingly simple question of "Who is a Jew?" gave rise to enormous legal as well as ideological problems.

Until the establishment of a sovereign Israel, the question of "Who is a Jew?" although philosophically debated among certain liberal and reform Jewish groups, had never been the focus of serious Jewish controversy. The codes of Jewish law had governed the determination of Jewish status for countless generations and were accepted as the rule. Since all definitions, moreover, were produced by non-Jews aiming to degrade the Jew, they carried almost permanently an overt or implied negative connotation to be followed by discrimination.[31] There was, therefore, no incentive for the Jews in the Diaspora to define themselves. On the contrary, being on the defensive and subject to ill treatment, persecution or at best only tolerated, Jews rejected any definition which singled them out.

In the independent Jewish State an historic change occurred leading to a tremendous paradox. A group which for millenia was held and often forced to be "the most exclusive of entities and yet, living in its sovereign state has been troubled by the impossibility to define who does and who does not belong to it"(Talmon:29). This paradox, originating in the complexity of the term "Jewishness," became acute as a direct development of the political independence of the Jewish state. In Israel, where Judaism is the dominant culture and Jews form the majority of the population, a definition of a Jew involves not only self-identity but his political identity as well. Instead of the previous wish of Jews in the Diaspora to conceal their identity in order to be accepted by the non-Jews around them and in sharp contrast to the justifying plea they held in the past, Jews in Israel seek for a positive definition to answer an immanent need. But since such definition reflects an inner need, various formulas are the natural outcome of a diverse society not necessarily holding to one traditional concept of Judaism. Along with the religious Orthodox viewpoint, which accepts the biological origin of the Jew at least on the maternal side as the only criterion to determine the Jewish status, since "no force in the world may or can possibly invalidate this principle which is the very basis of the totality of Judaism,"[32] the non-Orthodox view demands the inclusion of persons who sincerely wish to share the destiny and culture of the Jewish people. For them the Jews are foremost a nation, and national ties are the dominant factor that determines the Jewish identity (Liebman:10).

"History dictates a change . . . and the revolution of establishing a sovereign state calls for a revision of the values which [the Jews] have imbibed in [their] long exile" (*Rufeisen vs. Minister of the Interior*, 4, 16 PD 2428, 2441). Times have indeed changed and the "wheel has turned full circle." Yet on the other hand, the search after a new test of the Jewish identity "constitutes a complete denial of the continued existence of the Jewish people" (*Shalit*, Op. cit.:503), and might well change its composition. Accordingly, "there would be 'national' Jews—so declared by the State—and 'religious' Jews so identified by history" (Jacobvits:299). Thus the Jewish State, while reversing the flight from Judaism, has paradoxically provoked new tests for Jewish status and exposed the danger of disrupting the unity of the Jewish people.

It has rather been the concern for maintaining the unity of the Jewish people than agreement with the traditional attitude as such that is responsible for the wide consensus in Israel to keep the Jewish identity of the state. Although the majority of the Jewish population in the secular state of Israel does not observe the ritual laws and rejects any attempt to enforce religious decrees in daily life, yet the same secular majority acknowledges the covenant between religion and nation in Judaism and accepts religion as a factor for the determination of Jewish identity (see Liebman:9–13). On the other hand, it should be pointed out that this consensus does not conceal the deep ideological controversy regarding the substance and form of such Jewish identity, and its practical expressions in private and in public life (Dan-Yehiya:5–9).

In contrast to other nations and faiths that have long ago ceased to be troubled by arguments concerning national or religious status, accepting as final the ruling of their law codes, "Who is a Jew?" continues to be a dynamic matter in Israeli society where two conflicting definitions aspire to gain state recognition. Given the declared mission of the State—to gather in the world Jewry—and the legally established link of Jewishness and citizenship, a definition of Jew has a crushing impact on Israel's nationality policy. Whereas an American identity, for example, may only be developed as an outcome of the United States nationality, it is the opposite case with the Jewish citizens of Israel. For them it is their Jewish status that produces the prerequisite for Israeli citizenship, construing thereby the credo of the state of Israel as the fulfillment of the Jewish national destiny. It is therefore the "umbilical cord to historical Judaism" which binds the Jew to his Israeli identity: "There is one thing that is shared by all Jews who live in Israel . . . and that is that we do not cut ourselves off from our historical past nor deny our ancestral heritage" (*Rufeisen vs. Minister of the Interior*: 2438).

The fusion of Jewish and Israeli identity, although not complete, demonstrates the unique character of Israel's nationality, as against the concept of national identity in other national communities. If nationality laws reflect a state's constitutional ideology and outlook, those of Israel express the most basic and fundamental principles. There is indeed no doubt that it is easier for a Jew than a non-Jew to immigrate to Israel and to acquire its citizenship. This preference may perhaps open Israel to the charge that it discriminates on ethnic grounds, in favor of Jews. It should, however, be stressed that both the Law of Return and section 2(a) of the Nationality Law cannot be divorced from their historical context. The United Nations General Assembly approved a resolution on November 29, 1947, recognizing the right of the Jewish people to establish its state. It is easier for a Jew to acquire Israeli citizenship for the simple reason that Israel is primarily a state for the Jewish people. But this does not deprive the non-Jews. They may immigrate and may hold Israeli citizenship. Once Israeli nationality is obtained non-Jews and Jews enjoy equal status as citizens and are guaranteed "freedom of religion, conscience, language, education, and culture''(Declaration of the Establishment of the State of Israel). Israel's policy of open-doors applies wholly to Jews, yet non-Jews who wish to cast their lot with the Jewish state will not find its gates wholly barred.[33]

NOTES

1. See, entry into Israel Law, 5712–1952, section 11(6); 6 L.S.I. 159. Professor Rubinstein argues that in theory the Minister of the Interior has the power under this section to revoke an *oleh* visa in such cases, but in practice such authority has never been exercised. See: A. Rubinstein *The Consitutional Law in the State of Israel* (Tel-Aviv, 1973); p. 401.

2. HC 48/58, *Yoanovici vs. Minister of the Interior*, 12 PD 646; HC 94/62; *Gold vs. Minister of the Interior*, 3, 16 PD 1876; HC 442/71, *Lansky vs. Minister of the Interior*, 2, 26 PD 337. See as well, HC 186/62, *Veeder vs. Minister of the Interior*, 2, 16 PD 1547; HC 125/80, *Angel and Prizman vs. Ministry of the Interior*, 4, 34 PD 329.

3. President of the Court, Olshan, in *Yoanovice vs. Minister of the Interior*, p. 649. In this case, the petitioner, who was wanted by the French police, arrived in Israel under an assumed name, using another person's passport. He had been convicted in 1949 in Paris of having knowingly committed acts to the prejudice of the French national defense and was sentenced to five years' imprisonment. On arrival in Israel he applied for an *oleh* certificate and was rejected. He appealed to the High Court of Justice arguing that he could not be considered as having a criminal past if he had only been convicted once. The Court rejected this argument and confirmed the authority of the Minister of the Interior to invoke section 2(b)(3) in this case, due to the gravity of the offense committed.

4. The second fundamental principle is the ''law of the land'' (*jus soli*), by which citizenship is acquired by birth on the territory of a country without taking into consideration the nationality of the parents. Most countries apply a combination of both principles, placing emphasis on either one or the other.

5. The validity of such nationality will commence from the day of the grant of approval; the Nationality Law (Amendment no. 3) 5731–1971; 25 LSI 117. It should be noted that when the original bill was introduced in 1950 some Knesset members suggested a similar amendment, which was rejected. See, for example, Z Warhaftig, MD, *Divrei Ha'Knesset*, 6 (1950);2042: ''Our experience has proved that in many cases many lives could have been saved had there been a Jewish State, and had it been possible to grant Israeli citizenship to a Jew who could not realize his *aliya*.''

6. In order to ensure that no Jew settling in Israel should be stateless, opting-out of Israeli nationality does not apply to a person born in Israel after July 14, 1952, but only to an immigrant who is also a foreign national. The four cases are: ''(2) to a person of full age . . . and while still a foreign national who declares that he does not wish to become an Israel national; (3) to a minor of foreign nationality born outside of Israel whose parents have made a declaration . . . and included him therein . . . '' [The Nationality Law, Amendment 2, 1968]; ''(4) to a minor of foreign nationality born outside Israel who comes to Israel as an *oleh* without his parents . . . and his parents declare . . . that they do not wish him to become an Israel national . . . , (5) to a person born in Israel neither of whose parents was registered in the Population Register at the time of his birth'' [The Nationality Law, Amendment no. 4, 1980].

7. With regard to the immigrant's status during the interim period, despite the length

of time since 1968, it seems that under the 1968 Amendment nationality will be granted within the waiting period unless the immigrant renounces it, and not at the end of that period. The reason for this was not to impair his former nationality and thus leave him without any nationality at all. For a different opinion, see M. D. Gouldman, "Recent Changes in Israel's Nationality Law," *Israel Law Review* 4 (1969):554, who argues that in fact the Amendment did not supply any answer in regard to the immigrant's status during the three-month period. The Amendment in 1980 enables the Minister of the Interior to accept an opting-out declaration "made within a period of three months after the expiration of the three-month . . . if it appears to him that the delay . . . was due to causes over which the declarant had no control"—section 5(f).

8. 112/53 *Makara vs. Minister of the Interior*, 2, 7 PD 955, p. 957. In an earlier case HC 174/52 *Hussein vs. Governor of Acre Prision*, 2 6 PD 897, Justice Cheshin, delivering the majority opinion, held that "Palestine citizenship no longer exists, nor has it existed either in the territory of the State of Israel . . . or anywhere else in the world, following the establishment of the State in part of Palestine and the annexation of the other parts by other states" p. 901. It is worth mentioning that Palestine nationality was also terminated in those territories of Palestine that were annexed to Jordan. Unlike the Israel Nationality Law, the Jordanian law excluded Jewish residents completely from the right to nationality. See A. Rubinstein, "Israel Nationality," pp. 68–69.

9. HC 122/58, *Kalman vs. Minister of Defence et al.*, 2 12 PD 1884; HC 296/80, *Bocubeza vs. State of Israel* 1 34 PD 492. In Israel, the Defence Service Law—5719–1959 (Consolidated Version) 13 LSI 328—imposes the duty of military service on all persons of military age i.e., 18. The result could sometimes mean that such a person, visiting Israel as a tourist, might be "caught" and taken into army service. In order to overcome this difficulty, internal instructions were issued by the Head of Recruitment Center, which provided a special arrangement for Israeli nationals who reside or were born abroad. Under these provisions such nationals are not only exempt from service for as long as they remain abroad, but are permitted to leave Israel without being drafted. However, it is doubtful whether these regulations are legal as it is difficult to determine on what basis the Head of the Recruitment Center has the authority to proclaim an exemption of this kind. Israeli Arabs are excluded from military service for obvious reasons, through the exercise of administrative discretion and not due to specific provisions in the Law.

10. The conditions for naturalization are as follows: "(1) the applicant is in Israel; (2) he has been in Israel for three years out of five preceding the day of the submission of his application . . . ; (3) he is entitled to reside in Israel permanently; (4) he has settled or intends to settle in Israel; (5) he has some knowledge of the Hebrew language; (6) he has renounced his prior nationality or has proved that he will cease to be a foreign national upon becoming an Israel national"—section 5(a).

11. This Amendment, unlike the 1968 Amendment, keeps the District Court from the process. Under the 1968 Amendment it was the District Court, on application of the Minister of the Interior, that was empowered to revoke one's nationality. The 1980 Law, however, leaves it all to the Executive.

12. In HC 31/53, *Mustafa vs. General i/c Northern Command*, 1, 7 PD 587; Justice Olshan stated: "In every case . . . The Minister may, at his discretion, grant or refuse a certification of naturalization"—at p. 588. See also HC 145/51, *Abu Ras vs. Military Government of the Galilee*, 2, 5 PD 1476. It should be noted that the Minister of the Interior is empowered to exempt from compliance those who meet some or all of the

conditions, such as: a person who has served in the Israel Defence Army, a person who has lost a child in such service, or has performed a significant act to further the security or economy of Israel, a spouse of an Israel national—sections 6, 7. But it should be remembered that any exemption is not automatically given; it is in the Minister's discretion to decide.

13. Akzin, "Problems of Constitutional and Administrative Law," in *International Lawyers Convention in Israel, 1958* (Jerusalem, (1959): p. 184. See also Gideon Hausner, "Rights of the Individual in Court," *Israel Law Review*, 9 (1974):486; where he states: "Religion and nationality constitute two interwoven threads which together form the bond that binds a Jew to his people. A separation of these two threads will leave Jewish identity hanging on one thread." See also, Iztak Englard, "The Relationship between the Jewish Law and the State," *Molad* 197/198 (December) 1964:702–12 (in Hebrew); re: his view: "The unity of religion and nationhood is deeply rooted in the Jewish outlook," at page 702.

14. See Amnon Rubinstein, "Law and Religion in Israel," *Israel Law Review* 2 (1967):380–414; see especially conclusions at page 414. See also J. Tedeschi, "Who Is a Jew?" *Ha'Praklit* 19 (1963):101 (in Hebrew). It should be noted, however, that in the sphere of personal status, religious courts of the three religions have exclusive jurisdiction in matters of marriage and divorce. See Rabbinical Courts Jurisdiction (Marriage and Divorce) Law, 5713–1953; 7 LSI 139. See also M. Chigier, "The Rabbinical Courts in the State of Israel," *Israel Law Review* 2 (1967):147–81; J. S. Shiloh, "Marriage and Divorce in Israel," *Israel Law Review* 5 (1970):479–98.

15. HC 10/48, *Ziv vs. Gubernik*, 1 PD 85; Justice Zmorah at page 89: "[The Declaration] contains no element of constitutional law which determines the validity of any ordinances and laws." See also, HC 73/53; 87/53, *Kol Ha'am vs. Minister of the Interior*, 2, 7 PD 871.

16. Justices Silberg and Kister opinions in HC 58/68, *Benjamin Shalit and Others vs. Minister of the Interior and Another*, 2, 23: pp. 502, 547. See also, J. Katz, "The Jewish Character of the Israel Society," in his *Jewish Nationalism: Essays and Studies* (Jerusalem, 1979):86–101 (in Hebrew); and Justice Agranat in *Yerder vs. Chairman of the Central Committee for the Sixth Knesset*, op. cit., p. 385.

17. The word "nationality" here is an inadequate translation of the Hebrew *le'om*—which might be translated as nationhood, ethnic grouping, people, or folk. Although the word "nationality" in English applies to both nationhood and citizenship, as a translation here of *le'om* it should never be confused with citizenship.

18. The proposal was raised by Knesset members of the Religious Party and was rejected by all Committee members, including Z. Warhaftig, also of the Religious Party. See "Unpublished Protocols of the Constitutional, Legislation and Juridical Committee," July 5, 1950. Law of Return, 1950, File Knesset Archives, Jerusalem.

19. The Minister of the Interior, Israel Bar-Yehuda, informed Brother Daniel that while personally he would like to grant him his visa, he could not officially approve the request since he had converted to Christianity and therefore was not a Jew. The legal source for his refusal were the new directives issued by the Ministry of the Interior on January 1, 1960, which made "nationality" (*le'om*) and religion indivisible for Jews in Israel.

20. The Minister of the Interior suggested a regular naturalization procedure, which Brother Daniel agreed to undergo only after losing his case in Court. He was granted citizenship in August 1963. The majority: Justices Silberg, Landau, Manny, and Berinson.

Justice Cohen—the only one to dissent—was in favor of upholding the petition and confirming the order.

21. All the Justices were ready to assume that if the term "Jew" in the Law of Return was construed according to the *hallacha*, then Rufeisen had to be deemed "Jew" for the purposes of the Law and the order *nisi* confirmed. See Justice Silberg at p. 2437; Justice Cohen at p. 2440; Justice Landau at p. 2444; Justice Berinson at p. 2452. It is worth mentioning, however, that this premise was not free of criticism. See, for example, S. Merron, "Apostate: Jew or Person of Double Religion," *Ha 'Praklit* 23 (1967): p. 164 (in Hebrew); S. H. Shaki, *Who is a Jew in the Laws of the State of Israel*, (Jerusalem, 1976), 1:154–169 (in Hebrew).

22. The question of "Who is a Jew?" was not limited to the Law of Return. It arose many times when one of the parties to a marriage was not regarded as a Jew: HC 359/66, *Gitiye vs. The Chief Rabbinate and Jerusalem Religious Council*, 1, 22 PD 290. The matter arose recently when thousands of Falashas were brought to Israel from Ethiopia or when, in the late 1950s, Spanish Chuetas—whose ancestors were forcibly converted to Catholicism in the 15th Century but who secretly maintained their ties with Judaism—came to Israel but were refused recognition as Jews by the Orthodox Rabbinate. See Joseph Schechtman, "Marranos in Israel," *American Zionist* (April 1967) 15–16. Another case was that of the "Black Hebrews," who in December 1969 arrived in Israel requesting automatic citizenship under the Law of Return. In fact, this matter was only recently decided by the Supreme Court which ordered their deportation. See, HC 482/71, *Clark vs. Minister of the Interior*, 1, 27 PD 113. See also David Bleich, "Black Jews: A Halakhic Perspective," *Tradition* 15 (Spring/Summer 1975):59–60; Robert G. Weisbrod, "Israel and the Black Hebrew Israelites," *Judaism* 29 (Winter 1975):23–38.

23. Cases before the Supreme Court sitting as a High Court of Justice are usually heard by three judges only. Section 3 of the Courts of Law, 1957 (11 LSI 157) provides that the Supreme Court shall, at any sitting, be composed of three judges. The President of the Court, or his Permanent Deputy is, however, authorized to direct that the proceedings of a certain case shall be heard by a greater, uneven number of judges.

24. *Israel Digest* 1, no. 17 (December 12, 1958):2–3. The official letter is reproduced in Baruch Litvin and Sidney B. Hoenig, *Jewish Identity: Modern Responses and Opinions on the Registration of Children of Mixed Marriage*, (N.Y.,1969):11–15. On the basis of these opinions the Special Cabinet Committee—consisting of the Prime Minister, the Minister of the Interior, and the Minister of Justice—formulated their recommendations to the Israeli Government.

25. The majority consisted of Justices Cohen, Sussman, Berinson, Witkon, and Manny; in the minority were: President Agranat and Justices Silberg, Kister, and Landau. The judgment was delivered on January 23, 1970, after nearly two years of hearings, consisting of some 132 printed pages. And see *Shalit vs. Minister of the Interior*:478–79; and *Selected Judgments*:36–37. It may be noted that during the course of the hearings the Court took the unusual step of approaching the Government with a proposal to delete the entry of *le'om* from the Population Registry, but in November 1968 the Government rejected the proposal, leaving the Court to determine the issue. See *Divrei Ha'Knesset* 56 (1970):725.

26. President Agranat at p. 575–81; Justice Kister at p. 541–42, 553–54, 556–70; Justice Silberg at p. 493–96, 498–99; Justice Landau at p. 518–21, 531. *Selected Judgments*, pp. 153–58, 48–49, 53–56, 109–48, 37.

27. Commenting on the Shalit decision, B. Akzin remarked that the Court's decision was the only one possible under the circumstances prevailing in Israel. See B. Akzin,

"Who is a Jew? A Hard Case," *Israel Law Review* 5(1970):259–63. See also, Ben-Moshe, "Reaction to the Shalit Case," *Congress Bi-Weekly* 37, no. 4 (March 6, 1970):4–5; and Robert Alter, "The Shalit Case," *Commentary* 50, no. 1 (July 1970):55–61.

28. See A. Maoz, "Who is a Jew—Much Ado About Nothing," *Ha'Praklit* 31 (1977):271–310 (in Hebrew); P. Shifman, "Validity of non-Orthodox Conversion to Judaism Under the Law of Return," *Mishpatim* 7 (1975):391 (in Hebrew); S. H. Shaki, *Who Is a Jew in the Laws of Israel*, 1 (Jerusalem, 1976): 178–84 (in Hebrew).

29. The 1970 Amendment did not specifically prohibit the recognition by Registration authorities of conversions to Judaism by non-Orthodox rabbis, performed abroad. In the recent case of HC 230/86, *Miller vs. Minister of the Interior* (as yet unpublished), who was converted to Judaism by a Reform rabbi, the High Court of Justice ruled (December 2, 1986) that the petitioner should be registered as "Jewish" under the *le'om* entry. See *Ha'Aretz*, December 3, 1986; p. 1. As for conversions performed in Israel, an unrepealed ordinance of the British Mandate period assigned such authority to the Orthodox rabbinate.

30. See, for example, S. Ginossar, "Who is a Jew: A Better Law," *Israel Law Review* 5 (1970):264:67; B. Akzin, "Who is a Jew—A Hard Case," *Ibid.*:259–69; M. Shava, "Comments on the Law of Return (Amendment no. 2), 5730–1970 (Who is a Jew?)," *Tel-Aviv University Studies in Law* 3 (1977):140–153. HC 147/70, *Standerman vs. Minister of the Interior*, 1, 24 PD 766; HC 630/70, *Tamerim vs. The State of Israel*, 1, 26 PD 197; HC 18/72, *Shalit vs. Minister of the Interior*, 1, 26 PD 334.

31. In regard to the relevance of the negative definition to anti-Semitism, see Shaul Esh, *Studies in the Holocaust and Contemporary Jewry* (Jerusalem, 1973):128, note 38, where he refers to Raul Hilberg, *The Destruction of European Jews* (Chicago, 1961):43, 640–41, who stated that as a rule the idea of the extermination of the Jews started with the negative definition attached to them. See also Kurt Wawrzinek, *Die Entstehung der Deutshen Antisemiten Parties, 1873–1890* (Berlin, 1927): 29, 32, 83. Dr. Wawrzinek emphasized the crucial relevance of the definition of Jews to the anti-Semitic German parties in the late nineteenth century.

32. Rabbi Jehudah Lieb Maimon, in a letter to Prime Minister David Ben-Gurion, 26 Kislev, 5719 (December 8, 1958), in *Jewish Identity, Modern Responses and Opinions*, op. cit., p. 20. See also letters by Isaac Herzog, Chief Rabbi, Ibid., p. 19, and by Shlomo Goren, Chief Rabbi Israel Defence Forces, Ibid., pp. 37,49.

33. As, for example, the case of the refugees from Vietnam. On January 7, 1979, the Israeli Cabinet issued a resolution permitting the entrance of 100 refugees: "The State of Israel as a Jewish State Cannot Leave the Helpless Refugees to the Mercy of the Sea," *Davar* January 8, 1979, p. 1 (in Hebrew).

6

Venezuelan Immigration Policy and Politics

DANIEL HELLINGER

What countries in Latin America have been most influenced by immigration? Perhaps Argentina or Brazil spring to mind most readily, but since World War II no Latin American country has been influenced by immigration as much as Venezuela. Venezuela was the only Latin American country in the 1970's to take measures to attract European immigration. Today, a majority of Venezuela's immigrants are from Latin America, but hundreds of thousands of Europeans also entered. They and their descendants have left a distinct mark on the demography of the country.

In 1970, Venezuela already had the second highest percentage of foreign-born citizens in its population, second only to Argentina's 9.5 percent, and well above the 3.4 percent counted in Panama and Paraguay, the next closest countries. The officially counted population born abroad rose from 47,704 in 1941, to 541,563 in 1961, to 596,455 in 1971, to 1,039,106 in 1981 (Pellegrino, 1985:398). These figures indicate that the foreign-born population exceeded 13.8 percent of the total population. Foreign-born workers accounted for approximately 13.3 percent of the unemployed in 1984 (Berglund and Hernández, 1985:29,60). These figures do not fully measure the impact of immigration, however, because undocumented workers are undoubtedly underestimated and because there now exists a second generation of natives who are sons and daughters of immigrants.

Beginning with its first immigration law of 1831, Venezuela has sought to use immigration policy as a conscious, planned tool for development. The goals of immigration policy have been to populate the interior, fill labor shortages that cannot economically be filled through education and training, and to expand

The indispensable study upon which much of this chapter is based is *Las de afuera* (*The Outsiders*) by Susan Berglund and Humberto Hernández Caliman. However, the overall interpretation and any errors contained herein are my own responsibilty.

opportunities for native Venezuelans. Since 1935 governments controlled by modernizing elites have seen a controlled immigration policy as a critical aspect of their plans to "sow the petroleum," that is, to use revenues from export earnings to develop the country. Evidence is abundant that immigrants have played a key role in the transformation of Venezuela, but there is little evidence that that policy has successfully affected immigration in the ways envisioned by the government.

The Venezuelan experience provides a relevant case study of immigration policies in Third World nations pursuing developmental goals, but the experience also has entailed a problem familiar to many developed nations: undocumented and illegal immigration. Hundreds of thousands of Colombians have migrated eastward since World War II, especially between 1974 and 1981 when Venezuela's economy experienced fantastic growth due to the rise in oil prices. Now, in an era of economic contraction, Venezuela must cope with the demographic impact of this flow, even as the flood itself is receding.

Undoubtedly Venezuela will not be the last Third World country to face immigration problems promoted by the boom and bust nature of an economy highly dependent on the export of primary goods. What framework helps us best understand the factors that have shaped Venezuelan policies and determined their effectiveness?

A fruitful approach to understanding the limits and consequences of Venezuelan immigration policy is offered by "world systems theory," most frequently associated with the work of Immanuel Wallerstein (1974). This approach locates national economies either toward the center or toward the periphery of the world economy. Those at the center (or "core") enjoy considerably more autonomy in shaping their development than those in the periphery. However it is not clear that even the core nations have had great success in effecting demographic shifts, whether domestic or international, through policies aimed directly at population movement. More logically, world systems theory suggests that the uneven development of the world economy determines the basic contours of the world population. Nations located more toward the core are poles of attraction for immigration, and changes in the global economic system can shift the flow of population movement from one region to another.

While much attention has been directed at the flow of migrants from more peripheral nations toward central ones (e.g., from southern Europe northward; from Mexico to the United States), less attention has been paid to international migration patterns within the periphery—unless the movement is the result of war or natural calamity (Afghanistan–Pakistan, Central America, parts of Africa). Venezuela presents the case of a country that has been a pole of attraction for immigration, while not itself a "core nation." Nor is it on the extreme periphery. Venezuela occupies a semi-peripheral role in the world economy because its main export, oil, plays a crucial role in the world economy and because it has experienced a significant degree of industrialization.

Before the arrival of the transnational petroleum companies in the 1920s,

Venezuela occupied an extremely peripheral position in the world economy as a supplier (and a relatively insignificant one at that) of cacao, coffee, and ranching products to the central, industrial economies of northern Europe and (later) North America. Venezuela's rural economy, underdeveloped social system, and violent politics offered few inducements to potential emigrants from other countries, even from southern Europe, a peripheral region that would later became the most important source of immigrants between 1935 and 1973. Colombia and the Caribbean were hardly more developed than Venezuela and might plausibly have provided immigrants, but Venezuela's elites had little interest in attracting immigrants from these countries. The history of Venezuela's immigration policies through 1935 consists of its futile attempt to attract immigrants from countries located closer to the core of the world economy—in other words, from Europe.

As a result of oil and the social and economic transformations that it wrought, Venezuela's relationship with other parts of the periphery changed. Its relationship with parts of Southern Europe and Colombia became one of greater equality; emigrants from these countries began to view Venezuela's economy more opportunistically. Venezuela's elites envisioned a strategy of development that required amounts of labor and certain skills that could not be met domestically, and immigration policy reflects this. Still, this policy was never fully effective in regulating the waves of immigration, particularly when it reached a crescendo during the oil boom of the 1970s. The end of that boom, more than policy, has finally stemmed the tide of immigration.

Recent studies of undocumented Colombian workers deported by Venezuela illustrate this underlying dynamic. The origins of the deportees are disproportionately regions of Colombia where the workforce has been most drastically affected by world economic forces: from Medellín, where the decline of the textile industry has raised unemployment among both skilled and unskilled workers; from Bolivar, where a crisis in the fishing sector and decomposition of the prevailing peasant social and economic system is well advanced; from Norte de Santander, a frontier state that has never developed important industries to retain labor; from Boyaca and Santander, where agriculture is characterized by tenant farming and little social development.

At the top of the list is Valle, hundreds of kilometers from the border, where the growth of the commercial sugar cane industry has forced peasants off the land. The common pattern is for peasants to leave for the capital city of the province; subsequently the original migrants then relocate a second time to Venezuela or urban inhabitants, whose employment prospects and wages are negatively impacted by the internal migration, emigrate themselves. In either case Venezuela appears as a pole of attraction offering the prospect of a better life (Pellegrino, 1984:751–753). Ironically, the same force (rising oil prices, a factor external to Venezuela's own economy) that made Venezuela a pole of attraction, has been a significant force in reducing economic opportunities in many regions that have provided immigrants.

This suggests that on the one hand Venezuela's problem with undocumented immigration is comparable to that faced by the United States in its relationship with Mexico—that is, one caused by the gap between the levels of economic and social development in two neighboring countries. On the other hand, one Colombian scholar appropriately warns of an important difference: "Suffice it to say," he writes, " . . . that the inequalities between Mexico and the United States represent a classic case of a periphery–center relationship within a world system model, while those between Colombia and Venezuela today correspond to an inter-periphery relationship" (Murillo-Castaño, 1984:2–3). Immigrants in Venezuela are likely to confront opportunities and limitations more like those in the country from which they have emigrated. Population movements among countries in the semi-periphery and periphery, as in the case of Venezuela and Colombia, are much more likely to be sensitive to changes in the world economy than those between the center and periphery, as in the case of the United States and Mexico. It is doubtful that immigration policy alone, especially that of any one nation, can greatly influence international movements of population in either case.

It is not my contention that world systems theory fully accounts for the content and effectiveness of immigration policy. Factors such as geography, transportation, and communications cannot be discounted. Venezuela shares a 2,219-mile border with Colombia, a nation with which it shares a common language and many common historical and cultural characteristics. Family and economic ties draw Venezuelans and Colombians together in the Andean region, and the border has a relatively developed transportation infrastructure. By contrast, on Venezuela's southern and eastern frontiers are nations with distinct cultural, ethnic, and linguistic characteristics. The areas adjacent to these borders, which are often ill-defined, are largely unpopulated, with poor transportation.

The demographic center of Venezuela is metropolitan Caracas, far from any land border, with 1,037 people per square kilometer. While the western part of the country is closer to the national average of 15.98 per square kilometer, the immense Bolivar region bordering with Guyana and Brazil has but 2.88 persons per square kilometer (Berglund and Hernández, 1985:23). On the north is the Caribbean. There are few close, densely populated islands comparable to the Greater Antilles and Cuba, and the United States, a central economy, acts as an effective competing pole of attraction for Caribbean immigrants.

Venezuela's immigration experience has also been shaped by political conditions—both within its own borders and in global regions that are potential suppliers of immigrants. Often, however, political conditions themselves respond to developments in the world system. Endemic instability such as Venezuela experienced in the nineteenth century was directly linked to its vulnerability to intervention by the governments of core nations and the poor prospects for nation building offered by social and economic conditions typical in the periphery. On occasion policy has been shaped by calculations about which political factions would benefit from immigration; however this has always proved to be a short-term influence.

The remainder of this study analyzes the evolution of Venezuelan immigration policy—its goals, effectiveness, and impact during several periods, each defined by changes in Venezuela's location in the world system. The first period, from colonial times until 1935, covers the extended period during which Venezuela's position in the world system was extremely peripheral. Although oil revenues had already become an economic force by 1920, only after the death of General Juan Vincent Gómez, whose dictatorship began in 1908, did governments begin to plan actively how to use this new-found wealth. Immigration policy was part of that process.

The second period considered begins in 1935 and ends in 1973. During this period the rising importance of oil in the world economy propelled Venezuela closer to the dynamic core of the world system; from a rural, agriculturally-based society, Venezuela was transformed into a predominantly urban semi-industrialized one. Immigration policy became concerned not merely with filling labor shortages, but with the problem of integrating immigrants with the native population and with channeling immigration to geographic regions and economic sectors where they might contribute to development and expand opportunities for natives. Toward the end of the period the problem of undocumented and illegal immigration became a serious political issue.

The period 1974 to 1979 was one of boom. Venezuela became more than just another part of the semi-periphery; it became a pole of economic growth and powerful magnet to emigrants in the periphery and semi-periphery. By contrast, since 1979 Venezuela has experienced economic retrenchment and the legacy left by a decade of demographic upheaval. No longer is the problem one of attracting or discouraging immigration; the problem is dealing with the legacy left by a decade of demographic upheaval.

IMMIGRATION IN THE PERIPHERY: VENEZUELA, 1500–1935

The early colonial period is best characterized as one of "conquest" rather than "migration." After the consolidation of Spanish rule, the arrival of additional Spanish subjects and the transport of African slaves became factors in shaping what became the native population of independent Venezuela. Indians in the Western region contributed to the demographic mix. Venezuela's population has been described, as a result of this heterogeneous base, as "cafe con leche." A predominant social myth in Venezuela is that the mixture has left a racially tolerant society; in truth immigration policy has been influenced by racism from the start.

The first immigration law passed in 1831 was partly motivated by the fear of landowners that black immigration from the Carribbean might shake the foundations of slavery. Even after the abolition of slavery in 1854, racist sentiments were embodied in discriminatory provisions, including overt discrimination against non-white immigration in the law of 1936, which continues to be the basic law of immigration today. Just before a coup in 1948, a reformist government proposed to bring the immigration laws into conformity with the United Nations Universal Declaration on Human Rights. Even then, the offensive clauses were to be replaced with others authorizing the government to take measures to deter immigration from countries with "lower standards of living," a provision aimed specifically at Caribbeans. Finally, racist criteria were removed in 1966 (Berglund-Thompson,1980).

Of course, attracting white European immigration meant inducing emigration from a part of the world economy located closer to the core. A few economic and social statistics should demonstrate the underdeveloped character of Venezuelan society, whose dependent place as a supplier of agricultural goods, such as cacao and (later) coffee placed it on the margins of the world system, even toward the end of the era. As late as 1936, average life expectancy in Caracas, the capital, was only 36 years. Sixty percent of the adult population was illiterate; there were only 3,653 hospital beds to service 3.3 million Venezuelans. Industrialization had barely begun, with slightly over 20,000 persons listed as economically active in manufacturing, mostly in small, cottage industries. Between 1891 and 1926 the rate of population growth was at its maximum less than one percent 0.8 percent per year (Berglund-Thompson, 1980:13–16).

Conditions were even worse during the nineteenth century. Horrible sanitary conditions combined with poor health care to make life in Venezuela, particularly in the interior, repulsive to immigrants. Those who came often found a hostile social environment as well. With the exception of a brief respite under the dictatorial rule of General Antonio Guzmán Blanco, from 1870 to 1888, the nineteenth century saw Venezuela wracked by bloody civil wars. Population data are crude at best, but estimates are that Venezuela's population actually declined by several hundred thousand during each of several periods of bloody civil conflict, especially during the Federal War of 1859–1863 (Izard, 1970:9).

Besides the obvious threat to life itself, the civil strife also discouraged immigration because Europeans who might have farmed the interior found little security for land ownership in the anarchic conditions that prevailed. There was a constant threat from quarrelling *caudillos* ("men on horseback"), ambitious elite who lured land hungry peasants into their quasi-private armies to contest one another for political power and to enlarge their own estates. Not surprisingly, the Guzmán Blanco era was the only one during which immigration policy, which sought European immigrants to settle Venezuela's vast, underpopulated interior, saw any success—modest though it was (Berglund, 1982:959–961).

Given these realities, it is hardly surprising that immigration policy failed. The 1873 census indicated that 29,000 foreigners were resident in Venezuela; by 1936 the figure was only 45,484 (cited in Berglund, 1982:959).The failure was not in the laws, which (leaving aside the matter of racial discrimination) were often farsighted. The 1855 law envisioned resettlement centers dispersed throughout the country to help immigrants settle in the interior. Several laws empowered the government to seek immigrants in Europe through advertising and contracts with workers overseas. The 1874 law allowed entrepreneurs to go to Europe and contract immigrants directly. A French observer of immigration policy in Venezuela once remarked: "If migratory movements were regulated by laws and decrees, Venezuela would be the South American country most populated by immigrants" (quoted in Berglund and Hernández, 1985:19).

All these efforts ultimately failed because of the inhospitable conditions in the interior and the low administrative capacity of the state, which had few economic or manpower resources to implement legislation. Venezuela had no employment service nor other agencies to help immigrants adjust to their new country. The country did not even have a border patrol. Even if money had been available to implement the resettlement centers envisioned in the 1855 provision, civil war erupted and made the provision impractical.

Venezuelan immigration policy was shaped not by domestic reality, but by the influence of "positivism," an imported philosophy that seemed to offer Venezuelan elites, like their counterparts elsewhere in South America, a ready-made solution to indolence and underdevelopment. A Venezuelan critic complained that politicians seemed to think that it was " . . . possible to populate the empty country with strong strokes of the pen, not perceiving that the immensity of our territory, without means of communication and industries, makes it like the Sahara, that our physical environment is ravished by powerful epidemics and endemic plagues" (quoted in Berglund, 1982:959). Unfortunately, Venezuelan elites saw in immigration the most important tool for rectifying the very conditions that made their efforts to attract immigrants futile in the first place. Their racism compounded the problem.

Reflecting a national inferiority complex that persisted even after World War II, elites saw immigration as a way of "whitening" the population, what one official publication in 1876 called a "transfusion of blood." In 1900, ruminating on the apparent success of the immigration law of 1891, which explicitly banned nonwhite immigration, one Venezuelan oligarch expressed relief that the country had blocked an invasion by" . . . Chinese, and other yellows, blacks, Africans, and all other foreigners of inferior and decrepit races" (Wright, 1979).

Immigration was even seen as a solution to dictatorship. The most influential exponent of positivism in Venezuela, Laureano Vallenilla Lanz, argued that the brutal dictatorship of Juan Vincente Gómez, which he characterized as "democratic caesarism," was necessary because of Venezuela's cultural inferiority. He felt that such caesarism could be made obsolete by immigration. Not surprisingly, Gómez himself had little interest in this notion; his lack of interest in European immigration was shaped more by his immediate economic interests than by ideology. Although positivism fell into disfavor after the death of Gómez, Venezuelan intellectuals and politicians continued to reflect its influence (Sosa, 1974). In fact, a later dictator, Gen. Marcos Pérez Jiménez (1948–1958) placed the son of Vallenilla Lanz, who shared his father's ideas, in charge of immigration policy.

While Gómez resisted change, the growth in production and export of oil guaranteed that it would come. From 121,000 barrels of oil produced in 1917, production expanded to 136 million barrels by 1929. The percentage of the state budget derived from oil revenues rose from 1.4 percent in 1920 to 28.7 in 1935, and the proportion would be even higher if the indirect effect on government revenues (especially customs taxes on goods imported to meet rising consumer demand) were counted. (Wright, 1979:7; Márquez, 1977:66–71). Despite the depression, production rose to 148.5 million barrels by 1935. During this same period agricultural export production, especially coffee in the Andes, Gómez's home region, actually declined. But by 1920 Gómez (having seized power in 1908) had already consolidated his dictatorship, and the new revenues only aided him in constructing a powerful new state.

The state's share of profits earned from oil take the form of a rent—that is, the state, acting as a landlord, requires a fee for access to its natural resource. Even after nationalizing the oil industry, thereby making the producer and the landlord the same legal person, part of what appears as profit in the oil industry has little to do with labor or capital. Better technology and investments can increase profits, but an underdeveloped country like Venezuela must rely on the transnational corporations for necessary technology and for access to overseas markets. The earnings of its industry still greatly depend on its ability to demand a price for access to its national resource and on the natural productivity of the wells—in other words what economists call "ground rent" (Márquez, 1977).

The goal of all Venezuelan governments since Gómez has been to develop the country by using rent derived from oil exports for investment. Petroleum rents also provided the state for the first time the possibility of developing an effective administrative apparatus, a sine qua non for an effective immigration policy, which modernizers saw as one that would attract European immigrants and induce them to populate the interior, supplying needed skills, and creating new opportunities for native Venezuelans. But rents also raised an alternative that was barely possible before —the idea of sowing petroleum revenues to improve the quality of the domestic workforce through education, training, and social development.

The political possibility of pursuing either policy was virtually nonexistent under Gómez. His reign is the only lengthy one in Venezuelan history during which the government sought to discourage immigration—an irony considering that positivism was used by the dictator's apologists to justify his rule. Gómez was a product of the Andean coffee oligarchy and throughout his rule retained the outlook of his social class, the landed oligarchy. Corrupt and vicious, he ruled the country as a virtual fiefdom. He used control of the government to funnel oil revenues into his own pockets and those of his cronies.

Gómez and his sycophants purchased vast landed estates, which were then run not as efficient capitalist enterprises but as traditional *haciendas* and plantations, with peasants bonded to the land by debt, tradition, and force. Colonization schemes designed to attract Europeans to the interior were to Gómez nothing more than opportunities to place more land in the hands of his family and supporters. Gómez and the oligarchy saw only limited use for immigration: to supply labor for the oil industry and the ports and to supplement the agricultural labor supply being drawn to the oil camps and cities in search of better opportunities and a higher standard of living. Neither Gómez nor the oligarchy desired to compete with European immigrants or modern capitalist farms.

Ironically the only immigration law, that of 1918, that has been implemented with any degree of effectiveness prevailed during this era during which European immigration was viewed unfavorably. The 1918 law allowed Gómez, who viewed foreigners as potential troublemakers, to place many administrative obstacles in the path of immigrants, but it also allowed the government to issue exemptions, which Gómez used to serve the limited needs of the oil companies and oligarchy. Hence 6,000–11,000 blacks from the Antilles arrived to work on the landed estates and the docks, an effort not to disturb the system of cheap labor on the haciendas. Gómez also permitted the oil companies to contract and import several thousand additional Caribbean workers (Tennessee, 1979:98–103).

The companies brought thousands of these workers to the oil camps because they could speak English and often brought needed skills with them. Caribbeans were offered better wages and opportunities than Venezuelans, who developed the derogative term "*musiues*" to refer to these immigrants. In 1928, one of the demands of the nation's first oil workers strike, provoked in part by the companies' dismissal of 4,000 Venezuelan workers, was for the deportation of Caribbean employees, to which the government partially acceded. In 1929 a decree was published that required foreign, "colored" workers to carry an identity card that showed their legal right to move from place to place. The Ministry of Internal Affairs justified the decree because " . . . the primordial element to be considered in those who come to settle in Venezuela is race." The Ministry considered welcome only that race" . . . which raises by its fusion the physical, intellectual and moral level of the Venezuelans." Many Caribbean workers had entered the country originally under highly restrictive dispensations given to the oil companies, and they could not qualify for the card (Berglund-Thompson, 1980:24).

When Gómez died in 1935, the foreign-born population totaled but 45,484 persons, just 1.3 percent of the total population. An estimated 18,000 of these were Colombians living in the border region between the two countries. In reality, they were more like migrants than immigrants. After 1935, Venezuelan immigration policy would be determined by the outcome of a tug of war among the landed oligarchy, the middle class, the rising bourgeoisie, and the nascent working class. The first of these elements was doomed to ever-decreasing power after the death of the dictator, and the immigration door swung open even more widely as the landed obligarchy faded.

After Gómez, immigration policy would earnestly seek agricultural colonization and other modernizing goals. As industrialization became more feasible, choices had to be made concerning the relative merits of relying on domestic education and training or supplying labor needs through immigration. Oil revenues provided the state with resources by which it could develop the capacity to administer immigration laws more effectively, but in the end, the flow of immigration was affected less by policy than by factors outside of the state's control—specifically, the emergence of Venezuela as a pole of economic growth and opportunity in the global economy.

IMMIGRATION POLICY DURING A PERIOD OF TRANSITION, 1935–1973

The period from 1935 to 1973 is bounded on the one side by the death of Gómez and on the other by the fantastic boom in oil prices that made Venezuela a magnet for immigration in the 1970s. Over the course of nearly four decades, Venezuela shifted from the extreme periphery of the world economy toward a privileged position in the semi-periphery. With the exception of a brief period (1958–1961) in which immigration was discouraged, it is a period in which immigration policy steadily shifted away from the goal of merely settling the interior to that of attracting human resources needed for specific developmental goals.

By 1935 there had emerged in Venezuela a small but critically situated bourgeoisie, a middle class, and a labor union movement. The period from 1936 to 1944 is one in which there is a political struggle between modernizing elites and traditional elites, each attempting to influence the reformist, but unelected governments of Generals Eleázar López Contreras and Isaías Medina Angarita. The legal foundation for many of the current social and economic policies prevailing today was laid during this early period.

In 1936 López Contreras, responding to peasant violence, strikes, and street demonstrations aimed at Gómez's family and cronies, brought moderate, reformist elements into his government. He expanded political freedoms and presented the first coherent program of development ever offered by a Venezuelan government: the "February Program." Immigration was part of the program, and two pieces of legislation, the Immigration and Colonization Act of 1936 and the Aliens Act of 1937, became the basic laws governing immigration and foreign residence in Venezuela. though modified many times over by executive decree, they remain so today.

Only labor, influenced by the opportunistic use of immigrants by the oil companies, pressed for limiting immigration. But the result of this pressure was a restriction placed in the new Labor Law limiting the proportion of the workforce in any one enterprise that could be foreign to 25 percent. The expanding economy mitigated the pressures to close the doors to immigration.

Much to the frustration of Venezuela's younger generation of middle class and labor union leaders, the landed oligarchy exerted enough influence on López

Contreras that the period of reform and democratization proved short lived, although neither López Contreras nor his successor, Medina, ever implemented the kind of arbitrary, brutal measures by which Gómez smothered dissent and social change. One consequence of the conservatism of López Contreras was that he discouraged immigration of Spaniards fleeing civil war and the Franco regime. López regarded Republicans as likely allies of his leftist opponents, all of whom he regarded as Communists. Medina, who succeeded López Contreras in 1941, was more tolerant of dissent, but European emigration to Venezuela was discouraged by the disruption of trans-Atlantic transportation caused by submarine warfare during World War II.

Anti-semitism of the sort usually found in an overwhelmingly Christian country was also a factor. In a poll conducted in 1948, 81 percent of the respondents said they preferred that Jews not come to Venezuela. In the same survey 73 percent rejected Asiatics, and 66 percent rejected blacks (Berglund-Thompson, 1980:37). Between 1933 and 1947, the government reluctantly agreed to allow approximately 7,500 Jews to enter the country (although it is possible that additional Jews entered the country by lying about their religion) (Berglund-Thompson, 1980:73). Fortunately, the rising generation of political elites was less prejudiced, and it was their pressure and editorializing that pushed the door ajar, especially for Jews.

The end of World War II saw a change of government. In 1945 young officers, disgruntled over lack of professionalization in the military, approached a recently founded political party, called *Acción Democrática* (AD), with a plan to over-throw Medina, who was resisting demands for direct, free elections. AD was led principally by reformers who as students had organized demonstrations in 1928 against the Gómez regime and had been bitterly disappointed by López Contreras. AD and the Communist Party emerged as the first modern, mass-based parties in the country's history. Although many of the *adecos*, including their brilliant leader Rómulo Betancourt, had been Communist or radical leftists in the 1930s, the *adecos'* principal demand now was for free elections and reform, not the establishment of socialism. They agreed to act in concert with the military, and the coup was successful. Elections were held, and AD won overwhelmingly. The new government proceeded to plan an ambitious program of social and economic reform in a period known as the "*trienio*" (because it lasted three years).

The hallmark of *adeco* policy in immigration was a more active and organized attempt to recruit European immigrants, especially from Southern Europe, in-cluding Spaniards fleeing the Franco regime. Unfortunately, the *adeco* experi-ment was never fully tested because the military grew restless again. In 1948 a *golpe* inaugurated a ten-year period of military rule, which had many of the same characteristics of the hated Gómez dictatorship. The new dictator, General Marcos Pérez Jiménez, although he had been one of the officers who conspired with AD against Medina, characterized reformers, such as the *adecos*, as dan-gerous, violent revolutionaries, tools of international communism. Like Gómez, he enjoyed the support of the U.S. embassy and the oil companies. His regime was notorious for its extreme brutality, including assassinations, disappearances, torture, exile and arbitrary imprisonment.

The dictatorship was corrupt, brutal, and inefficient, but unlike the Gómez regime it was not the expression of a landed oligarchy. In any case, Pérez Jiménez could hardly hold back the forces of social and economic transformation underway in Venezuela, and at least rhetorically he cast himself as a populist ruler committed to the industrialization of the country. Similarly, his attitude toward immigration was different from his predecessors. Pérez Jiménez put the younger Vallenilla Lanz in charge of immigration policy as Minister of Internal Affairs (under Medina Vallenilla had headed the agency responsible for settling immigrants) (Berglund-Thompson, 1980:47–58).

Whereas Gómez had closed the immigration door, and his successors left it ajar, the new regime threw it wide open. Between 1946 and 1959, an average of 30,000 Europeans per year entered Venezuela. Pérez Jiménez cultivated them as a political base, making aliens eligible to vote in a plebiscite, held in 1958, through which he hoped—by fraud, intimidation, and buying of votes—to win, and thus prolong his rule. Government-financed immigrant associations—especially Portuguese, Italian, and Spanish—published full page ads praising the government, helping to feed a nativist backlash against immigrants after the overthrow of the dictatorship. Many immigrants shared the general disgust with the hated dictatorship prevalent among native Venezuelans, but were hardly in a position to resist its power.

One of the first acts of the junta that replaced Pérez Jiménez in 1958 was to close immigration to all but family members, a decision supported by labor and by most of the population, but opposed by the Chamber of Commerce, which felt it would provoke a labor shortage (Berglund-Thompson, 1980:51–58). The mild xenophobia toward foreigners was reinforced by an economic recession that reinforced labor opposition to immigration. Labor was the core constituency for AD, and after the 1958 elections were won by AD, the new president, Rómulo Betancourt, retained the restrictions.

Besides changes in policy, economic recession, and negative public attitudes, immigration was discouraged by civil unrest. Many students and radical labor leaders, inspired by the Cuban Revolution and feeling betrayed by Betancourt's failure to keep promises of more profound economic and social reform, resorted to guerrilla warfare. The war was marked by terrorist tactics on both sides, and Venezuela hardly appealed to Europeans as a promising destination. The result was not only a slower influx of refugees, but a net loss, as many immigrants left the hostile environment.

However, as the civil war subsided and Venezuela settled into a more peaceful and constitutional mode of government, marked by the emergence of a multiparty system, transfers of power between AD and its main opposition (the Christian Democrats), and the resuscitation of Venezuela's oil-lubricated economy, entries began to increase. But a new dynamic was underway. Most of the rest of Latin America was slipping further into economic and political crisis. Although Europeans began to come again, other Latin American countries were now providing the majority of new arrivals. Between 1936 and 1961, 850,000 foreigners officially entered the country. More than double that figure entered between 1961 and 1973 (Berglund-Thompson, 1980:viii; Berglund and Hernández, 1985:43,48,85). However, it is important to keep in mind that many who arrived did not come as immigrants intending to establish permanent residence.

Table 6.1 indicates overall tendencies in the movement of foreigners as revealed by registration statistics. One reason for using these figures rather than a count of the official immigration visas granted is that most immigrants (i.e., those foreigners entering the country with the intention of taking up residence) did not enter under the provisions of the 1936 Immigration Act, which is highly restrictive, especially toward non-Europeans, non-Catholics, and people of color. Instead, most immigrants entered, as they do today, illegally (in which case they do not appear in these figures until they acquire a legal status later) or legally under the provisions of the 1937 Aliens Act, which is less discriminatory and provides multiple categories of visas. Many Colombians entered originally on nothing more than a tourist visa.

Looking at Table 6.1, it is important to note the high number of new registrants in two of the selected years, 1955 and 1957, reflecting the attempt of Pérez Jiménez to build a base of support among the immigrant community. The figures for 1960 and 1963 illustrate the impact of the nativist backlash. Even by 1973 the net influx as well as the number of new registrants had not nearly returned to the 1948 level. However, the numbers of entries and exits steadily rose from the 1963 low, indicating that many workers entered temporarily rather than as immigrants. The rise in the number of seasonal or temporary foreign workers led to the coining of the term "*golondrinas*", which carries the double meaning of "swallow" and "vagabond" in Latin America. Although official immigration has not returned to the maximums reached in the 1950's, foreigners were becoming a larger proportion of the workforce.

Although the high point of immigration corresponds to the Pérez Jiménez period and the low point to the early years after his overthrow, the flow of migration was probably more responsive to the overall process of social and economic transformation, a process that went forward whether governments were democratic or dictatorial, corrupt or efficient, hostile or favorable to the working class, disposed or indisposed toward immigration.Literally hundreds of statistics could be used to illustrate this passive revolution; a few will have to suffice. The most startling change, one with considerable impact on the country's demographic profile and indicative of its allure to other Latin Americans, was the decline in the rate of mortality, from 32.9 deaths per thousand annually during 1930–1934, to 16.1 during 1945–1949, to 8.9 during 1955–1959. By 1976, the figure had reached 7.1 per thousand. The infant mortality rate declined from

Table 6.1.

Official Registration of Foreign Residents ("cedulas" issued) and Entry and Exit of Foreigners in Venezuela, Selected Years

Years	Entries	Exits	Net influx	Number of new registrants
1936–47[1]	203,657	183,802[1]	19,855[1]	n.a.
1941–47				50,712
1948	71,902	34,164	37,004	38,319
1949	72,902	46,489	26,404	35,866
1955	137,416	79,874	57,542	75,153
1957	150,361	104,305	46,056	65,397
1960	127,567	127,946	-379	28,958
1963	103,876	105,309	-1,433	23,685
1964	125,758	111,829	13,929	23,713
1969	204,880	189,223	15,657	24,974
1973	394,662	372,140	22,522	29,966

[1] *Figure may underestimate immigration because exit data does not discriminate between Venezuelans and foreigners during this period.*

Source: Berglund and Hernández [1985: 43, 48, 58, 60], selected years from tables.

77.1 in 1950 to 36.1 in 1968 (Brito Figueroa, 1975:804; Bolivar Chollet, 1974:362–371).

Venezuela's demography was marked not only by immigration and a revolution in life expectancy and health, but by a massive movement from countryside to city. The Venezuela of 1936 was 71.1 percent rural; that of 1969 was 74.9 percent urban. In 1941, 53.1 percent of the workforce was employed in the primary (mining and agricultural) sectors; by 1968, nearly half were engaged in services and another 22.3 percent were employed in manufacturing and construction. Except for a brief period around 1960, when unemployment hovered around 13 percent (and contributed to anti-immigration sentiments in the population), the official unemployment rate hovered around 6–7 percent throughout the postwar period. Between 1950 and 1970 alone, despite the years of corrupt and inefficient dictatorship and the recession of the early 1960s, the income per inhabitant (adjusted for inflation) more than doubled (by a factor of 2.24). Venezuela had gone from one of the poorest countries in the hemisphere to the wealthiest south of the United States (Aranda, 1985:229).

Fueling this growth was, of course, the oil industry. Annual production was 154.6 billion barrels per year in 1936, and it expanded almost constantly until it reached a peak of 1.353 trillion by 1970. As Table 6.2 indicates, petroleum already represented the lion's share of export earnings for Venezuela by 1935, and by 1960 agricultural exports, the staple of the economy during the nineteenth century, had barely reached the level of the 1920s. In dollars, the total paid to the government reached $968 million in 1957, and after a modest decline through 1961, resumed a steady upward trajectory until it reached $1.755 billion by 1971 (Aranda, 1985:111; Tugwell, 1977:243).

This influx of revenues from ground rent had significant implications for the employment structure in the country and, therefore, for immigration policy. As Table 6.3 indicates, agricultural employment was more or less stable throughout the entire period, and the mining and petroleum industries, capital intensive by nature, did not absorb large numbers of new workers. The dramatic increases were registered in manufacturing, construction, and services. Immigrants played a major role in all three areas, and also in agriculture. Petroleum earnings raised demand for agricultural products, but domestic producers had to compete with imports and to cope with urban jobs that offered higher wages and drove up the price of domestic, agricultural labor. Immigrants filled some of the void.

As it was between 1936 and 1948, Venezuela had an official policy of selective immigration designed to meet labor shortages. With the expansion of the state bureaucracy and services made possible by export earnings, it might seem that prospects for success should have been bright. However, having the resources for an effective bureaucracy and actually creating one are not the same.

Progress was slow. For example, despite authorization for providing services for immigrants, no employment office was created throughout this period. The Plaza Bolívar in Caracas became an open air market for immigrant labor. The 1936 "Law of Immigration and Colonization" specifically mentioned artisans, industrial workers, and mechanics as desirable immigrants, but the agency cre-

Table 6.2.
Exports of Petroleum and Agricultural Products

Year	Total	Petroleum	Agriculture
1925-30	551,526	395,131	151,953
1930-35	650,831	573,754	67,404
1935-40	861,976	790,795	55,306
1940-45	988,250	917,900	46,900
1945-50	2,442,820	2,355,720	85,844
1950-55	4,768,390	4,583,990	168,019
1955-60	7,800,140	7,285,580	192,947

Source: Compiled by Sergio Aranda B. [1977: 166].

Table 6.3
Economically Active Population (thousands of persons)

	1941	1950	1961	1971
Agriculture	635	704.7	721.2	655
Petroleum, mining	23.5	49.3	45.6	55
Manufacturing	164.8	167.7	246.9	573
Services	377.2	586.5	947.3	1646
Construction	39.6	91.1	81.5	186
Total	1240.1	1599.3	2042.5	3115

Source: Compiled by Sergio Aranda B. [1985: 229]

ated to implement the Act, the Technical Institute for Immigration and Colonization (ITIC), dedicated itself to the formation of agricultural colonies. The Act empowered the state to take active measures (ranging from subsidies to services) to attract immigrants, and it prohibited the establishment of any fees for entering the country. It authorized the government to provide for training and assistance in relocating, and to provide employment offices and legal assistance to immigrants in disputes they might have with exploitative employers (Berglund and Hernández; 1985:93–136).

During the *trienio*, AD developed ambitious plans to use the ITIC to meet the original goals, but in 1949 the dictatorship took control of immigration affairs from the ITIC and placed it in the hands of the National Agrarian Institute (IAN). On the one hand this represented a return to the policy of populating the interior, but the effective policy of the dictatorship was to allow anyone to enter the country under the provisions of the 1937 Aliens Act. This legislation was never intended to deal with immigration; it contained no provisions for training or locating the newcomers, nor were any implemented. Its original purpose was to serve as nothing more than a control law to limit and define the rights of aliens. Nonetheless, the vast majority of immigrants who entered the country legally came under its provisions. The seminal study by Berglund and Hernández (1985:35–37) shows that 90 percent of the professionals, semiprofessionals, and technicians who emigrated to Venezuela between 1966 and 1975 entered under provisions of the Alien Act, not the Immigration Law.

For this reason, Berglund and Hernández identify the Office for the Identification and Regulation of Foreigners (DIEX) as the most important policy making agency in the area of immigration even though DIEX is not responsible for administering immigration laws. DIEX regulations in 1954 and 1955 illustrate that the Venezuelan immigration door was not only open but flapping during the dictatorship. For Italy, Portugal, Spain, the United States, Canada, and Lebanon, to receive a visa to enter Venezuela as a transient one only had to be younger than 35, have no criminal record, and have a certificate of good health. When the transitional government of 1958 wanted to slam the door, it issued a circular through the Ministry that limited entry to family members of foreigners already in the country.

Most Venezuelan intellectuals saw selective immigration as necessary for development, and even when studies contradicted their views they clung tenaciously to the idea. For example, a major study informed the *trienio* government that Europeans would not be easily induced to settle in the countryside. The authors advised that if health and education were improved, immigration would not be necessary (cited in Berglund-Thompson, 1980:46). In fact, later studies of a model colonization scheme at Turen (in the southwest) showed that it had cost the government $5,000 for every foreign family, but only $3,000 for every Venezuelan family located in the colony (Kritz, 1975:520).

But the leading *adecos* were not disposed to listen. An element of positivism remained in the notion that, especially in agriculture, immigrants would provide the necessary example to shake traditional Venezuelan peasants and landlords out of their indolence. President Romulo Gallegos had represented in his novels the need to civilize the barbarian interior. Rómulo Betancourt had been greatly influenced by the ideas of the leading Venezuelan economist, Alberto Adriani, whom he served as secretary in 1936 while Adriani was a member of the cabinet of López Contreras. Adriani had estimated that every immigrant would save Venezuela 10,000 bolivars (Berglund-Thompson, 1980:26–27). Neither Betancourt nor Gallegos indulged in the kind of national denigration that characterized nineteenth century positivism in Venezuela, and each spoke out against the racist content of immigration laws and policies. But each also believed that immigration was required not merely to fill labor shortages, but diffuse modern values into Venezuelan culture.

Public attitudes toward immigration were mixed. Venezuela's first scientific public opinion poll focused on this topic in 1948. A sample drawn from the ten largest cities were asked their opinions. More than three quarters of the respondents answered "yes" to the questions, "Should immigration be encouraged?" and "Will your economic position improve because of immigration?" Only 30 percent said they thought that Venezuelans were "better workers" than foreigners, with 26.1 percent seeing them as "the same", and a plurality of 42.5 percent answering "no". But a plurality opposed liberalizing naturalization procedures or permitting immigration on a large scale. This seems to indicate that public opinion was prepared for a selective immigration policy, not the waves that were to arrive over the next ten years (cited in Berglund-Thompson, 1980:36–37).

There have been several excellent studies of the pattern of immigration to Venezuela (Kritz, 1975; Berglund-Thompson, 1980; Berglund and Hernández, 1985; Sassen-Koob, 1979). It would be a daunting task to summarize them in just a few paragraphs, so we will only examine the broadest patterns. This means that we must pass lightly over some aspects less relevant to our central concern: the interaction between policy and trends. It is worth noting, however, that some of the most powerful entrepreneurial families (Boulton, Cisneros, Newmann, Volmerrs) are originally of immigrant stock. Much of the traditional elite was killed off in the murderous civil wars of the nineteenth century; it was almost inevitable that a high proportion of Venezuela's modern elite would arise from immigrants. Smaller waves of immigration tied to short-term political factors have also left a mark, obscured by the larger pattern. Many followers of the Cuban dictator Batista fled from Cuba to Venezuela after the 1959 Revolution; a few became key parts of the security apparatus that carried out counter-insurgency tasks during the 1960s.

The best indication of the demographic impact of legal immigration (covering the minority who entered as immigrants and those who entered under the Aliens Act and later legalized their status) is the census data. This seems to indicate that through 1971 immigration was marked by a decidedly European character, as Table 6.4 indicates. The data indicate that from 1936 to 1961, the proportion

Table 6.4.
Distribution of the Foreign-Born Population, by Ethnic Origin, 1936–1971 (in percentages)

Region and Country	1971	1961	1950	1941	1936
N (000's)	599	526	207	50	47
Americas	39.9	26.0	33.4	47.4	49.0
Colombia	30.0	18.1	21.8	34.0	41.3
Cuba	1.7	1.4	1.9	2.4	0.8
U.S.	1.9	2.4	5.6	7.2	4.7
Other	6.3	4.1	4.1	3.8	2.2
Europe	55.8	70.2	64.9	49.9	48.6
Spain	24.5	31.4	18.3	13.9	12.2
Italy	14.6	23.0	21.3	6.3	5.6
Portugal	11.4	8.0	5.3	1.3	0.1
Other	5.3	7.8	20.0	48.4	30.7
Other	1.7	3.8	1.7	2.7	2.4

Source: Adapted from Mary Kritz (1975: 523). Originally from Venezuelan censuses.

of European immigrants was steadily rising. However, the 1971 census shows a shift back toward the Americas, particularly Colombia. In fact, by 1971 the overall immigration pattern may have already shifted away from Europe because by this time illegal Colombian immigration had become an issue, with estimates of their number ranging from 400,000 to 500,000. Nonetheless, the data do show that Venezuela was attracting a high number of European immigrants throughout the period. Was this European influx a result of policies pointed toward that goal, or was this the result of the increasing attractiveness of Venezuela to Southern Europeans, themselves living in a semi-peripheral part of the global economy?

There are several indications that the immigration flow was not obeying policy so much as larger economic forces. None of the goals of immigration —population of the interior, transference of skills to the rural population, nor improvement of opportunities for native Venezuelans—seems to have been furthered by immigration. None of the three censuses of 1950, 1961, or 1971 found more than 12.6 percent of the foreign-born population living in primarily agricultural regions, where 35–45 percent of Venezuelans lived. Each census found more than half of all immigrants in the Caracas area. Three quarters of all Spanish and Portuguese immigrants settled in Caracas. In 1961, foreign-born workers were 33.8 percent of the labor force in Caracas. Colombians were most likely to be found in western states closer to their native country. Legal and illegal Colombians alike were more likely to be replacing Venezuelans in low-paying agricultural occupations rather than contributing new entrepreneurial or technical talent (Kritz, 1975:525–528).

An examination of the occupational distribution of foreigners and natives in the workforce in 1961 indicates the role that immigrants were playing. Although less than 5 percent of foreign workers were managers, they occupied more than half of all managerial positions in the workforce. (Berglund-Thompson, 1980:99). Overall, 35.5 percent of male foreign workers held white collar jobs, compared with just 18.5 percent of Venezuelan males. Immigrants were also found in blue collar occupations in higher proportions. Fewer than a quarter of immigrant workers were in agriculture—about a tenth of those from Spain and Italy. In contrast, 43.4 percent of Venezuelans in the workforce held farm jobs. Among female workers, the foreign-born and domestic workforces matched more closely, with approximately 23 percent of each found in domestic work, and only a slight difference in the percent found among office workers. Venezuelan women were more likely to be restaurant workers, while foreign-born women were more likely to find jobs as tailors (Kritz, 1975:533–536).

This period corresponds to a period of massive migration among native Venezuelans as well. The 1961 census found that 1,500,000 Venezuelans were not living in the state of their birth. A survey of immigrants based on a sample drawn from 1961 indicated that the educational level of Immigrants was considerably higher than both migrating and non-migrating Venezuelans. The unemployment rate among immigrants was always nearly half of the rate among

Venezuelan workers (Berglund-Thompson, 1980:97, 121; Kritz, 1975). It appears that immigration was neither transforming agriculture so that rural life would improve for peasants, nor was it increasing opportunities in the cities for peasants who migrated. It suggests that immigration has allowed Venezuela's economy to grow despite a failure by Venezuelan elites to adequately prepare its own domestic labor force to contribute to this growth.

Most students of Venezuelan immigration have reached the same conclusion. Kritz (1975) finds that immigrants tended to compete with Venezuelans for economic opportunities created by economic expansion. Instead of diffusing the benefits of their higher educational level, Europeans used it principally to replace Venezuelans in commercial enterprise, skilled occupations, professional services, and managerial positions. Colombians and other Latin American immigrants were not as educated as the Europeans, but had more formal schooling than Venezuelans migrating from the countryside and competed with the latter for jobs in construction and manufacturing, sectors in which migrants have traditionally found early employment. Foreigners held more than a quarter of all construction jobs in 1961; and government investigators found that 30 percent of 14,000 firms visited were in violation of the provision of the Venezuelan law requiring that no more than 25 percent of the labor force in an establishment be foreign-born—a fact that is magnified by the fact that most commercial and manufacturing establishments employed less than 100 workers, the minimum threshold before the law becomes applicable (Kritz, 1983:541).

Berglund draws similar conclusions based on her analysis of the 1961 pattern (see Table 6.5):

If the Venezuelan government was indeed trying to up-grade the labor force by means of immigration, it would seem given the predominence of certain occupations then they had not accomplished their goal. Yet . . . the impact of immigration depends in great part on the receiving society. Although most immigrants were not skilled workers, they did on the average have more years of formal education than the Venezuelans. In addition, foreigners had the reputation for being responsible, hard workers. To quote one commentator: "Foreigners know their labor and Venezuelans know their labor law." (Berglund-Thompson, 1980:96–97).

Venezuelan immigration policy during this entire period 1936–1973 was guided by the developmentalist assumptions of the generation of political elites that ruled the country. Their goal was the development of a fully-integrated, autonomous economy, but the Venezuelan bourgeoisie was not prepared to make a radical departure from capitalism in order to develop the economy in the interest of the poor majority. A good example was the refusal of Venezuela to abandon the commercial treaty, signed in 1939 when the country had virtually no industrial infrastructure, which conceded preferential tariff rates to the United States for guaranteed entry of Venezuelan exports. The combination of this treaty and an overvalued bolivar (due to the high price of oil) ensured that commercial activity

Table 6.5.
Foreign-Born Participation in the Work Force: 1961 Census

Economic Activity	Total Workforce	Total Foreign Foreign	% Foreign of Total	% of Foreign Workforce
Agriculture	759,785	39,617	5.2	11.7
Petroleum, Mining	53,540	7,300	13.6	2.1
Artisan, Manufacturing	287,344	77,367	26.9	22.8
Construction	131,001	35,378	27.0	10.4
Utilities	23,326	2,341	10.0	.7
Commerce, Finance	297,458	72,465	24.3	21.3
Transport, Communicatns	117,648	16,629	14.1	4.9
Services	548,298	77,201	14.1	22.7
Not specified	132,891	10,449	7.9	3.1
First time looking for work	21,140	850	4.0	.3

Source: Berglund-Thompson (1980: 96), Table 11. Originally from 1961 census.

and services would be the preeminent areas of economic opportunity for natives and immigrants alike. No immigration law could compensate for the distorted form of economic growth produced by dependency; no immigration law could hold back the wave of immigrants coming to take advantage of that growth.

This is not to say that immigrants made no important contributions. In rural areas and smaller towns, Europeans and some Latin Americans provided professional skills and services—barbers, bakers, mechanics, retail merchants, accountants—that helped improve the quality of life. But most Europeans and more educated immigrants settled in Caracas and simply magnified a problem afflicting so much of Latin America, the concentration of population and services in the capital city. Their chic restaurants and shops dominate the main shopping and tourist district, Chacaito and Sabana Grande, today (Berglund–Thompson, 1980:127–128).

Had little else changed, it is likely that Venezuela's immigration experience would have come to an unexceptional end sometime after 1973. In fact, in 1973 Venezuela was poised on the brink of a spectacular economic roller coaster that would illustrate how dynamic demographic exchange in the periphery can be.

IMMIGRATION POLICY DURING BOOM AND BUST

Between 1972 and 1974 state revenues in Venezuela increased by 250 percent as a result of the rise in oil prices emanating from the crisis in the Mideast. From 1974 to 1976, economic investment doubled, and then kept rising until it reached a plateau in 1978; state investments tripled. Manufacturing grew at a rate of 11.2 percent in 1974 and 13.2 percent in 1975. Employment increased steadily, leaving an average annual unemployment rate of only 5.5 percent. By the late 1970s; one million workers were added to an original workforce of 3.7 million.

Then, from 1978 to 1983, the economy actually contracted, showing a negative (−4.8 percent) growth rate for the GNP, a rise in official unemployment to 14 percent, and a steady decrease in real wages. While oil prices were plunging, the government faced a $32.3 billion debt, the product of vigorous borrowing during the boom and the continued dependence on imports to satisfy domestic demand. In 1983, the government decided to allow the bolivar to fluctuate against the dollar, and it quickly rose from an exchange rate of 4.3 bolivars to the dollar to 13. By 1987, it had more than doubled again. In 1986 the economy recovered somewhat, but financial reserves had nearly been exhausted, the debt had actually grown slightly larger, and continued economic growth in 1987 was unlikely.

During the first part of this period Venezuela acted as a pole of attraction for immigration. From 596,455 foreign-born counted in the 1971 census, the count rose to 1,039,106 in 1981, according to preliminary published results. The size of the European-born population showed a slight decline from 1971 (from 329,850 to 323,192), and there was a massive increase in the number of foreign-born workers who originated from Latin America. Whereas Latins constituted a minority of foreign-born residents counted in the 1971 census, in 1981 they constituted over 65 percent of resident foreigners. Among the 653,850 Latin Americans counted, 491,463 originated from Colombia.

Unlike the case in 1961 and 1971, most of the Latin American immigrants were settling in the Caracas areas and in the heavily populated and industrialized North Central area. A majority (59 percent) of the Colombians, unlike most other immigrant groups, were women. Like females among their illegal counterparts, they were absorbed more by domestic service (41 percent) than any other area of the economy. Given the shift in their geographic location, it is not surprising that Colombians are over-represented in the industrial workforce. Whereas only 28.5 percent of Venezuelan workers were found in this category, it accounted for 38 percent of Colombians. They tend to be more highly educated than their Venezuelan counterparts, though less so than European immigrants. Whereas 25 percent of those who entered the country in the 1980s came as farmers, only 18 percent of those who came in the 1970s declared farming as their occupation (Pellegrino, 1985:399–400, 406).

It was the hope of Venezuelan policymakers that immigration would supply much of the labor necessary to sow the oil bonanza and nurture sustained economic growth once it ended. Carlos Andrés Pérez (CAP) was elected President in December 1973, and when the bonanza arrived, CAP responded with his ambitious five-year development plan, calling for an increasingly technologically diversified economy with 900,000 new jobs. The education and training budget was tripled, but planners recognized that it could not supply the need for so vast a transformation as envisioned in the plan and that at least 273,000 additional workers would have to be added. In 1975, CAP created a Selective Immigration Program and signed onto the Inter-governmental Committee for European Migration in 1976 to recruit new workers—following a precedent pursued once before by a Venezuelan government in 1948. He later created a National Human Resources Council, giving it final say over how many and which foreign workers would be allowed to enter the labor market (Grace-Plaza, 1979:53–54).

As the figures reviewed above indicate, most of this effort came to naught. Business groups blamed government red tape for the lack of European immigration, and it probably did not help that Venezuela had (and continues to have) among the most difficult naturalization laws (making prospects of citizenship dimmer for potential immigrants) and among the least favorable set of legal rights for resident aliens in all of Latin America. But the problem was deeper. By 1979, Venezuelan consulates in Colombia were granting an average of 5,000 tourist visas monthly to Colombians—and few were really interested in the "natural wonders" of their neighbor (Grace-Plaza, 1979).

Approximately one third of male immigrants found work in the manufacturing sector, but there is little indication that they contributed disproportionately to skilled occupations. A study of the educational level of immigrants from all the major countries of origin shows that neither the European nor Latin American immigrants had in the majority completed secondary school, and fewer than half of all immigrants brought with them any secondary education at all. Educational levels were slightly above Venezuelan levels, but hardly enough to make a difference. Berglund and Hernández fear that Venezuela may experience what a Canadian study revealed: that the workforce became less, not more, skilled as a result of immigration (Berglund and Hernández, 1985:31).

In addition to legal immigration (again, mostly entering under the 1937 Aliens Act), Venezuela experienced a phenomenon familiar to the United States: massive illegal immigration. As the economy cooled off in 1979 and entered an actual decline after 1981, Venezuelan policymakers began to pay more attention to the phenomenon, and it emerged as a significant social issue. The Christian Democratic government, which had to cope with the consequences of the economic downturn, decided to take advantage of a provision of the Andean Pact, an international agreement on trade and economics signed by the prior AD administration. The government used a provision on movement of labor to decree in May 1980 an amnesty for illegal aliens who registered. Hence an important and potentially controversial policy initiative to deal with illegal immigration was implemented without congressional approval.

In the following four month period, 266,795 immigrants over the age of eight registered—probably indicative of approximately 300,000 total immigrants. In the subsequent crackdown, no more than 200 illegal aliens were rounded up and deported. Some Venezuelan observers have interpreted these numbers as evidence that the illegal immigration problem has been exaggerated by politicians eager to court the labor vote (Serbin, 1982; Roy, 1983). Indeed, there were alarmists claiming that as many as 2 million illegal Colombian aliens were living in Venezuela. The amnesty certainly puts such claims to rest, but it would be wrong to take it as an accurate count of illegal immigrants. DIEX reported 163,462 deportations during the period 1970–1980 alone, indicative of a much larger population of *indocumentados* than that which registered or was caught. Also, surveys of those who registered show much lower proportions of illegals in agriculture and manufacturing than other studies of indocumentados have found, an indication that many of the poorest and least-educated did not register. The best estimates are that there were somewhere in the neighborhood of 700,000–900,000 illegal aliens before the registration and before the economic downturn in 1980 (Pellegrina, 1984, 1985; Sassen-Koob, 1979; Berglund and Hernández 1985; Murillo-Castaño, 1984).

With the economic crisis, it is probably safe to assume that many legal and illegal immigrants have left Venezuela, but no extensive studies indicating trends since 1980 have been published. Official data on entries and exits show a net emigration of 130,000 persons between 1980 and 1983 (España, 1986:401–403), but this takes into account only those who have left documentation upon their departure.

Obviously the pattern of Venezuelan immigration in this latest period has defied government policy and obeyed the larger forces at work in the world economy. It is worth recalling that during much of the period of boom in

Venezuela, the rest of the continent was experiencing recession, caused in part by the same phenomenon that was super-heating the Venezuelan economy—rising oil prices. Hence, unlike the immigration problem perplexing Mexico and the United States, the flow of migrants out of Colombia was not related to an enduring, entrenched gap between the level of development of neighboring economies. Colombia's demographic profile resembles Venezuela's in many respects, including age distribution and physical quality of life (Diaz Briquets, 1983:64). Before the oil boom, most Colombian emigration, as we noted earlier, was more in the nature of migration along the border region.

The oil boom wrenched the Venezuelan economy toward the dynamic center of the global economy and temporarily distorted the regional equilibrium. The demand for labor and the overvalued Venezuelan bolivar manifest the distortions. In 1978, one Colombian study (although based on a very small sample) documented the enormous gap between the real wages for similar occupations in the two countries (see Table 6.6). Salesmen and service workers in Venezuela could expect to earn four times what they could gain in Colombia; skilled workers, construction workers, and agricultural workers could make well over double, mechanics well over triple. Not without reason, the Colombian government began to seek ways of preventing a drain on its own skilled labor force, and it also had to cope with more than 100,000 deportees dropped on its border by DIEX during the 1970s.

Today Venezuela's most serious problem is not how to attract immigration, but how to deal with the large numbers of legal and illegal immigrants in the country, who now compete with Venezuelans in an era of economic contraction. One does not detect an atmosphere of xenophobia in the country today, yet the immigration problem, particularly that aspect concerning indocumentados, remains. Not surprisingly, employers are least anxious about the presence of foreign workers. To them, the Venezuelan worker has become lazy, overpaid, and overprotected. In 1981, during a bitter general strike in the textile industry, union leaders accused employers of violating the 25 percent limitation on employment of foreign-born workers. This industry is situated in the North Central region, which was the destination of large numbers of Colombian migrants in the 1970s, including a large group who were driven by economic crisis out of the Medellín area where textiles is the crucial industry. There are no studies confirming that such migrants were a factor in the labor dispute, but it certainly is plausible.

The Venezuelan working class is not the only sector that has an interest in regulating the flow of immigrant labor. In 1976, about one fourth of all immigrants in Caracas were employed in commerce—and anyone who has visited the country will testify that there was an enormous contraband trade, another consequence of the overvalued bolivar. An estimated 20 percent of foreign workers are "self-employed" (España, 1986:402). The hundreds of thousands of shops, stalls, and eateries in Caracas operate on a low volume and high profit margin, and pressure from contraband goods sold by street vendors has always been perceived by them as a constant threat. When the economic crisis hit and squeezed

Table 6.6.

Average Monthly Income of 400 Colombian Migrants to Venezuela by Occupation in Colombia before Migrating and in Venezuela in 1978 (U.S. dollars)

Occupation	Earnings in Colombia	Earnings in Venezuela
Skilled Workers	130	357
Construction Workers	121	332
Mechanics, Technicians	119	395
Office Workers	101	419
Salesmen	88	364
Service Workers	79	170
Agricultural Workers	72	347
Total	99	

Source: From Diaz Briquets (1983: 66), Table 3.

them further, native and established foreign merchants pressured municipal authorities to crack down on street vendors, who are disproportionately of foreign origin. (Ironically, as the bolivar has declined in value in spectacular fashion, it is Colombian entrepreneurs who face competition from immigrant smugglers.) In contrast, the Venezuelan labor movement has been temperate in its demands, placing the emphasis on enforcement of the legal limitations in hiring of foreign-born workers rather than urging mass round-ups and deportations.

The economic crisis has especially severe consequences for female immigrants, who tend to be less well educated and powerless in their employment as domestic servants. Clusters of zinc and cardboard shanties dot the mountainsides walling the Caracas valley, and tens of thousands of Colombian women and their families eke out a bare existence. Unlike men, who often migrated to earn money either for savings or to send back to their families at home, these women endured great hardships and dangers to enter the country, and return is less of an option (Pinto, 1981).

Recently immigrants have been scapegoated by no less than President Jaime Lusinchi who accused Colombians of fomenting street rioting in Caracas and Mérida in 1987. More restrained concerns have been raised by students of immigration who have pointed out that large waves of immigrants may distort the national culture. Berglund and Hernández warn that the Andean Pact, to which Venezuela is a signatory, could force Venezuela into a more liberal immigration policy than is suitable for its labor market (Berglund and Hernández, 1985:28–40, 134–136). A few religious activists and left political activists have suggested that enhancing the ability of non-citizens to organize themselves into unions and economic associations might deter Venezuelan employers from substituting immigrants for Venezuelans in the workforce. The recent surge of civil unrest in Colombia has raised the prospect of a massive influx of political refugees that will present new challenges to policy makers and overwhelm a labor market already marked by high unemployment and the lowest minimum wage in South America.

The Venezuelan flash flood of immigration has precedent in the experience of Latin America's other great experiment in immigration, Argentina. The great tide of Latin American and European immigrants who came to that country at the turn of the century were also attracted by a booming economy based on export of a primary good (beef), and when the waters receded it was also in the context of an economic crisis, provoked by a decline in the price of the export and by a huge foreign debt (Felix, 1987:11–12). As in Venezuela, government planners had hoped to attract immigrants to populate the interior, but socially and geographically the interior proved repulsive, and most immigrants ended up concentrated in the central, capital city, Buenos Aires.

During the anarchy and underdevelopment of nineteenth century Venezuela, a nation on the outer periphery of the world system, elites viewed immigration as one of the keys to moral, economic, and political rejuvenation, and the result was a national inferiority complex that has marked Venezuelan policy to this day. Even as Venezuela assumed a relatively privileged position in the world economic order and gained greater resources for implementing and administering policies, immigration was viewed more than anything else as a way of compensating for national failings. When the immigration flow finally came, it overwhelmed the capacity of a state that had enormous financial resources at its disposal. When the wave receded it had little to do with state policy and more to do with economic trends external to its own control.

In some respects, the Venezuelan experience with immigration corresponds to policy dilemmas in the core nations of the world economy. Xenophobia, competition between foreign and native labor, and political manipulation of the immigration issue are apparently not limited to the immigration experience of core nations. But there are also differences. If Venezuela's experience is any guide, immigration in the periphery is usually set in the context of a quest for development. This means more than just substituting immigrants for shortages in the domestic labor supply, it means using immigration policy to increase the opportunities for the native population.

Perhaps the similarities and differences are clearest in regard to undocumented immigration. On the one hand, the gap between Venezuela and its neighbors was pronounced enough to produce an immigration problem that North Americans can readily understand. However, if what the United States confronts in Mexican immigration is a steady flow of immigrants progressively rising above flood stage, what Venezuela experienced was more like a flash flood, followed by slowly retreating waters. The Venezuelan experience adds to the evidence that immigration in the modern world obeys more the forces of the capitalist world economic system than it does the policies of individual states.

Bibliography

Abramov, S.Z. "The Danger of the Religious Split in Jewry," *Midstream* 12, no. 8 (October 1966):3–13.

Abrams, Elliot, and Franklin S. Abrams. "Immigration Policy—Who Gets in and Why?" *Public Interest* 38 (1975):3–29.

"Abuse of Immigration Law Feared by Some Hispanic Groups," *New York Times*, March 1, 1987, p. 31.

"A Flood to a Trickle," *The Economist*, March 21, 1987, p.22–27.

"Aids Test Required for Immigrants Here," *Cumberland Times/News*, Saturday, August 29, 1987, P. 2.

Akzin, Benjamin, "Problems of Constitutional and Administrative Law," in *International Lawyers Convention in Israel, 1958*, Jerusalem: Post Press, 1959.

———, "Who is a Jew?: A Hard Case," *Israel Law Review* (1970):259–63.

"Aliens Become More Diverse Over Decades," *Washington Post*, Sunday, June 10, 1984; pp. A1,16.

"Aliens Facing $185 Fee on Amnesty," *New York Times*, March 16, 1987; p. 15.

"Alien Legalization Project Seeks Volunteer Helpers," *Maryland Church News*, June 1987; pp. 1, 8.

"Alien Smuggling Ring Cracked in San Diego," *Washington Post*, Sunday, September 28, 1987; p. A–18.

Allen, Leslie. *Liberty: The Statue and the American Dream*, New York: Statue of Liberty– Ellis Island Foundation, National Geographic Society, 1985.

Almond, Gabriel, and Sidney Verba, *The Civic Culture*, Princeton: Princeton University Press, 1963.

Alon, M. (ed.), *The Principles of Jewish Law*, Jerusalem: Encyclopedia Judaica, 1975.

Alter, Robert, "The Shalit Case," *Commentary* 50, No. 1 (July 1970): 55–61.

"Amnesty Program Means Phony Document Business Will Flourish," *Cumberland Sunday Times*, Sunday, November 2, 1986; p.A–16.

"Amnesty Sending Fearful Aliens for Help, Only Some of It Useful," *New York Times,* January 15, 1987; pp. B–1, 7.

Appleyard, R. T. *British Emigration to Australia,* Canberra: Australian National University, 1964.

"A Push to Delay Deportation of Aliens," *Washington Post,* July 26, 1987; p. 4.

Aranda, B. Sergio, *La Economia Venezolana,* Venezuela: Editorial Pomaire, 1977, 1985.

"A Refugee's Despair," *Newsweek,* November 17, 1986; p. 12.

Arocha, Zita, "Illegals Fill Day Care Jobs," *Washington Post,* August 16, 1987; pp. A–1, 16.

———, "Immigration Law Backer Declares Success Amid Others' Doubts," *Washington Post,* November 6, 1987; p. A–12.

"Asian Indians Operating Many U.S. Hotels, Motels," *Cumberland Times/News,* Thursday, September 12, 1985; p. 36.

Australian Ethnic Affairs Council, *Australia as a Multi-cultural Society: Submission to the Australian Population and Immigration Council on the Green Paper, "Immigration Policies and Australia's Population"* Canberra: *Australian Government Publishing Service,* 1977.

Australian Population and Immigration Council, *Immigration Policies and Australia's Population: A Green Paper,* Canberra: Australian Government Publishing Service, 1976.

———, *A Decade of Migrant Settlement: A Report on the 1973 Immigration Survey* Canberra: Australian Government Publishing Service,1976.

Bach, Robert L. "Mexican Immigration and the American State," *International Migration Review* 12 (Winter 1978):536–58.

Baker, Kendall, Russell Dalton, and Kai Hildenbrandt. *Germany Transformed: Political Culture and the New Politics,* Cambridge: Harvard University Press, 1981.

Bar-Ya' acob, M. *Dual Nationality.* London: *Stevens,* 1961.

Beals, Carleton. *Brass Knuckle Crusade.* New York: Hasting House, 1960.

Beetham, D. *Transported Turbans: A Comparative Study of Local Politics,* Oxford: Oxford University Press, 1970.

Ben-Gurion, D. "Letters," *Congressional Weekly* 26, no. 1 (January 5, 1959).

Ben-Moshe, Zvi. "Reactions to the Shalit Case," *Congressional Bi-Weekly* 37, no. 4 (March 6, 1970):4–5.

Bennett, Douglas C. "The Enforcement of Immigration Policy and the Meaning of Citizenship," Paper Delivered at the 1985 Annual Meeting of the APSA, New Orleans, August 29, 1985.

Bennett, Marion T. *American Immigration Policies: A History,* Washington, D.C.: Public Affairs Press, 1963.

Benyon, J. "Spiral of Decline: Race and Policy," in Z. Layton-Henry and P. Rich (eds.), *Race, Government and Politics in Britain.* London: Macmillan, 1986.

Berglund-Thompson, Susan. "Las Bases Sociales y Economicas de las Leyes de Inmigracion Veneozolanas, 1831–1935," *Boletin de la Academia Nacional de la Historia* 65 (260, 1982):951–962.

———. The "Musiues" in Venezuela: Emigration Goals and Reality 1936–1961. Dissertation, University of Massachusetts, 1980.

———, and Humerto Hernandez Caliman, *Los de Afuera: un Estudio Analitico del Proceso Migratorio en Venezuela,* 1936–1985. Caracas: Central de Estudios de Pastoral y Assistencia Migratoria (Cepam), 1985.

Bernard, William S. (ed.), *Immigration Policy: A Reappraisal*. New York: Harper and Bros., 1950.

Bernsen, Sam, "Updating the Immigration Law," In Lydio Tomasi (ed.), *In Defense of the Alien*, New York: Center for Immigration Studies, 1987; pp. 203–208.

"Bilingual Education's Dilemmas Persist," *Washington Post*, Sunday, July 7, 1985; pp. A1, 12–13.

Billard, R. "Ethnic Minorities and the Social Services," in Khan, V. S. (ed.), *Minority Families in Britain*, New York: Macmillan, 1979.

Billington, Ray A. *The Origins of Nativism in the United States, 1800–1844*, New York: Arno Press, 1974.

Birrell, Robert, et al. *Populate or Perish? / The Stresses of Population Growth in Australia*, Sydney: Fontana/Australian Conservation Foundation, 1984.

Blainey, Geoffrey, *All for Australia*, Sydney: Methuen Haynes, 1984.

Blakeney, Michael, *Australia and the Jewish Refugees, 1933–1948*, Sydney: Croom Helm, 1984.

Bleich, David "Black Jews: A Halachic Perspective," *Tradition* 15 (Spring/Summer 1975):59–60.

Bolivar Chollet, Miguel J. "El Comportamiento Demographico en el Subdesarrollo: El Caso Venezolano," in D. F. Maza Zavala, et al. (Eds.), *Venezuela, Crecimiento Sin Desarrollo*. Caracas: Editorial Nuestro Tiempo, 1974; pp. 343–380.

Bonacich, Edna, "Advanced Capitalism and Black/White Relations, A Split-Labor Market Interpretation," *American Sociological Review* 41 (February 1976):34–41.

"Border Patrol Goes on Alert," *Washington Post*, July 26, 1987; p. 21.

Borrie, W. D. "British Immigration to Australia," in A. F. Madden and W. H. Morris-Jones (eds), *Australia and Britain: Studies in a Changing Relationship*, Sydney: Sydney University Press, 1980.

————, *Immigration: Australia's Policies and Prospects*, Sydney, 1949.

————, *Population Trends and Policies: A Study in Australian and World Population*, Sydney: Australian Publishing Company, 1948.

————, et al. *A White Australia: Australia's Population Problem*, Sydney: Australian Publishing Company, 1957.

————, and Ruth Rodgers, *Australian Population Projections, 1960–1975: A Study in Changing Population Structure*, Canberra: Australian National University, 1961.

Bouvier, L. F. *The Impact of Immigration on U.S. Population Size*, Washington,D.C.: Population Reference Bureau, 1981.

Brewster, Lawrence. *The Public Agenda: Issues in American Politics*, 2nd. Ed. New York: St. Martin's Press, 1987; pp. 194–235.

Brito Figueroa, Federico, *Historia Economica y Social de Venezuela*, Tomo III. Caracas: Universidad Central, 1975.

Brown, C. *Black and White Britain*, London: Heinemann, 1984.

Bryce-LaPorte, R. S. (ed.) *A Scrapbook on the New Immigration*, New Brunswick, N.J.:Transaction Books, 1981.

Brye, David L. (ed.), *European Immigration and Ethnicity in the United States and Canada: A Historical Bibliography*. Santa Barbara, Ca.:Clio Press, 1983.

Buber, Martin. *The People and the World*. Jerusalem: The Zionist Library, 1961.

Burton, H. "Historical Survey of Immigration and Immigration Policy," in F. W. Eggleston, et al.(eds.), *The Peopling of Australia*, Melbourne: Macmillan, 1933.

Butler, D. and D. Stokes. *Political Change in Britain*, London: Macmillan, 1969.

Butz, William, et al. "Demographic Challenges in America's Future," R–2911-RC, Santa Monica, Calif.: The Rand Corporation (May 1982), 40 pp.

Calwell, Arthur A. *Immigration: Policy and Progress*, Canberra: Department of Immigration, 1949.

"Canada Moves to Stem Increasing Flow of Aliens Seeking Refuge," *New York Times*, February 21, 1987; p. 30.

Central Office of Information, *Immigration in Britain: Notes on the Regulations and Procedures*, Reference Pamphlet No. 164, HMSO, 1981.

Charlwood, Don. *The Long Farewell*, Ringwood: Allen Lane, 1983.

Cheetham, J. "Immigration," in A. H. Halsey (ed.), *Trends in British Society Since 1900*, London: Macmillan, 1962.

Chigier, M. "The Rabbinical Courts in the State of Israel," *Israel Law Review* 2 (1967):147–81.

Chiswick, Barry R. (ed.). *The Gateway: U.S. Immigration Issues and Policies*. Washington, D.C.: American Enterprise Institute, 1982.

Cohen, H. "The Law of Return," *Gesher* (December 1972):96–117.

———, "The Spirit of Israel Law," *Israel Law Review* 9 (1974):456.

Cohen, S. A., and E. Dan-Jehiya (eds.), *Comparative Jewish Politics*, II. Ramat-Gan: Bar Ilan University Press, 1985.

Cohodas, Nadine, "Immigration Law Brings Anxiety, Ambiguity," *Congressional Quarterly*, (May 2, 1987):838–841.

"Conferees Agree on Vast Revisions in Laws on Aliens," *New York Times*, Wednesday, October 15, 1986: pp. A–1, B–11.

Congressional Quarterly Weekly Report (October 18, 1986):2595–2598, 2612–2613.

Congressional Research Service, The Library of Congress, "Alien Eligibility Requirements for Major Federal Assistance Programs," Washington, D.C.: Library of Congress (January 9, 1981).

———, "Illegal/Undocumented Aliens," Issue Brief No. IB74137, Washington, D.C.: Library of Congress (September 14,1981).

———, "Immigration and Refugee Policy," IP0164. Washington, D.C.: Library of Congress (October 1981).

———, "Immigration and Refugee Policy," MB81244. Washington, D.C.: Library of Congress (September 16, 1981).

———, "The Immigration and Nationality Act–Questions and Answers," Report No. 81–65 EPW. Washington, D.C.: Library of Congress (March 10, 1981).

———, "Refugees in the United States: The Cuban Emigration Crisis," Issue Brief No. IB80063. Washington, D.C.: Library of Congress (August 6, 1981).

———, "U.S. Immigration and Refugee Policy: A Guide to Sources of Information," Research Guide JV6201. Washington, D.C.: Library of Congress (February 26, 1982).

Conradt, David P. *The German Polity*, 2nd Ed. New York: Longman, 1982.

Conservative and Unionist Central Office. *The Conservative Manifesto, 1979*, London, 1979.

———, *The Right Road for Britain*, London, 1949.

Conservative Research Department. *The Campaign Guide, 1987*, London, 1987, pp. 397–401.

Cornelius, Wayne, and Ricardo A. Montoya. *America's New Immigration Law: Origins, Rationales and Potential Consequences*. San Diego, Cal: Center for U.S.–Mexican Studies, UC-SD, 1983.

————, "Illegal Mexican Migration to the United States: Recent Research Findings and Policy Implications," *Congressional Record* (July 13, 1977):H7061–7068.

Craig, Gordon A. *Germany, 1866–1945*, New York: Oxford University Press, 1978.

Craig,Richard B. *The Bracero Program: Interest Groups and Foreign Policy*. Austin: University of Texas Press, 1971.

Crewdson, John. *The Tarnished Door*. New York: Times Books, 1983.

Cross, Harry E., and James Sandos. *Across the Border*. Berkeley: Institute of Government Studies, 1981.

"Closing the Golden Door," *Time*, May 18, 1981, p. 24.

Dahrendorf, Ralf. *Society and Democracy in Germany*. New York: Doubleday, 1967.

Dan-Yehiya, E. *Religion in Israel*. Jerusalem: Information Center, 1975.

Department of Education and Science. *Education for All*, London: HMSO, 1985.

Department of the Environment. *Census Indicators of Urban Deprivation*.London, 1976.

Department of Immigration and Ethnic Affairs, *Committee of Review on Migrant Assessment: Statement of Findings, July, 1981*, Canberra, 1981.

————, *1788–1978: Australia and Immigration: A Review of Migration to Australia*, Canberra: Australian Government Publishing Service, 1978.

"Developments in the Law—Immigration Policy and the Rights of Aliens," *Harvard Law Review* 96 (1983):1268–1465.

Diaz Briquets, Sergio. *International Migration Within Latin America and the Carribbean*, Staten Island, NY: Center for Migration Studies, 1983.

Divine, Robert A. *American Immigration Policy, 1924–1952*, New Haven: Yale University Press; 1957.

Divrei Ha' Knesset (Knesset Records).

Dugan, Michael, and Joseph Szwarc, *There Goes the Neighborhood: Australia's Immigrant Experience*, South Melbourne: Macmillan, 1984.

Dunlevy, James A., and Henry A. Gemery, "Economic Opportunity and the Response of 'Old' and 'New' Migrants to the United States," *Journal of Economic History* 38, no. 4 (1978):901–917.

Edinger, Lewis J. *Politics in Germany*. Boston: Little, Brown, 1977.

"Eight Maryland Companies Cited for Illegal Alien Violations," *Cumberland Times/News*, Monday, November 30, 1987; p. 3.

England, Iztak, "The Relationship Between the Jewish Law and the State," *Molad* (December 1964):702–12.

Esh, Shaul. *Studies in the Holocaust and Contemporary Jewry*. Jerusalem: Institute of Contemporary Jewry, The Hebrew University of Jerusalem, 1973.

España, Luis Pedro. "La Problacion Venezolano," *Revista SIC* 49 (November 1986):401–403.

Esser, Hartmut, and Hermann Korte. "Federal Republic of Germany," in Tomas Hammer (ed.), *European Immigration Policy: A Comparative Perspective*. Cambridge: Cambridge University Press, 1985; pp. 165–205.

Federal Ministry of the Interior. *Record of Policy and Laws Related to Foreigners in the Federal Republic of Germany*, Bonn: Government Printing Office, 1985.

Feldstein, Stanley, and Lawrence Costello (eds.). *The Ordeal of Assimilation: A documentary History of the White Working Class, 1830s to 1970s*. Garden City, NJ: Doubleday, 1974.

Felix, Asher, and Peter Elman (eds.). *Selected Judgments of the Supreme Court of Israel*. Jerusalem: Ministry of Justice, 1971.

Felix, David, "Alternatives Outcomes of the Latin American Debt Crisis," *Latin American Research Review* 22, no. 2 (1987):3–46.

Ferris, Elizabeth (ed.). *Refugees and World Politics.* New York: Praeger Publishers, 1985.

Fragomen, Austin T., Jr. "Alien Employment," *International Migration Review* 13, no. 3 (1979):527–31.

———. "Permanent Resident Status Redefined," *International Migration Review* 9, no. 1 (1975):63–68.

Franklin, Frank G. *The Legislative History of Naturalization in the United States.* New York: Arno Press, 1969.

Freeman, G. P. *Immigrant Labour and Racial Conflict in Industrial Societies,* Princeton: Princeton University Press, 1979.

Frenkel, J. "The Declaration and Its Meaning," *Há Praklit* 5 (1949):99–100.

Gallaway, Lowell E., et al. "The Distribution of the Immigrant Population in the United States: An Economic Analysis," *Explorations in Economic History* 11, no. 3 (1974):213–26.

Garrod, J. A. *The English and Immigration,* Oxford: Oxford University Press, 1971.

Garza, E. (Kika) De La, et al. "Should People Stay Home? Regulation and Free Movement and Rights of Establishment Between the U.S., Canada, and Mexico," *American Society of International Law* 68 (1974):38–58.

Gaugler, Ernst, et al. *Auslaender in deutschen Industriebetrieben.* Cologne: Happ Verlag, 1978.

General Accounting Office "Information on the Enforcement of Laws Regarding Employment of Aliens in Selected Countries." Washington, D.C.: U.S. Government Printing (August 31, 1982).

German Information Center. *Deutsche Nachrichten,* New York (Selected Issues, 1982–1986).

Geschwender, James A. *Racial Stratification in America.* Dubuque, Iowa: William C. Brown, 1978.

Ginossar, S. "Who is a Jew: A Better Law," *Israel Law Review* 5 (1970):264–67.

Glazer, Nathan (ed.), *Clamor at the Gates: The New American Immigration,* San Francisco: ICS Press, 1985.

Gordon, Charles, "The Need to Modernize Our Immigration Laws," *San Diego Law Review* 13 (1975):1–33.

Gordon, Charles E., and Harry N.Rosenfield. *Immigration Law and Procedure.* Revised. New York: Matthew Bender, 1980.

Gouldman, M. D. *Israel Nationality Law.* Jerusalem: The Hebrew University of Jerusalem, Faculty of Law. Institution for Legislative Research and Comparative Law, 1970.

———, "Recent Changes in Israel's Nationality Law," *Israel Law Reviews,* 4 (1969).

Grace-Plaza, Francine, "When Too Much Isn't Enough," *Business Venezuela* (May/June 1979):53–61.

Green, Stephen, "Immigration, Politics," *The Cumberland Times/News,* November 1, 1984, p. 13.

Hammar, Tomas (ed.), *European Immigration Policy: A Comparative Study.* Cambridge, England: Cambridge University Press, 1985).

Harper, Elizabeth J. *Immigration Laws of the United States.* 3rd ed. Indianapolis: Bobbs-Merrill, 1975.

Hart, Jeffrey, "Illegal Immigration," *Cumberland Evening Times,* Monday, July 22, 1985; p. 8.

Harwood, Edwin, "Can Immigration Laws Be Enforced?" *Public Interest* 17 (Summer 1983):105–23.

Hausner, Gideon, "Rights of the Individual in Court," *Israel Law Review* 9 (1974).

Helbush, Terry J. "Aliens, Deportation and the Equal Protection Clause," *Golden State University Law Review* 6 (Fall 1975):23–77.

Hewlitt, S. "Coping With Illegal Aliens," *Foreign Affairs* 60 (1981):358–78.

Higham, John (ed.). *Ethnic Leadership in America.* Baltimore: Johns Hopkins University Press, 1978.

————. *Send These To Me.* New York: Atheneum, 1975.

Hilberg, Raul. *The Destruction of European Jews.* Chicago: Quadrangle Books, 1961.

"Hill Revises Immigration Law," *Washington Post,* Saturday, October 18, 1986, pp. A–1, 7–8.

"Hispanic Americans Haven't Found Their Pot of Gold," *Washington Post National Weekly Edition,* May 28, 1984; pp. 9–10.

Holborn, Hajo, *A History of Modern Germany,* New York: Knopf, 1970.

Holt, Harold E., et al. *Australia and the Migrant: Papers Read at the 19th Summer School of the Australian Institute of Political Science, Canberra, 1953,* Sydney, 1953.

Hoskin, Marilyn, "Integration and Nonintegration of Foreign Workers: Four Theories," *Political Psychology* (1984): 661–685.

"House Approved Compromise Bill on Illegal Aliens," *New York Times,* Thursday, October 16, 1986, p. B–15.

"House Passes Compromise Immigration Bill," *Washington Post,* Thursday, October 16, 1986, p. A–5.

Hugo, Graeme J. *Australia's Changing Population: Trends and Implications.* Melbourne: Oxford University Press, 1986.

Hutchinson, Edward P. *Legislative History of American Immigration Policy, 1798–1965.* New Brunswick, NJ: Rutgers University Press, 1970.

"Illegal Aliens: Invasion Out of Control," *U.S. News and World Report,* January 29, 1979, pp. 38–43.

"Illegal Migration's Fact of Life, Study Concludes," Washington Post, November 15, 1987, p. 18.

Illich, Richard. *The Human Rights of Aliens in Contemporary International Law.* Manchester, England: Manchester University Press, 1984.

"Immigration: Has Our Melting Pot Boiled Over?" *Washington Post,* October 18, 1987, pp. D1, 4.

"Immigration Law Alone Can't Work," *Chicago Sun-Times,* April 10, 1987, p. 42.

"Immigration Reform, Control Act Impacts Farmers in State," *Cumberland Times/News,* September 24, 1987, p. 15.

"Immigration Rules Called Hard on Poor," *Washington Post,* April 9, 1987, p. A–22.

"Immigrants in Washington," *Washington Post Magazine,* April 10, 1983.

"Immigrants: The Changing Face of America," *Time* (Special Edition, July 8, 1985).

"Immigration Bill Approved; Bars Hiring Illegal Aliens, But Gives Millions Amnesty," *New York Times,* Saturday, October 18, 1986, pp. A–1, 8.

"Immigration Bill: How a 'Corpse' Came Back to Life," *New York Times,* Monday, October 13, 1986, p. A–16.

"Immigration Bill Mixed Blessing for Aliens," *Washington Post,* Sunday, June 24, 1984, pp. C 1, 7.

"Immigration Issue Heats Up Again," *Washington Post,* Sunday July 28, 1985, p. A–15.

"Immigration Legislation Voted Down," *Cumberland Times/News,* Saturday, September 14, 1985, p. A–1.

"Immigration Measure Produces Sharp Division in House Hispanic Caucus," *Washington Post,* Sunday, March 18, 1984, p. A–2.

"Immigration Reform: A Mess on the Border," *Newsweek,* December 22, 1986, p. 27.

"Immigration Reform and Control Act," HR 1510, 98th Congress, First Session (the Simpson–Mazzoli Bill). Washington, D.C.: U.S. Government Printing Office, 1983.

Inglehart, Ronald P. *The Silent Revolution,* Princeton: Princeton University Press, 1977.

———, and Paul R. Abramson, "Generational Replacement and the Future of Post-Materialist Values," *Journal of Politics* 49 (1987):231–241.

"INS Tries New Approach," *Washington Post,* August 23, 1987, pp. A–1, 18–19.

"Is Hatred of Japanese Making A Comeback?" *Washington Post,* Sunday, July 7, 1985, pp. B–1, 4.

Izard, Miguel, *Series Estadisticas Para la Historia de Venezuela.* Merida: Universidad de Los Andes, 1970.

Jones, Maldwyn Allen. *American Immigration.* Chicago: University of Chicago Press, 1960.

Katz, J. *Jewish Nationalism: Essay and Studies.* Jerusalem; The Zionist Library, 1979.

Keely, Charles. *U.S. Immigration: A Policy Analysis.* New York: Population Council, 1979).

Keely, Charles, "Illegal Migration," *Scientific American* 246 (March 1982):31–37.

Knickrehm, Kay M. "Congress, the Executive, and Immigration Policy," Paper Delivered at the Annual APSA Meeting, New Orleans, August 29, 1985.

Kraines, Oscar. *The Impossible Dilemma: Who Is a Jew in the State of Israel.* New York: 1976.

Krane, Ronald E. *International Labor Migration in Europe.* New York: Praeger, 1979.

Kritz, Mary, M. *U.S. Immigration and Refugee Policy: Global and Domestic Issues.* Lexington: Lexington Books, 1983.

———, "The Impact of International Migration on Venezuelan Demographic and Social Structure," *International Migration Review* 9 (Winter 1975):513–534.

Kubat, Daniel. "Introduction," in Daniel Kubat (ed.), *The Politics of Migration Policies,* New York: Center for Migration Studies, 1979, pp. xvii–xxx.

LaBonte, Christine, et al. *Arbeitsbedingungen und Arbeitsmotivation auslaendischen Arbeiter,* Berlin: Wissenschaftszentrum, 1975.

Lawrence, D. "Prejudice, Politics and Race," *New Community* 7, No. 1 (1978/79):44–55.

Laws of the State of Israel (L.S.I.).

Layton-Henry, Z. *The Politics of Race in Britain,* London: Allen and Unwin, 1984.

Leibowitz, A. "The Refugee Act of 1980: Problems and Congressional Concerns," *Annals of the American Academy of Political and Social Science* (1983):163–171.

LeMay, Michael. *The Struggle for Influence.* Lanham, MD: University Press of America, 1985.

————. *From Open-Door to Dutch-Door: An Analysis of U.S. Immigration Policy Since 1820*. New York: Praeger Publishers, 1987.

Lewins, Frank H. *The Myth of the Universal Church: Catholic Migrants in Australia*, Canberra; Australian National University, 1978.

Liebman, Charles, S. "The 'Who Is a Jew'? Controversy: Political and Anthropological Perspectives," in S. A. Cohen and E. Don-Yehiye (eds.), *Comparative Jewish Politics*, vol. 2. Ramat-Gan, 1985.

Litvin, Baruch, and Sidney Hoenig. *Jewish Identity: Modern Responses and Opinions on the Registration of Children in Mixed Marriage*. New York: P. Feldheim, 1969.

Livingston, Robert G. (ed.), *West German Political Parties*, Baltimore: American Institute for Contemporary German Studies, 1986.

"Living With a New Law," *Cumberland Times/News*, September 10, 1987, p. 14.

London, H. I. *Non-White Immigration and the "White Australia" Policy*, Sydney: Sydney University Press, 1970.

Louvish, Misha, "Who Is a Jew?" *Israel Digest* 15 (July 21, 1972).

Lungren, Daniel, "Immigration Reform: If Not Now, When?" *Washington Post National Weekly Edition*, September 24, 1984, p. 28.

MacRae, Verena. *Gastarbeiter: Daten, Fakten, Probleme*, Munich: Verlag Beck, 1980.

Madgwick, R. B. *Immigration into Eastern Australia, 1788–1845*, Sydney: Sydney University Press, 1969.

Manning, B. "The Congress, the Executive and Intermestic Affairs: Three Proposals," *Foreign Affairs* 55 (1977):306–324.

Maoz, A. "Who Is a Jew—Much Ado About Nothing," *Ha'Praklit* 3 (1977):271–310.

"Marcos' Filipinos Flock to America," *Cumberland Times/News*, Wednesday, July 17, 1985, p. 7.

Markus, Andrew, and M. C. Ricklefs, *Surrender Australia? . . . Geoffrey Blainey and Australian Immigration*, Sydney: Allen and Unwin, 1985.

————, *Fear and Hatred; Purifying Australia and California, 1850–1891*. Sydney: Hale and Iremonger, 1979.

Marquez, Angel. *Las Ganancias Extraordinarias y la Soberania Nacional*. Caracas: Comision Ideologica de Ruptura, 1977.

"Marriages of Convenience," *Washington Post*, Sunday, October 21, 1984, pp. A–1, 18–19.

"Maryland Growers Assisting with New Immigration Laws," *Cumberland Sunday Times*, July 19, 1987, p. C–12.

Massey, Douglas S. "Understanding Mexican Migration to the United States," *American Journal of Sociology* 92 (May 1987):1372–1403.

McCarthy, Kevin, "Immigration and California: Issues for the 1980s," P–6846. Santa Monica, CA: The Rand Corporation (January 1983),11 pp.

————, and R. Burciaga Valdez, *Current and Future Effects of Mexican Immigration in California*, R–3365-CR. Santa Monica, CA: The Rand Corporation (May 1986), 104 pp.

McClellan, Grant S. (ed.), *Immigrant, Refugees, and U.S. Policy*, New York: H. W. Wilson, 1981.

McKenna, George. *A Guide to the Constitution—That Delicate Balance*. New York: Random House, 1984.

Mehrlaender, Ursula, "Federal Republic of Germany," in Daniel Kubat (ed.), *The Pol-

itics of Migration Policies. New York: Center for Migration Studies, 1980, pp. 145–162.

Mehrlaender, Ursula, et al. *Situation der auslaendischer Arbeitnehmer und ihrer Familienangehorigen in der Bundesrepublik Deutschland*, Bonn: Friedrich-Ebert Stiftung, 1981.

"Melting Pot Boiling from Racial Tension," *Cumberland Evening Times*, Tuesday, January 10, 1984, p. 5.

Mendes-Flohr, Paul, and Jehuda Reinharz (eds.). *The Jews in the Modern World: A Documentary History*, New York: Oxford University Press, 1980.

"Mexico's People Boom," *Cumberland Evening Times*, Friday, October 4, 1985, p. A10.

Miles, R., and A. Phizacklea. *Labour and Racism*. London: Routledge Kegan-Paul, 1980.

Miller, Mark J., and Philip L. Martin. *Administering Guest Worker Programs: Lessons from Europe*. Lexington: Lexington Books, 1982.

Miller, Mark J. *Foreign Workers in Europe: An Emerging Political Force*, New York: Praeger, 1981.

Milne, Frances, and Peter Shergold (eds.), *The Great Immigration Debate*, Sydney: Federation of Ethnic Community Councils of Australia, 1984.

Ministry of Labour. *Report of the Working Party on the Employment in the United Kingdom of Surplus Colonial Labour*, London: Ministry of Labor Papers, 26/226/7503, Public Records Office, 1948.

Montero, Darrel. *Vietnamese Americans*. Boulder, Co: Westview Press, 1979.

Moore, R., and T. Wallace, *Slamming the Door: The Administration Of Immigration Control*, London: Martin Robertson, 1975.

Morris, M. *Immigration—The Beleagured Bureaucracy*. Washington, D.C.: The Brookings Institution, 1985.

"Much Major Legislation Approved in Final Days," *Washington Post*, Sunday, October 19, 1986, p. A–17.

Murillo-Castano, Gabriel. *Migrant Workers in the Americas: A Comparative Study of Migration Between Colombia and Venezuela and Between Mexico and the United States*, San Diego: University of California, Monograph Series 13, 1984.

Murphy, Caryle. "Sanctuary: How Churches Defy Immigration Law," *Washington Post National Weekly Edition*, September 17, 1984, pp. 8–9.

National Population Inquiry, *Population and Australia: A Demographic Analysis and Projection*, Canberra: Australian Government Printing Service, 1975.

"New Law Leaves Immigrants Confused and Fearful," *New York Times*, February 21, 1987, p. 29.

"New Rules for a Human Tide," *The Economist*, January 17, 1987, p. 29.

Nicolinakos, Marios. *Die Internationalisierung des Arbeitsmarktes innerhalb der EG*, Berlin: Wissenschaftzentrum, 1976.

Noelle-Neumann, Elisabeth, (ed.), *The Germans: Public Opinion Polls 1967–1980*, Westport, Conn.: Greenwood Press, 1981.

North, David S. "The Growing Importance of Immigration to Population Policy," *Policy Studies Journal* 6, no. 2 (1977):200–207.

North, David S., and Allen LeBel. *Manpower and Immigration Policies in the United States*. Washington, D.C.: U.S. National Commission for Manpower Policy, Special Report 20, The Commission, 1978.

North, David S. *Immigration and Income Transfer Policies in the United States: An*

Analysis of a Nonrelationship. Washington, D.C.: New Trans Century Foundation, 1980.

———. *Seven Years Later: The Experiences of the 1970 Cohort of Immigrants in the U.S. Labor Market.* Washington, D.C.: New Trans Century Foundation, 1978.

O'Farrell, Patrick, *The Irish in Australia,* Kensington; New South Wales University Press, 1987.

Office of Population Census and Surveys, *Labour Force Survey, 1983 and 1984,* London: HMSO, 1986.

Orback, William. *The American Movement to Aid Soviet Jews,* Amherst, MA: University of Massachusetts Press, 1979.

Palfreeman, A. C. *The Administration of the White Australian Policy,* Melbourne: Melbourne University Press, 1967.

Panich, Catherine. *Sanctuary? Remembering Postwar Immigration.* Sydney: Allen and Unwin, 1988.

Papademetriou, Demetrious G., and Mark J. Miller (eds.), *The Unavoidable Issue,* Philadelphia: Institute for the Study of Human Issues,1984.

"Paper Provides Homeland News to Indian Immigrants," *Cumberland Times/News,* Wednesday, July 17, 1985, p. 7.

Parlin, Bradley W. "Immigrants, Employers, and Exclusion," *Society* 14, no. 6 (1977).

Pellegrino, Adela, "The Recent Evolution of Immigration in Venezuela, " *International Migration,* 23, no. 3 (1985):397–412.

———, "Venezuela: Illegal Immigration from Colombia," *International Migration Review* 18 (Fall 1984):748–766.

Peters, Ronald M., Jr., and Arturo Vega, "The Role of House Democratic Party Leaders on Non-Party Position Legislation with Partisan Consequences: The Immigration Bill," Paper Presented at the 1986 Meetings of the American Political Science Association, August 28–31, 1986, Washington, D.C.

Pinto, A. "Undocumented and Illegally Resident Migrant Women in Venezuela," *International Migration* 19, nos. 1/2 (1981):241–262.

Piore, Michael. *Birds of Passage: Migrant Labor and Industrial Societies.* New York: Cambridge University Press, 1979.

Pitkin, Thomas M. *Keepers of the Gate.* New York: New York University Press, 1975.

"President Endorses Immigration Proposal," *Washington Post,* Friday, October 17, 1986, p. A–4.

Price, Charles A. *The Great White Walls Are Built,* Canberra: Australian National University Press, 1974.

———(ed.), *Australian Immigration: A Bibliography and Digest,* No. 1, Canberra: Department of Demography, Institute of Advanced Studies, Australian National University, 1966.

——— (ed.), *Australian Immigration: A Bibliography and Digest,* No. 2, Canberra: Department of Demography, Institute of Advanced Studies, Australian National University, 1970, 1971.

———(ed.), *Australian Immigration: A Bibliography and Digest, 1979,* No. 4, Canberra: Department of Demography, Institute of Advanced Studies, Australian National University, 1979.

——— (ed.), *Australian Immigration: A Review of the Demographic Effects of Post-War Immigration Upon the Australian Population,* Research Report No. 2, National Population Inquiry, Canberra: Australian Government Publishing Services, 1976.

————, (ed.), *The Demography of Post-War Immigration,* Canberra: Department of Demography, Institute of Advanced Studies, Australian National University, 1976.

————, and Jean I. Martin (eds.), *Australian Immigration: A Bibliography and Digest,1975,* No. 3,Canberra: Department of Demography, Institute of Advanced Studies, Australian National University, 1976.

" 'Productive' Congress Wraps Up," *Washington Post,* Sunday, October 19, 1986, pp. A–1, 16–17.

"Quiz Traps Fraudulent Immigrants," *Cumberland Sunday Times,* November 3, 1985, p. A–3.

Racial disadvantage: Fifth Report of the Home Affairs Committee, 1980/81. House of Commons, 424–1, London: HMSO, 1981.

"Raids Nab High-Pay Aliens, Make Jobs, Outrage Clergy," *Washington Post,* May 2, 1982, p. A–10.

Ratcliffe, P. *Racism and Reaction: A Profile of Handsworth,*London: Routledge Kegan-Paul, 1981.

"Reaction to Immigration Bill is Sharply Split," *New York Times,* Thursday, October 16, 1986, p. B–15.

"Reagan Said to Favor Signing New Aliens Bill," *New York Times,* Friday, October 17, 1986, p. A–2.

Reimann, Horst, and Helg Reimann. "Federal Republic of Germany," in Ronald Krane (ed.), *International Labor Migration in Europe,* New York: Praeger, 1979, pp. 63–87.

Research Institute on Immigration and Ethnic Studies, "Caribbean Immigration to the United States," RIIES Occasional Papers, No. 1. Washington, D.C.: Smithsonian Institution Press, 1983.

————, "Female Immigrants to the U.S." RIIES Occasional Papers, No. 2. Washington, D.C.: Smithsonian Institute Press, 1981.

————, "Pacific Migration to the U.S." RIIES Bibliographic Studies, No. 2. Washington, D.C.: The Smithsonian Institute Press, 1977.

————, "Quantitative Data and Immigration Research," RIIES Research Notes, No. 2. Washington, D.C.: Smithsonian Institute Press, 1979.

————, "Recent Immigration to the United States: The Literature of the Social Sciences," RIIES Bibliographic Studies, No. 1. Washington, D.C.: The Smithsonian Institute Press, 1976.

————, "Return Migration and Remittances: Developing a Caribbean Perspective," RIIES Occasional Papers, No. 3. Washington, D.C.: The Smithsonian Institute Press, 1982.

Rex, J., and S. Tomlinson. *Colonial Immigrants in a British City,* London: Routledge Kegan-Paul, 1979.

"Right Versus Right: Immigration and Refugee Policy in the United States," *Foreign Affairs* (Fall 1980).

Rischin, Moses (ed.), *Immigration and the American Tradition.*Indianapolis: Bobbs-Merrill, 1976.

Rist, Ray C. *Guestworkers in Germany,* New York: Praeger, 1978.

Rivera, Jose A. "Aliens Under the Law: A Legal Perspective," *Employer Relations Law Journal* 3 (Summer 1977):12–37.

Roberts, Hew (ed.), *Australia's Immigration Policy,* Perth: University of Western Australia Press, 1972.

Rose, E. J. B., et al. *Colour and Citizenship*, Oxford: Oxford University Press, 1974.

Rosenblum, Gerald. *Immigrant Workers: Their Impact on American Labor Radicalism*. New York: Basic Books, 1973.

Roucek, Joseph S., and Bernard Eisenber (eds.), *America's Ethnic Politics*. Westport, Conn.: Greenwood Press, 1982.

Royal Commission on Population, Cmnd 7695, London: HSMO, 1949, pp. 226–7.

Rubinstein, Amnon, "Israel Nationality," *Tel Aviv University Studies in Law* 2 (1976).

———, "Law and Religion in Israel," *Israel Law Review* 2 (1967):138–414.

———, *The Constitutional Law in the State of Israel*. Tel Aviv, 1973.

Sassen-Koob, Saskia. "Economic Growth and Immigration in Venezuela," *Economic Growth and Immigration*, 13 (Fall 1979):455–474.

Scanlon, Joseph, and G. Loescher, "Mass Asylum and Human Rights in American Foreign Policy," *Political Science Quarterly* 97 (1982):39–56.

Scarman, Lord. *The Brixton Disorders* April 10th–12th 1981: *Report of an Inquiry*, Cmnd 8427, London: HMSO, 1981.

Schander, Edwin R. "Immigration Law and Practice in the U.S.: A Selective Bibliography," *International Migration Review* 12, no. 1 (1978):117–27.

Schechtman, Joseph B. "Marranos in Israel," *American Zionist* (April 1967):15–16.

Scholem, G. *Explications and Implications: Writings on Jewish Heritage and Renaissance*. Tel-Aviv: Am Oved, 1975.

Schuck, Peter H. "The Transformation of Immigration Law," *Columbia Law Review* 84, no. 1 (January 1984):39–56.

Select Commission on Immigration and Refugee Policy, *Final Report*, Washington, D.C.: U.S. Government Printing Office, 1981.

Serbin, Andres. "The Venezuelan Reception," *Caribbean Review* 11, no. 1 (1982):42–45.

Shaki, S. H. *Who is a Jew in the Land of Israel*, Jerusalem: Mosad H'Rhav Cooke, 1976, pp. 154–69.

Shava, M. Z. *Tel Aviv University Studies in Law*, Tel-Aviv: Tel-Aviv University, Faculty of Law, 1977, pp. 140–53.

Sherington, Geoffrey, *Australia's Immigrants, 1788–1978*, Sydney: Allen and Unwin, 1986.

Shifman, P. "Validity of Non-Orthodox Conversion to Judaism Under the Law of Return," *Mispatim*, 7 (1975).

Shiloh, J. S. "Marriage and Divorce in Israel," *Israel Law Review* 5 (1970):479–98.

Sieghart, Mary Ann, "Border Patrol: A Revolving-Door Policy," *Washington Post National Weekly Edition*, September 17, 1984; p. 7.

"Simpson Tackles Immigration Reform Again," *Minneapolis Star and Tribune*, Monday, June 24, 1985, p. A10.

"Simpson: the 'Anglo' Behind the Immigration Bill," *Washington Post*, Sunday, October 19, 1986, pp. A–8, 9.

Smith, D., and J. Gray. *Police and People in London*, London: Gower, 1985.

———, *Racial Disadvantage in Britain*, New York: Penguin Books, 1977.

Sosa A., Arturo. *La Filosofia Politica del Gomecismo: Estudio del Pensamiento de Laureano Vallenilla Lanz*. Barquisimeto, Venezuela: Centro Gumilla, 1974.

"Spotlight on Immigration Bill's Cost," *Washington Post*, Sunday, October 12, 1986, p. A–4.

Staley, Joseph, "Law Enforcement and the Border," in Richard D. Erb and Stanley R.

Ross (eds.), *United States Relations With Mexico*. Washington, D.C.: American Enterprise Institute, 1981, pp. 106–120.

"State Panel Faults Enforcement of New Federal Immigration Law," *New York Times*, March 16, 1987, p. 15.

Stoller, Alan (ed.), *New Faces: Immigration and Family Life in Australia*, Melbourne, 1966.

Stolzenberg, Ross M. "Occupational Differences Between Hispanics and Non-Hispanics," N–1889-NCEP. Santa Monica CA: The Rand Corporation, July 1982, 107 pp.

Strange, Steven L. "Private Consensual Sexual Conduct and the 'Good Moral Character' Requirement of the Immigration and Nationality Act," *Columbia Journal of Transnational Law* 14, no. 2 (1975):357–81.

Studlar, D. "Policy Voting in Britain: The Coloured Immigration Issue in the 1964, 1966 and 1970 General Elections,"*American Political Science Review* 72 (1978):46–72.

"Study Shows Indochina Refugees Doing Well," *Cumberland Times/News*, Wednesday, July 24, 1985, p. 5.

"Successes Outweigh Failures in First Year of Amnesty Program," *Washington Post*, November 6, 1987, p. A–12.

"Suit Alleges Amnesty Law Puts Many Aliens in Limbo," *New York Times*, February 7, 1987, p. 6.

"Surge in Bogus Papers Predicted in Wake of Change in Alien Law," *New York Times*, Monday, October 20, 1986, pp. A–1, 24.

Talmon, J. L. "Who Is a Jew?" *Encounter* 24 (May 1965).

Tannahill, J. *European Volunteer Workers in Britain*, Manchester: Manchester University Press, 1958.

Tanton, John. *Rethinking Immigration Policy*. FAIR Immigration Paper I. Washington, D.C.: Federation for American Immigration Reform, 1980.

Taylor, Philip. *The Distant Magnet: European Emigration to the U.S.A.* New York: Harper and Row, 1971.

Tedeschi, J. "Who Is a Jew?" *Ha' Praklit* 19 (1963).

Teitelbaum, Michael S. *Latin Migration North: The Problem for U.S. Foreign Policy*. New York: Council on Foreign Relations, 1985.

————. "Rights Versus Rights: Immigration and Refugee Policy in the United States," *Foreign Affairs* 59 (1980):21–59.

Tennassee, Paul Nehru. *Venezuela: Los obreros petroleros y la lucha por la democracia*. Caracas: E.F. I. Publicaciones, 1979.

"The Gatekeepers," *Wall Street Journal*, Thursday, May 9, 1985, pp. 1–2, 7.

"The New Immigrants," *Newsweek*, July 7, 1980, pp. 26–31.

"The State of Israel as a Jewish State Cannot Leave Helpless Refugees to the Mercy of the Sea," *Davar*, January 8, 1979, p. 1.

"Thousands Eligible for Alien Amnesty Across Maryland," *Cumberland Times/News*, Tuesday, November 11, 1986, p. A–10.

"Tortilla Curtain Fails to Stem Tide of Illegal Aliens," *Washington Times*, Monday, May 13, 1985, p. 8a.

Trade Union Congress, *Annual Report*, London, 1955.

"Tragedy Spotlights Immigration Rise," *Milwaukee Journal*, July 12, 1987, p. 1.

"Trying to Reform the Border," *Newsweek,* October 27, 1986, pp. 32,35.

Tugwell, Franklin. "Petroleum Policy and Political Process," in John Martz and David Myers (eds.), *Venezuela: the Democratic Experience,* New York: Praeger, 1977, pp. 237–254.

"2,800 Illegal Aliens Arrested in a Weeklong Border Sweep, " *New York Times,* Monday, October 20, 1986, p. A–20.

"U.S. Border Patrol Going 'High Tech'," *Cumberland Times/News,* Thursday, October 17, 1985,p. 23.

"U.S. Canada Border Guarded by Mechanical Sentries," *Cumberland Sunday Times,* October 25, 1987, p. A–7.

United States Commission on Civil Rights, *The Tarnished Door: Civil Rights Issues in Immigration.* Washington, D.C.: U.S. Government Printing Office, 1980.

United States Congress, House of Representatives, "Immigration Reform and Control Act of 1983" (Mazzoli Bill), HR 1510, 98th Congress, 1st Session, February 17, 1983:1–163.

U.S. Congress, Senate, Committee on the Judiciary. *The Immigration and Naturalization Systems of the United States.* Washington, D.C.: U.S. Government Printing Office, 1950.

U.S. Department of Justice, Immigration and Naturalization Service, "1979 Statistical Yearbook of the INS." Washington, D.C.: U.S. Government Printing Office, 1980.

"U.S. Hispanics 'Melting' But Not Prospering," *Washington Post,* Sunday, May 13, 1984, pp. A–1, 8.

"U.S. Immigration Bill Assailed," *New York Times,* Sunday, October 19, 1986, p. A–12.

U.S. Immigration Commission. "Brief Statement of the Investigations of the Immigration Commission, With Conclusions and Recommendations and Views of the Minority," U.S. Senate Doc. 747, 61st Congress, 3rd Session. Washington, D.C.: U.S. Government Printing Office, 1910/11.

U.S. Interagency Task Force on Immigration Policy. *Staff Report.* Washington, D.C.: Departments of Labor, Justice, and State, March 1979.

U.S. President's Commission on Immigration and Naturalization. *Whom Shall We Welcome: Report.* Washington, D.C.: U.S. Government Printing Office, 1953.

U.S. President's Select Commission on Immigration and Refugee Policy. *U. S. Immigration Policy and the National Interest: Final Report.* Washington, D.C.: U.S. Government Printing Office, March 1, 1981.

———. *U.S. Immigration Policy and the National Interest: Staff Report.* Washington, D.C.: U.S. Government Printing Office, April 30, 1981.

"U.S. Recession Export That Could Cripple Mexico's Economy," *Cumberland Times/ News,* November 26, 1987, p. 5.

Van Roy, Ralph. "Venezuela's Indocumentados," *Migration News,* 32 (Jan.–Mar. 1983):19–23.

Vecoli, Rudolph, and Joy K. Lintelman. *A Century of American Immigration, 1884–1984.* Minneapolis: University of Minnesota Continuing Education and Extension, 1984.

Vialet, Joyce. "A Brief History of U.S. Immigration Policy," *Report 80–223 EPW.* Washington, D.C.: Education and Public Welfare Division, INS, December 1980.

Vittoz, Stan. "World War I and the Political Accommodation of Transitional Market

Forces: The Case of Immigration Restriction," *Politics and Society*, 8, no.1 (1978):49–78.

"Waiting Anxiously: Amnesty Seekers Hope to Prevent Family Separation," *Dallas Morning News*, Monday, January 4, 1988, pp. A–13, 15.

Wallerstein, Immanuel. *The Modern World System: Capitalist Agriculture and the Origins of the European World-Economy in the Sixteenth Century*. New York: Academic Press, 1974.

Wallraff, Guenter. *Granz Unten*, Cologne: Kiepenheuer and Witsch, 1985.

Walshaw, R. W. *Migration to and from the British Isles: Problems and Policies*, London: Cape, 1941.

Walters, Robert, "Immigrants and Jobs," *Cumberland Times/News*, Friday, October 25, 1985, p. 8.

Wareing, J. *The Changing Pattern of Immigration Into the United States, 1956–1975*," *Geography* 63, no. 3 (1978):220–224.

Wawriznek, Kurt. *Die Entstehung der Deutschen Antisemiten Parteies, 1873–1890*. Berlin; 1927.

Weisbrod, Robert G. "Israel and the Black Hebrew Israelites," *Judaism* 29 (Winter 1975):23–38.

Weisman, Alan, "Mexican Hearts. California Dreams," *Los Angeles Times Magazine*, September 7, 1987, p. 7–28.

Weissbrodt, David. *Immigration Law and Procedure*. St. Paul, Minn.: West Publishing Co.. 1984.

West Indian Children in Our Schools: Interim Report of the Committee of Inquiry into the Education of Children from Minority Groups, Cmnd 8273, London: HMSO, 1981.

"Where the Family Comes First," *Parade Magazine*, June 2, 1985, pp. 4–6.

White, Jerry C. *A Statistical History of Immigration*. Immigration and Naturalization Reporter, vol. 25 (Summer 1976).

Wilkes, John (ed.), *How Many Australians? Immigration and Growth*, Australian Institute of Political Science, 37th Summer School, Canberra, 1971.

Williamson, Jeffrey G. "Migration to the New World: Long Term Influences and Impact," *Explorations in Economic History* 11, no. 4 (1974):357–89.

Wilpert, Czarina. *Die Zukunft der zweite Generation*, Koenigstein: Verlag Anton Hain, 1980.

Wilson, Paul R. *Immigrants and Politics*, Canberra: Australian National University Press, 1973.

Wright, Winthrop, "Race, Nationality, and Immigration in Venezuelan Thought, 1890–1937," *Canadian Review of Studies in Nationalism* 6, No. 1 (1979):1–12.

Yzaquirre, Raul, "What's Wrong With the Immigration Bill," *Washington Post National Weekly Edition*, December 12, 1983, p. 29.

Ziegler, Benjamin M. *Immigration: An American Dilemma*. Lexington, MA: D.C. Heath, 1953.

Index

About the Contributors

MICHAEL C. LEMAY is a Professor of Political Science at Frostburg State University. He received his Ph.D. from the University of Minnesota. He has taught at the University of Wisconsin Milwaukee and at the Seido Juku Institute in Japan. His research and publications have dealt with minority group politics and public policy. He has published in the *American Politics Quarterly, National Civic Review,* and *Teaching Political Science.* He is author of: *The Struggle for Influence: The Impact of Minority Groups on Politics and Policies in the U.S.* (1985), and *From Open Door to Dutch Door: An Analysis of U.S. Immigration Policy Since 1820* (1987). This chapter is based on a paper presented at the Midwest Political Science Association Meeting in Chicago, April 1987.

GREGORY TOBIN is Senior Lecturer in American Studies, Flinders University of South Australia. He received his Ph.D. from the University of Texas at Austin. He is interested in the comparative study of aspects of the social history of the United States and Australia, including problems of regional and ethnic identity. He is author of *The Making of a History: Walter Prescott Web and "The Great Plains" (1976).*

ZIG LAYTON-HENRY is Senior Lecturer in Politics at the University of Warwick, Coventry, England. He received his Ph.D. from the University of Birmingham. He has taught at the University of Birmingham, the University of Brunel, and the Open University, and has served as a Visiting Senior Research Fellow at the SSRC-s Research Unit on Ethnic Relations, University at Aston. His publications include (ed.) *Conservative Politics in Western Europe* (1982); *The Politics of Race in Britain* (1984); (ed.) *Race, Government and Politics in Britain* (1986); *The Political Challenge of Migration for Western European States* (forthcoming); and *The Campaign for Black Sections of the Labor Party* (forthcoming). He authored a chapter on British immigration policy in Tomas Hammer (ed.), *European Immigration Policy: A Comparative Study* (1985). His *The Politics of Race in Britain* is soon to be released in a new edition by Cambridge University Press, England. He has authored numerous scholarly journal articles and papers.

MARILYN HOSKIN received her Ph.D. from the University of California at Los Angeles. She has been a Fulbright Senior Lecturer at the University of Mannheim, West Germany, and is currently Associate Dean and Associate Professor of Political Science at the State University of New York at Buffalo. Her research and publications have focused on political socialization, the determinants of public support for political parties, and the integration of immigrants in Western democracies. She has published in *The American Journal of Political Science, Comparative Politics, International Migration*, and *Political Psychology* on immigration topics, and has contributed to a number of edited volumes in this area. Her current work is a comparative study of government initiative and public attitudes toward the absorption of new immigrant minorities.

ROY C. FITZGERALD earned his J.D. degree from the State University of New York and is currently completing his Ph.D. in Political Science there. He has contributed chapters to volumes on ideological shifts in Anglo-American democracies and has published in *Law and Social Policy*. He is currently working on a study of the relationship between economic perceptions, economic conditions, and political preferences in Western democracies. Hoskin and Fitzgerald's chapter was presented as a paper at the Midwest Political Science Association Meeting in Chicago, in April 1987.

BAT-AMI ZUCKER is Professor of History at Bar-Ilan University, Israel. She specializes in U.S. constitutional and political history. She has published in Israeli journals, German *Amerikastudien/American Studies*, and *Simon Weisenthal Center Annual*. Her current work deals with U.S. aid to Israel and the media's perspective—exemplified by *The New York Times* and *The Washington Post*. Her chapter is based on a paper presented at the Midwest Political Science Association Meeting in Chicago, April 1987.

DANIEL HELLINGER is Associate Professor of Political Science at Webster University, St. Louis, Missouri. He is presently working on two forthcoming books: a text on U.S. politics (coauthor, Dorsey), and *Venezuela: Oil, Development, and Dependency*. His articles on Latin America have appeared in *Western Political Quarterly* and *Latin American Perspectives*. This chapter is a revised version of a paper presented at the 1987 Meeting of the North Central Council of Latin Americanists in Northfield, Minnesota.